EXPECTING EXCELLENCE
in Urban Schools

D1567411

I would like to dedicate this book to my wife, Lessie, and children Nassor, Kamya, Imani, and Jelani Jr. This project could not have been possible without you. I would also like to dedicate it to my grandparents, Ethel and Lawrence Thompson, and mother, Adrienne Smith, for believing in me and helping to shape a strong academic foundation for me. I appreciate the time you put in to assist me. And finally I would like to dedicate it to Uncle Lawrence Thompson, for helping me to become the man I am today.

EXPECTING EXCELLENCE
in Urban Schools

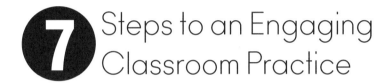 Steps to an Engaging
Classroom Practice

JELANI JABARI

Foreword by Marcia L. Tate

CORWIN
A SAGE Company

CORWIN
A SAGE Company

FOR INFORMATION:

Corwin
A SAGE Company
2455 Teller Road
Thousand Oaks, California 91320
(800) 233-9936
www.corwin.com

SAGE Publications Ltd.
1 Oliver's Yard
55 City Road
London EC1Y 1SP
United Kingdom

SAGE Publications India Pvt. Ltd.
B 1/I 1 Mohan Cooperative Industrial Area
Mathura Road, New Delhi 110 044
India

SAGE Publications Asia-Pacific Pte. Ltd.
3 Church Street
#10-04 Samsung Hub
Singapore 049483

Printed in the United States of America

A catalog record of this book is available from the Library of Congress.

ISBN 978-1-4522-5780-8

Acquisitions Editor: Jessica Allan
Associate Editor: Kimberly Greenberg
Editorial Assistant: Heidi Arndt
Production Editors: Cassandra Margaret Seibel
                 and Melanie Birdsall
Copy Editor: Cate Huisman
Typesetter: C&M Digitals (P) Ltd.
Proofreader: Caryne Brown
Indexer: Sue Nedrow
Cover Designer: Karine Hovsepian
Permissions Editor: Karen Ehrmann

This book is printed on acid-free paper.

SUSTAINABLE FORESTRY INITIATIVE
Certified Chain of Custody
Promoting Sustainable Forestry
www.sfiprogram.org
SFI-01268
SFI label applies to text stock

13 14 15 16 17 10 9 8 7 6 5 4 3 2 1

Contents

List of Tables and Figures — xi

Foreword — xiii
Marcia L. Tate

Preface — xv

Acknowledgments — xxi

About the Author — xxiii

1. **The Engaging Educational Practice** — 1

What Is Student Engagement? — 4
The Elements of Engagement — 5
The Challenge of Creating Engagement in HUMS — 6
The Barrage of Mismatches — 8
Developing an Engaging Educational Practice — 8
What Does an Engaging Educational Practice Consist of? — 9
Rationale for Developing an Engaging Practice — 10
Laying the Foundation for Creating the Practice:
    Sales Situations in the Classroom — 12
THEORETICAL FRAMEWORK: UNDERLYING REASONS FOR
    THE ESSENCE OF ENGAGEMENT — 13
Chapter Summary — 15
Actionable Professional Learning — 17

2. **Inspect to Inspire: Become a Scholar of Your Students** — 19

Preparing Student-Centered Pedagogy — 19
Studying While Teaching: Creating a Pipeline of
    Continuously Flowing Information — 20
Techniques for Becoming a Scholar of Your Students — 21
    Listen—Then List — 22
    The 5/3 Rule — 23

Mining Student Writing 23

Utilizing Interest Inventories 26

Administering a Learning Profile 27

Utilizing Student Surveys to Inform and
Improve Instruction 27

Basics of Designing Your Student Survey 29

Open-Ended Versus Closed-Ended Questions 29

Addressing the Issue of Time 29

Analyzing and Using Your Survey Results 31

How Else Can Feedback Be Elicited? 32

Chapter Summary 32

Actionable Professional Learning 33

3. **Nurture Their Attributes: Turn Commonly
Perceived Deficits Into Classroom Deposits** 35

THEORETICAL FRAMEWORK: UNDERLYING REASONS
FOR BUILDING ON STRENGTHS 38

Turning Commonly Perceived Deficits
Into Classroom Deposits 39

Strong Penchant For Interacting With Others 40

Paroling Students From Seat Incarceration:
Using Movement as a Tool 41

What Other Assets Do Students in HUMS Bring to the Table? 45

Customizing Lessons With Student Personas 46

A Sample Chemistry Lesson 48

The Value of Personalized Presentations 49

The MOVE Checklist 50

The Focus on HUMS Students 50

Chapter Summary 52

Actionable Professional Learning 53

4. **Sew Success Into Your Instructional Fabric** 55

Why Should Placing Students in Positions
of Success Be a Priority? 56

THEORETICAL FRAMEWORK: UNDERLYING REASONS
FOR CREATING CLASSROOM WINS 57

How Can Success Be Sewn Into Your Instructional Fabric? 58

Begun by Spoken Words, Believed
by Sustained Support 59

Position Supportive Structures Throughout the
Learning Environment 60

Develop a Classroom Culture of
Collaboration Versus Competition 60

Negotiating Failure: Mold Missteps
    Into Learning Modules   61

Positioning Them to Get the Wins:
    Creating Instructional SOFAs   61
    Me Versus Me: Use Self-Growth as a
        Barometer of Progress   62
    Use Baseline Data to Clearly Define
        Students' Starting Points   63
    Establish Incremental Targets Along the
        Road to Goal Mastery   63
    Essential Pedagogical Approaches That Position
        Students to Succeed   64
    The Need to Support Teachers in Positioning
        Their Students for Success   65
    Practices That Create Barriers to Success in HUMS   66

Chapter Summary   67
Actionable Professional Learning   68

5. Partner to Make Emotional Connections   71

Aiming to Connect Versus Control   72
    The Power of Emotional Appeal   73
    Creating the Emotional Connections:
        Getting Critical Buy-In   74
    How Can I Emotionally Connect With My Students?   75
    Connecting When Your Background, Experiences,
        and Culture Are Completely Different From Theirs   77
    Attributes of Teachers Who Successfully
        Establish Emotional Connections   78
    Using Connections to Create Emotional
        Engagement   78
Why Emotional Engagement Should Be a First
    Priority in the Process   79
THEORETICAL FRAMEWORK: UNDERLYING REASONS FOR
    CREATING EMOTIONAL ENGAGEMENT   80
Building the Classroom Community: Cultivating the
    Culture for Emotional Engagement to Grow   81
    Essential Elements of the Classroom Community   83
    How Are Caring Classroom Communities Built?   83
Anchors of the Academic Experience: Creating and
    Sustaining Student–Teacher Relationships   84
    Why Student–Teacher Relationships?   87
THEORETICAL FRAMEWORK: UNDERLYING REASONS FOR
    BUILDING STUDENT–TEACHER RELATIONSHIPS   87

The Four Cs Process of Building Student–
  Teacher Relationships   89
The First C: Care   89
    Why Care?   89
    How Can You Show You Care?   90
The Second C: Communication   94
    Why Communication?   95
    Connecting Through Conversations   95
The Third C: Consistency   103
    Why Consistency?   104
The Fourth C: Commitment   105
    Why Commitment?   105
    How Is Commitment Evident in Your Teaching?   105
Providing the Assist: When You Find the Issue,
  You Find the Entrance   106
    How Can I Provide an Assist Given the
      Overwhelming Number of Other
      Things I'm Already Asked to Do?   110
Chapter Summary   112
Actionable Professional Learning   113

6. **Intersect Their Interests and Experiences With Instruction**   **115**

Beginning the Engagement When the Tardy Bell Rings   115
How Are Interests and Experiences Intersected
  With Instruction?   116
First Focus: Intersecting Interests and
  Experiences With Text   117
THEORETICAL FRAMEWORK: UNDERLYING REASONS
  FOR INTERSECTING STUDENTS' INTERESTS AND
  EXPERIENCES WITH INSTRUCTION   118
    Characteristics of Texts That Engage
      Students in HUMS   119
    The Bare Essentials: A Realistic Exposure   119
    Which Specific Texts Can I Use to
      Engage My Students?   120
    Is This the Only Genre of Text HUMS
      Students Should Be Exposed To?   134
In What Other Ways Can I Engage
  My Students With Text?   135
    Getting Highly Resistant Readers to Get Started   135
    Use an Entrée to Introduce the Lesson   135
    Introduce Culturally Relevant and
      Socially Significant Texts   136

Utilize Critical Literacy to Engage Students		136
Envelop Content in Popular Culture and Media Arts		136
A Few Other Suggestions for Engaging Students		137
How Will I Know If My Students Are Engaged With Text?		138
Creating Intersections in Mathematics		140
How Is Math Made Engaging by Successful Teachers of Mathematics?		141
Intersecting Mathematics, Science, and Social Science Content With Students' Interests and Experiences		141
Additional Strategies for Intersecting Interests and Experiences With Content		148
Using Their Love for Play as a Tool		148
Using Multimedia Tools		148
Using Closure as a Tool of Engagement		153
Chapter Summary		154
Actionable Professional Learning		155

7. Reflect on Practice as a Tool of Improvement — 157

Reflecting Versus Reflective Practice		158
Why Engage in Reflective Practice?		159
THEORETICAL FRAMEWORK: UNDERLYING REASONS FOR ENGAGING IN REFLECTIVE PRACTICE		159
Suggestions for Engaging in Reflective Practice		160
Why Video?		161
Using Video as a Tool of Reflective Practice		163
Chapter Summary		165
Actionable Professional Learning		166

8. Expect Nothing Short of Excellence — 167

Teacher Expectations and Their Importance in HUMS		168
THEORETICAL FRAMEWORK: UNDERLYING REASONS FOR ELEVATED TEACHER EXPECTATIONS		169
Assessing, Elevating, and Maintaining Expectations for Your Students to Excel		170
Assess Your Expectations While Reflecting on Practice		170
Survey Student Perceptions of Your Expectations		171
Develop a Clear Understanding of Adolescent Development		171
Stay Abreast of Exemplars Who Have Experiences and Backgrounds Similar to Those of Your Students		171

Provide Multiple Opportunities for
Exposure to Exemplars   173
Envision the Possibilities   174
Chapter Summary   174
Actionable Professional Learning   175

Appendix: Interest Inventory   **177**

References   **179**

Index   **191**

List of Tables and Figures

List of Tables

1. Changing Perceived Deficits Into Deposits   42
2. Essential Pedagogical Frameworks That Position
   HUMS Students for Success   65
3. Effectively Connecting Through Conversations as
   Communicative Tools of Relationship Building   98
4. Connecting by Assisting With Academic Issues   108
5. Connecting by Assisting With Personal Issues   109
6. Realistic Fiction Texts That Intersect Experiences of
   African American Students With Content   121
7. Realistic Fiction Texts That Intersect Experiences of
   Latino/a Students With Content   129
8. Engineering Intersections of Interests and Experiences
   With Mathematics   142
9. Engineering Intersections of Interests and Experiences
   With Science Content   144
10. Constructing Intersections of Interest and
    Experience With Social Studies Content   146
11. Intersecting Games With Content   149
12. Processes Utilized to Engage in Reflective Practice   164

List of Figures

1. Items That Could Be Included in Your Survey   30
2. Additional Considerations for Designing Your Survey   30

3. Frequently Perceived Deficits of HUMS Students   37
4. Effective Ways to Create Emotional Connections
   With Students   77

Foreword

In a day and age when excellence is espoused and yet dropout rates in inner city schools can approximate or exceed 60%, it is time for someone to write a book that provides more realistic answers than questions. Jelani Jabari has done just that in the publication you are about to read.

Good writers and teachers know that there are specific brain-compatible strategies that engage the reader and result in a comprehension and retention of any message. Jelani masterfully incorporates many of those strategies beginning with the mnemonic device that denotes the main concept of his book—*INSPIRE (inspect, nurture, sew, partner, intersect, reflect,* and *expect).* These verbs summarize the major concepts in this book. Other acronyms include *HUMS*—high-poverty, urban, largely minority schools—the target population that the book addresses, and *SOFAs*, or success opportunities for all.

Jelani's use of actual classroom vignettes to illustrate the concepts is a most effective use of the age-old strategy of storytelling. Through his stories, the reader learns how teachers actually change the lives of HUMS students through such actions as taking a personal interest in them, building caring relationships with them, and making content relevant by connecting it to real examples from their personal lives. Jelani's book even includes an inventory a teacher can use to discern the likes, dislikes, and personal interests of students.

Some chapters also include chunks of research that provide the theoretical framework for the concepts that he espouses. Other chapters give content-specific examples of how to connect the content to be taught with the interests and experiences of HUMS students.

Jelani is a masterful writer and wittily employs the brain-compatible strategies of using metaphors, analogies, and similes throughout the text to make his message plain. Some of my favorites are (1) *trying to teach without engagement is like trying to send a text message without a service provider,* and *teachers are the thermostats of classrooms in that they monitor the emotional, cognitive, and behavioral temperature of the learning environment.* When he discusses the value of incorporating movement into a lesson (a concept I wholeheartedly espouse, by the way), he writes about *paroling students from seat incarceration.* He even outlines a blueprint for turning students' *trip ups into triumphs.* I cannot think of a better way to express these thoughts!

One of the most important aspects of the book is the *Actionable Professional Learning* plan that closes each chapter. In other words, now that the reader has a conceptual understanding of the ideas detailed in the chapter, the learning plan enables the reader to actualize the concept in the classroom by responding to the questions in this section. Those of us who teach about adult learning theory know that this reflection is crucial to adult behavior change.

It is not often that you find a book that provides practical ideas for addressing one of the most pressing challenges of today's educators. This is exactly what Jelani does. In fact, he also gives the research behind why his ideas work and practical examples for implementing them. This is a must-have text for your professional library. I will certainly add it to mine!

Marcia L. Tate

Preface

Growing up, you've probably heard it a million times that *practice makes perfect*. Generally speaking, the more you do something, the better you get at it. Lawyers build successful law practices by successfully representing clients in court, providing sage legal advice, and drafting well-thought-out legal documents. Doctors with successful medical practices are able to consistently and accurately diagnose health challenges and prescribe the best course of treatment. However, much less widely does society hold the perception that K–12 educators who teach conduct an *educational practice.*

The use of knowledge to perform the duty of educating students defines an educational practice. Effective educational practices consist of practitioners who utilize research-based pedagogy to attain educational and social outcomes. They are defined by professionals who refine the quality of instruction through repeated planning, preparing, and presenting of material. Successful practitioners are able to consistently place learners in optimal situations of success by making the appropriate modifications and adjustments to instruction. The instruction is refined by self-reflection and feedback from the principal consumers of the curriculum—the students.

What does a highly *engaging* educational practice consist of? When you think of engaging students, elements such as time on task, students showing interest in a topic, or students showing excitement while completing a task may come to mind. Engaging educational practices are about sustaining student engagement whether the students are in or out of school. These practices are characterized by students who excitedly anticipate what the teacher has planned each day, interact effectively with their peers in the classroom, and most of all, enjoy the presence of the teacher. It's about enveloping students in an engaging educational experience.

To the point, the hallmarks of highly engaging educational practices are teachers who are able to consistently connect with students through strong emotional and intellectual bonds. It consists of committed educators whose main emphasis is to make learning about *students* and consistently place them in situations of success. As a guide to assist you in building your practice or making your existing practice more engaging, this book will provide you with a well-constructed seven-step process represented by the acrostic *INSPIRE:*

- **I**nspect to inspire: Become a scholar of your students.
- **N**urture their attributes: Turn commonly perceived deficits into deposits.
- **S**ew success into your instructional fabric.
- **P**artner to make emotional connections.
- **I**ntersect their interests and experiences with instruction.
- **R**eflect on practice as a tool of improvement.
- **E**xpect nothing short of excellence.

This process will assist you in transforming your practice from one that simply delivers instruction into one that provides a dynamically engaging educational experience. It will also assist you in enhancing the academic rigor in your pedagogy with methods for providing challenging tasks and content, meaningful real-world applications, and not only elevating but also sustaining expectations for all.

Organization of This Book

Chapter 1. The introductory chapter provides insight into the elements of engagement, what an engaging practice is along with the rationale for creating one, the theoretical framework supporting engagement, and similarities between teaching and sales situations.

Chapter 2. The first principle in the INSPIRE process, *Inspect to Inspire: Become a Scholar of Your Students,* is explored. Your success in creating a highly engaging practice rests on the effectiveness of processes that consistently inform you about your students. That is, tools, techniques, and strategies for gathering critical information about both personal and academic facets are examined. You'll receive specific guidance for designing your survey to elicit critical feedback and ultimately make the learning more student centered. These invaluable pieces of information serve as the foundation of the engaging practice.

Chapter 3. A common perception held in many high-poverty, urban, largely minority schools (HUMS) is that student deficits are largely responsible for achievement failures. This chapter explores ways to turn commonly perceived deficits among students into deposits of the learning community. Specific ways of affirming, legitimating, and harnessing what students bring to the learning community are examined.

Chapter 4. One of the biggest barriers that preclude emotional and behavioral engagement is the lack of academic success of students. Moreover, chronic failure has been cited as one of the biggest contributors to student misbehavior in classrooms. Strategies for creating a highly supportive learning environment with pedagogy that consistently places students in positions of success are examined.

Chapter 5. A recurring emphasis in many urban classrooms is the creation of an environment of control rather than one in which strong emotional ties are developed with students. The extent to which teachers in HUMS successfully engage their students is inextricably tied to the strength of such emotional connections. A plethora of specific techniques, tools, and strategies for successfully developing strong, yet essential, emotional bonds is examined.

Chapter 6. One of the most effective ways to engage students is to find a way to weave required academic content with their world. This chapter yields a wealth of timely insight on how to minimize boredom, apathy, and disinterest and connect student interests and experiences with the core content areas of English language arts (reading), mathematics, science, and social studies. How to intersect play (games) with content and use multimedia tools and closure as a means of engaging the students is explored.

Chapter 7. One of the surest ways to stay stagnant or render a practice ineffective is to infrequently engage in reflective practice. This chapter describes the fundamentals of reflective practice and provides techniques, such as video, for framing and reframing issues, learning from experience, and, as a result, improving your practice.

Chapter 8. Pervasively negative perceptions of the impoverished conditions of HUMS students and their communities often contribute to the subconscious lowering of academic expectations. Strategies for critically examining your current expectations, elevating them, and maintaining high expectations of HUMS students are explored.

Vignettes

Several key principles of this writing are illustrated through vignettes of three teachers as described below:

1. Ms. Klein, a 26-year-old teacher who grew up in a tony upper class midwestern suburb, has three years of teaching experience. She teaches fourth grade in a large urban elementary school in a midwestern city where 100% of the students qualify for free or reduced-price lunch. Most students' homes are headed by single parents who don't consistently participate in the school activities.
2. Mrs. Jones, a 31-year-old teacher who grew up in the same neighborhood and attended the same school in which she teaches, has eight years of teaching experience. She teaches seventh grade English language arts in a large northeastern urban city. The city has seen a precipitous decline in population as a changing economy shuttered many once-thriving steel mills. Several of her students have to walk by abandoned houses during their journey to and from school.
3. Mr. King, a 43-year-old teacher who grew up in the Great Plains, has five years of teaching experience. After being laid off from his midlevel management position when his former employer downsized, he returned to school to earn a teaching certificate. He relocated to the West Coast and teaches economics to 10th graders at an urban high school that is often marred by violence; its walls are marked by gang graffiti.

Actionable Professional Learning

Would you agree that when information is presented in books, other media, or professional learning workshops, the presentation too often ends with no meaningful way to extend the learning? That is, it doesn't answer the "so what?" or "what now?" or "how do I?" questions. To help you put ideas into practice, each chapter of this book concludes with a framework for you and your colleagues to engage in continual learning. In the last section of each chapter, Actionable Professional Learning, practical ways to critically reflect on, integrate, and improve the implementation of ideas over time are given to use within the framework of a teacher learning community.

When teachers are active participants in ongoing professional learning, such as professional learning communities (PLCs), their professional knowledge is continuously enhanced, and student learning improves. As Darling-Hammond (2008) poignantly noted,

"Teaching in which teachers have the opportunity for continual learning is the likeliest way to inspire greater achievement for children, especially for those whom education is the only pathway to survival and success" (p. 99). Moreover, knowledge is not only woven into the thread of teachers' daily experiences but is understood best when engaging in shared critical reflection with those with similar experiences (Buysse, Sparkman, & Wesley, 2003). Such teacher learning communities yield much needed collegial support as well as opportunities to learn from each other about ways to create the "richest opportunities for student growth" (Lieberman & Miller, 2011, p. 19).

As you're probably aware, collaboration is a cornerstone of PLCs. With the well-documented challenges of teaching in high-poverty underresourced urban schools, collaborative practices provide sorely needed collegial support. This book will encourage your team to utilize shared practices, critiquing of practice, collaborative inquiry, action research, and debriefing and dialoguing as vehicles of improvement.

Acknowledgments

Corwin gratefully acknowledges the contributions of the following reviewers:

Karen Kersey
Second-Grade Teacher
Kanawha County Schools
Charleston, WV

Ken Klopack
Art & Gifted Education Consultant
Chicago Public Schools
Chicago, IL

Jennifer Sinsel
Gifted Facilitator
Wichita Public Schools
Wichita, KS

About the Author

 **Jelani Jabari**, PhD, is founder and president of Pedagogical Solutions, LLC. Pedagogical Solutions partners with learning communities throughout the United States and abroad to both enhance pedagogical practice and improve academic achievement. His research interests include engaging pedagogy, academically rigorous instructional practices, and utilizing assessment as an instructional tool. He holds a BA in economics, an MA in curriculum and instruction, and a PhD in educational evaluation and research.

Jelani has had a stellar career that spans more than 20 years in the field of education. He thoroughly enjoyed serving more than ten years as a school teacher and three years as a school administrator. He has also served as university instructor and has consulted with the Michigan Department of Education. His exemplary work has led to presentations for the National Staff Development Council, National Middle School Association, International Society for Technology in Education, and a many other organizations.

Jelani wholeheartedly believes the capacities all children have to excel are unearthed when educators expect exemplary performance, position the students in situations of success, and inspire them to maximize their potential. Touching lives, positively impacting each other, and enhancing educational experiences for all students lies at the heart of the mission of a team of highly competent and wholeheartedly committed educators.

Jelani currently resides in southeastern Michigan with his wife and children.

1

The Engaging Educational Practice

In October 1994, I left a message on the district's substitute teaching hotline indicating that I was available to teach the next day. At 7 o'clock that evening, the call I received from the substitute office wasn't exactly the one I wanted. I was told that I would be going to one of the worst middle schools in one of the roughest areas of the city. In a panic, I called a friend who had some experience teaching in schools with students who could be *quite* the behavioral challenge.

I nervously said, "Mr. Houston, you know they're sending me over to M. L. King Junior High School. Those students are known to be among the *worst* behaved in the city. What should I *do?*" He paused and said,

> Some of the biggest mistakes teachers make when going into new situations is that they neglect to connect. One of the most important things you have to do is to temporarily ignore the academics and find ways to connect or bond with them first. First introduce a topic or idea that has meaning to them. Then try to frame as much content as possible around something they like, value, or have experienced or that is familiar to them from their community.

I wanted to ask him for more specific ideas, but respecting his time, I politely thanked him and ended the conversation. I pulled together the materials I could that evening and hoped it was good enough to help me *survive* the day.

The community of King Junior High had been blighted by riots occurring a few decades earlier and decimated by a steady decline in residents. Some blocks in the school community had as many abandoned houses as occupied homes. Bars protected the homes while bulletproof glass partitioned the store clerks from customers.

As I drove into the school parking lot, the unique design of the school caught my eye. Built like an impregnable fortress, it looked like an ideal prototype for a "supermax" type of maximum security prison. After what seemed an eternity, I finally made it through the long line of students waiting to go through the metal detector and to be searched by the security officers. The assistant principal, who was assisting with the search of students, introduced himself as I walked through the metal detectors.

Mr. Anderson, affectionately called "Mr. A" by the students, was a cordial gentleman in his early forties. Among the many hats he wore was that of coordinator of the assignment of substitute teachers. As we briefly talked in his office, he sternly looked down his nose through thin-rimmed glasses and asked me, "Son, do you think you're *really* ready for this?" He explained that I was to cover a classroom where one teacher had literally walked off the job during the middle of the period, her predecessor had quit after just one week, and the current teacher had been so frustrated at the end of the previous day that she had hinted she might try to seek a stress leave. "Yes sir!" I assured him, though I tried to cloak my anxiety and cover the intimidation caused by the uncertainty that lay ahead.

As we walked up the steps to the classroom I was to teach in, we heard loud noises long before we saw the students. Little did I know they were coming from the room in which I was to teach. Loud laughing, profanity-laced tirades, and other noises suggesting a party atmosphere could be heard coming from Room 232 as we strolled down the long, dimly lit corridor. When students saw Mr. A in the doorway, the basketball game played with wads of paper and the trash can stopped, conversations among students shifted to silence, and the boys who were horse playing returned to their seats. He eased some of my anxiety, which was no longer hidden, by assuring me he would be in to check on me periodically during the day. He said, "If things get out of hand, hit the 'panic button' (intercom) on the wall; this will signal me or security to come."

Having had the fortune of prior substitute teaching experiences where no lesson plans were left by the teacher of record, I knew that if I didn't come in with my own "stuff," I would be overwhelmed by student-induced stress. However, the teacher of record, Mrs. Washington, had indeed left a well-thought-out, meticulously planned algebra lesson for her seventh-grade classes. I started to write the first few variables from problems on the board but suddenly felt the breeze of a balled up piece of paper whiz by the back of my head. I had a feeling that the conversational murmur behind me would quickly turn into chaotic mayhem that would consume the classroom. I tossed the chalk on the ledge of the chalkboard and figured it would be much wiser to use the content I had prepared.

Clearing my throat as an attempt to get their attention, I said as loudly as I could, "Tupac Shakur. If you are a fan of the rapper Tupac, raise your hand." The majority of students raised their hands. "Who knows who Christopher Wallace is?" One of the students who had smiled blurted out, "Ah man, that's Biggie Smalls! Whadda you know about him, teach?" I explained that I had listened to a few of his songs and thought he was a talented lyricist. On that day, the content I had brought was a lesson on life and how to better negotiate the choice-consequence paradigm. For the rest of that period, I was surprised that the students hung on every word I uttered.

About halfway through the period, out of the corner of my eye, I glanced and saw Mr. A peek through the window of the door. He returned a few minutes later with a lady, who I later found out was the school principal, veering into the room with a look of amazement. Near the end of the period, a few students literally begged and pleaded to stay with me for an additional period.

At the end of the day, Mr. A called me down to his office. When I walked in, he introduced me to the school principal. They asked me what I had done to captivate and keep the attention of students who were notorious for their bad behavior. I explained that I simply went in and intentionally connected with the students through deliberately starting in their world. The principal and Mr. A both expressed how pleased they were with the job I had done of maintaining order in a chronically chaotic classroom. To my surprise, they offered me a long-term substitute teaching placement. I politely declined, explaining that I was assigned to teach at another school four days a week. At the beginning of the next school year, however, I accepted their offer and decided to give it a try.

I never thought that the little piece of advice from Mr. Houston would have such a profound impact on my career. After more than 20 years of experience with high-poverty urban schools, I have come to embrace the importance of making initial connections with students and enveloping content around them as the foundational pathway for successfully engaging them. Furthermore, I became inspired to intentionally make student engagement a defining element of my professional practice. As you probably already know, when students are engaged, teachers are less likely to be stressed by student misbehavior, and students are more likely to do well in class. As a result, I ravenously fed off their interest and enthusiasm to learn and became more engaged with the instructional process.

What Is Student Engagement?

Trying to teach without engagement is like trying to send a text message without a service provider. Without the service provider, you can type as many messages as you like, but when you try to send them, the intended receiver(s) never get them. In the classroom, messages sent to students are never received because of the missing service provider, student engagement. Student engagement is to achievement what reality programming is to network television ratings. In each case, without the former, the latter would significantly decline. You, like most teachers, probably know the importance of engaging students in the learning process. You know it's the green instructional "send" button that makes the learning go. However, increasing numbers of teachers struggle with not only what it is but also how to make it happen for them.

How do you define the term *student engagement?* I've asked participants this question many times during professional learning workshops. Most conceptualize engagement as observable actions carried out by students. The most common responses I hear are "the majority of students are on task," "really into the lesson," "act as if interested," and "show effort."

Though the forms and degrees of engagement may vary from classroom to classroom, you won't find effective learning happening without it. Though there is no universally accepted definition of student engagement (Appleton, Chrisenton, & Furlong, 2008), I define *academic engagement* as the extent to which students are interested in, emotionally involved with, and willing to participate in the task at hand. Although dissension exists regarding a concise definition, researchers monolithically agree that there are three principal dimensions or elements of student engagement.

The Elements of Engagement

Engagement is often conceptualized as having three main elements: the emotional, the cognitive, and the behavioral (Appleton et al., 2008). Simply put, it's about the interaction of students' feelings, thinking, and actions. These are not mutually exclusive; they are often thought of as interrelated parts that are fused together. For example, Fredericks, Blumenfeld, and Paris (2004) noted the following:

> The fusion of behavior, emotion, and cognition under the idea of engagement is valuable because it may provide a richer characterization of children than is possible in research on single components. Defining and examining the components of engagement individually separates students' behavior, emotion, and cognition. In reality these factors are dynamically interrelated within the individual; they are not isolated processes. (p. 61)

[handwritten marginal note: 3 factors are dependent on each other]

A fourth though lesser used component of engagement, reaction to challenge, entails how students use strategies to deal with difficulties, especially challenging situations of perceived failure (Klem & Connell, 2004). However, several bodies of work have examined the three dimensions separately, and much of the presentation of the topic in this book will follow suit.

Emotional engagement, sometimes called *psychological engagement*, refers to the connection students feel to your classroom and the important elements that compose this connection. It's about the extent to which students see you and your learning environment as warm, affectionate, and caring. The degree to which students feel close to people at school, feel that they are themselves valued members of the school community, and like being in school is the essence of emotional engagement. It's greatly impacted by the relationship teachers have with their students. Terms such as i*dentification, belonging*, and *school membership* fall under this umbrella.

[handwritten marginal note: what does a look like? interpreted]

Cognitive engagement is thought of as the degree to which students are willing to psychologically invest the needed "thinking energy" to learn (Connell & Wellborn, 1991). It includes students' understanding of the importance of the task at hand. When higher levels of cognitive engagement are present, students show more willingness to persist with complicated tasks and difficult-to-understand ideas, and to keep trying after experiencing failure. *[handwritten note: perseverance]*

Behavioral engagement refers to the current behavior patterns of students. It includes your students' desire to attend class, initiative to start tasks, attention to the task at hand, time on task, effort expended, and persistence shown, as well as the characteristics of how they respond to the you. Rates at which students complete homework, attend school, and are attentive in class indicate levels of behavioral engagement.

You may be thinking of the question teachers often ask: "Can my students be *fully* engaged if one or two of the above elements are missing?" Given that there is no agreed-upon definition of engagement, whether or not they have achieved full engagement is inconsequential. However, students can show evidence of one or two dimensions and not the third. For example, Mrs. Klein's fourth graders may be *interested* in a lesson about the plight of poverty and hunger-stricken children of Ethiopia but have no emotional involvement with the topic, and they may also be reluctant to participate in a lesson about it. Mrs. Jones's seventh graders may be highly interested in and passionately emotional about curfew times for teenagers but have no *intention* of completing any assigned tasks about it. Mr. King's sophomores may be willing to complete a required essay because it is necessary to pass the class and yet may have little interest in or emotional involvement with the project.

The Challenge of Creating Engagement in HUMS

Two of the biggest challenges in teaching are to successfully establish orderly, well-structured, learning environments that consistently produce substantive student achievement gains in high-poverty, urban, largely minority schools (HUMS). Many classrooms in HUMS have students who have greater-than-average chances of faring badly with respect to either school or developmental outcomes. That is, they are what Werner (1986) called students at risk. Contributing to the difficulty is that many students in HUMS, such as some African American students, simply don't identify with school (Taylor, 1991).

A failure to identify with school is at the root of issues such as inattentiveness during instruction, low persistence on tasks, minimal effort, high levels of truancy, and a host of other concerns. Rising participation of African American youth in gang activity, abuse of drugs, and youth violence, for example, has been attributed to the evolution of a subculture that simply doesn't identify with school (Taylor, 1991).

Some students are in desperate need of varying degrees of psychological support services, which the underresourced HUMS often inadequately provide. Therefore, mental health issues that masquerade as bad behavior frequently spill over into the classroom. Of further concern is the fact that too many students in these classrooms face daunting issues outside of school. Factors placing students in precarious positions at great risk of failure are ever present.

Many of these students are saddled with the responsibility of clothing and feeding younger siblings, ensuring their homework is completed, and walking them to and from school. Some are fearful of the journey between school and home because they must pass drug dens, abandoned abodes, or threatening thugs. Others are careful about creating close bonds with classmates because of the hurt they have felt from frequently changing schools. The burdens of these tremendously challenging life issues outside of school often make the job of engaging these students quite a formidable task.

To compound challenging home issues, many students at risk do not fare well academically. They are often teased by classmates over such issues as reading three levels below their grade. As they get older, they become numbed by repeatedly receiving poor grades, resist giving effort to persist, and eventually become resigned to a perceived inevitable fate of academic failure. As a result, many of these students find solace in successfully honing their ability to disrupt the learning process. Other impediments to engaging students in HUMS come into play as well.

An additional challenge that often negatively impacts a significant number of students in HUMS is the fact that academic achievement is not a number one priority in their homes. Because their parents struggle to make ends meet, may be intimidated by the school or the work sent home, or may even be indifferent toward the academic gains of their children, doing well in school and qualifying for higher education often takes a back seat in the home life of these students. A second grade HUMS teacher shared a story about a discussion around college she had with her students. One of her male students raised his hand and said, "Mrs. Howard, my momma told me I shouldn't worry about going to college because we can't afford it. She said don't talk about college 'round her no more!"

Some of the apathy is attributable to the perception of an inescapable condemnation to a life of being poor. Some families believe that because they have experienced generational poverty, it is inconceivable to think that any offspring can break the cycle. In other cases, poor prior academic experiences lead parents to myopically view education as a dead end with no meaning versus a means to an end.

The Barrage of Mismatches

Certainly you're familiar with the oft repeated definition of insanity: "doing the same thing over and over again and expecting a different result." As each school year begins in many HUMS districts, the way learning is structured in schools remains the same. This results in far too many students failing over and over again. In HUMS, an important mismatch exists between the students and the school structures, learning environments, and instructional techniques. For instance, it's been well documented that lecturing is at best a marginal teaching method, yet it's still the predominant method of delivery in far too many classrooms. Class periods are structured in a way that addresses the needs of the average student, while the needs of those who lie above and below the norm are infrequently met. The learning styles, or ways in which students in HUMS learn best, are often at odds with the delivery method most often used. Moreover, a smaller proportion of teachers are highly qualified than in other schools, and these teachers are less likely to be able to deliver pedagogy that adequately meets students' needs. All of these factors make it tremendously challenging to engage students in HUMS.

Developing an Engaging Educational Practice

Unfortunately, even in classrooms where academic engagement is a priority, the focus is on making a single activity more interesting or a given lesson more exciting. This is problematic because of its short-lived nature. Your students' attention may be momentarily captured by a short video clip but quickly turned elsewhere after they've viewed it. They may be instantly interested in learning about cancer, but interest may wane after they realize that the cost of completion is an up-front investment of intellectual energy. Their desire to participate may dwindle after they have been repeatedly dealt devastating blows by the fists of failure.

Developing an engaging educational practice diminishes the ills associated with capriciously implemented strategies of engagement that target isolated lessons or activities within lessons. An engaging practice is about creating a true learning experience. It's about embedding supportive structures into practice. It's about emphasizing the creation of emotional connections between student and teacher, and between peers. Such practices include integrated elements that sustain emotional, cognitive, and behavioral engagement.

Engaging educational practices are known for customized educational content for the unique learners in each room.

As stated, a key component of an engaging practice is emotional engagement of students with their teacher. In HUMS, this is a critical prerequisite for creating the engaging experience. Without this emotional connection, students are much less likely to do the required thinking or actions for a given task. The emotional bond is the link that gets students to move from intention into action. The emotional connection is the catalyst of the classroom. It drives the engaging reaction into existence with even your most challenging students. When you get the emotional connection, you improve the chances that students will *do* even when they *don't* feel like doing. Not only does sustained emotional engagement cultivate fertile ground for growing cognitive and behavioral engagement, but it also is an essential step in the development of an engaging educational practice.

What Does an Engaging Educational Practice Consist of?

You may be thinking, "What's the difference between academically engaging students and creating an engaging educational practice?" An engaging educational practice is more comprehensive in scope than academic engagement. Academic engagement is one, albeit essential, component of an engaging educational practice. When you deliver activities, lessons, or units of instruction that promote greater levels of emotional, behavioral, and intellectual involvement on the part of your students, you are engaging students academically. However, when you develop a system of processes that continuously promotes and sustains the emotional, intellectual, and behavioral engagement of your students, you're creating an engaging educational practice.

An engaging educational practice is known for the sustenance of the engaging experience. It's about having students experience *flow* where their levels of engagement lead to them becoming less aware of space and time (Csikszentmihalyi, 1990). Highly engaging practices are known to have students *find* new passions and interests and *lose* track of time. Engaging educational practices have collaborative structures in place that reduce the sense of isolation and alienation often associated with students who drop out of school, and these structures help students to become more socially competent as well.

Cornerstones of engaging educational practices are the use of research-based practices. Differentiated instruction and using assessment as an instructional tool for learning are examples of such practices in that they both significantly enhance the likelihood of learner success. Embedded structures to support the development of student academic and social competencies are in place. Furthermore, positive versus punitive behavioral supports are proactively used. A hallmark of these supports is that student buy-in is negotiated via student voice and choice. Reflective practice is another cornerstone, in that teachers reflect to refine and improve their instruction, and they have students reflect on strategies and techniques they used to learn.

Students' personal lives are a critical element of this pedagogical practice. Practices such as these are structured such that students are provided ample opportunities to chart the course of their learning. These practices are characterized by a customization of the overall educational experience uniquely around each student's interests, issues, preferences, and potential. Processes for planning, preparing, and presenting content are focused on creating engagement. An engaging practice is a system of interrelated methods that move the engagement forward. Unlike discrete practices, such as making individual lessons more academically engaging, an engaging educational practice comprehensively creates an engaging educational experience.

Rationale for Developing an Engaging Practice

What would happen to the temperature of your house during the winter if there were no ducts for hot air to move throughout the structure? Of course, you know that your home would be much cooler or perhaps downright frigid! The thermostat monitors the temperature and triggers the kindling of the fire in the furnace. It is then blown through the insulated ducts, which results in a warmer home. If one of the elements were missing, your house would not be properly heated. If you remove the blower from the furnace or the ductwork, for instance, only the area around the furnace would be warmed. In essence, there is a *system* in place for not only warming the home at a given moment but sustaining that warmth over time.

Teachers are the thermostats of their classrooms, in that they monitor the emotional, cognitive, and behavioral temperature of the learning environment. If the emotional temperature is too cool (boredom), they can *ignite* the learning with engaging instructional strategies and techniques, such as an energetic presentation of material. They also monitor elements such as pacing of the presentation and difficulty of material to make adjustments that are *just right*. However, engaging strategies delivered in isolation are not enough to sustain the engagement of one student, let alone a full class of 30, each of whom has a unique set of characteristics. There needs to be a system in place that structures practices in such a way that engagement is sustained.

An engaging educational practice is the system that *heats up* the students' educational experience. Collaborative processes are the ducts through which ideas, information, and support are mutually exchanged. Like the screws that connect ducts, structures for relationship building bond members of the caring learning community together. Supportive structures, such as peer-interactive strategies, surround the learning process like insulation surrounds the ducts. As a blueprint specifies the layout of the ducts for each home and the rooms within it, the teacher customizes the blueprint for learning for different classes and individual learners. In a word, an engaging educational practice provides a system for organizing interrelated practices that lead to engagement. It is needed to fully address the complex classroom elements; it not only creates engagement but sustains it over time as well.

Two statements I hear most often from teachers who struggle with student apathy and boredom are these: "My students just don't care" and "These kids just aren't motivated." I argue that *all* students *do* care. They care a great deal about many things, a majority of which aren't going on in enough classrooms. In my experience, I have found that in any given HUMS classroom, about 20% of students are intrinsically motivated. As you probably have observed, these are the ones who act as if they care about learning when, indeed, they don't. They hang onto every word that flies out of your mouth, remain engaged and on task even if your lesson is incredibly boring, and consistently give 110% effort. Then you have about 70% of students who are extrinsically motivated by something you do or give them. They are engaged and on task some of the time, but it takes a bit of effort to gain and sustain their attention and desire to learn. The remaining 10% of students are seldom engaged, rarely show that they care about any content or anything, and are classic case studies of apathy, disinterest, and boredom. Developing an engaging practice helps to consistently rekindle classroom flames for these latter two groups.

Part of the success in engaging students lies in incessantly doing your homework to uncover everything that touches them, makes them tick, and means the most to them. It lies in discovering how to "dress up" the process of learning in garments they would don on any day. The other part of that success comes from framing the learning around critically meaningful ideas, issues, and information. In classrooms with a smaller proportion of intrinsically motivated students, the extent to which students are engaged is inextricably linked to the teacher's ability to customize content around students. Creating an engaging educational practice minimizes levels of boredom and apathy through the creation of continuously evolving student-centered pedagogy.

Do you remember a time when more students than not would follow most of the rules and demands of teachers and school administrators? Indeed, there was a time where most students would willingly complete the majority of classroom tasks and comply with most rules (Modell & Elder, 2002). An engaging practice is called for given that you can no longer assume your students will come to school ready to comply with the majority of school mandates. Students in classrooms today are dealing with more challenging social issues. Pedagogy that addresses these issues is called for. Methods that pique interest and stimulate the desire for them to *want* to be there are essential to maintaining order as well as laying the foundation for engagement.

It will be no surprise to you that the pressure to increase standardized test scores in America's schools has never been greater. Improved standardized scores reflect enhanced pedagogy and other learning processes in the classroom. An essential first step in corralling attention and motivating students to, at the bare minimum, *begin* the process of learning is the establishment of an ongoing yet effective framework for engagement. Not only does the engaging practice greatly increase the chance that greater numbers of your students will become more academically and socially competent, but you will be less stressed, and you will also increase the chance that they will stay in school until graduation. Additional reasons for making engagement a priority are listed below.

Laying the Foundation for Creating the Practice: Sales Situations in the Classroom

With the understanding of the importance and benefits of student engagement as an important part of the teaching practice, why do so many teachers find it difficult to create engaging educational practices?

THEORETICAL FRAMEWORK: UNDERLYING REASONS FOR THE ESSENCE OF ENGAGEMENT

- One of the most pivotal factors affecting achievement in the classroom is student engagement. When students are highly engaged, it lowers the likelihood they will take part in risky behaviors (Connell, Halpern-Felsher, Clifford, Crichlow, & Usinger, 1995).
- There is a positive, strong link between engagement and performance across diverse populations of students (Finn, 1989; Finn & Rock, 1997).
- Academic engagement has been found to be an important factor in increasing the likelihood of educational success for low-income African American students (Connell, Spencer, & Aber, 1994).
- Understanding why students drop out of school is principally theoretically modeled by engagement (Appleton et al., 2008).
- At-risk students in HUMS are more likely to do well when engaged in school (Finn & Rock, 1997).
- Nearly 50% of high school students cite being bored in school each day (Yazzie-Mintz, 2010). Students who are male, nonwhite, or Asian, lower SES (socio-economic status), or special education have reported being less engaged than other students while in high school (Yazzie-Mintz, 2007).
- School engagement predicts a significant part of how students perform academically irrespective of gender, grade, cognitive ability, or mother's education (Sirin & Rogers-Sirin, 2005) and robustly predicts student success in school (Lee, 2012).
- When students are engaged, it aids their cognitive and social development (Finn, 1993; Newmann, Wehlage, & Lamborn, 1992).
- Engaged students have a greater chance than others of learning, graduating, and pursuing education after high school (Marks, 2000).
- Student engagement predicts student achievement and behavior in school. When students are engaged in school, they get higher grades higher test scores and are less likely to drop out. Between 40% and 60% of students experience chronic disengagement from school by ninth grade (Klem & Connell, 2004).
- Student engagement has been found to postpone pregnancy for high-school students (Manlove, 1998).
- The best place to begin school reform that improves the likelihood that poor African American students will succeed in school is student engagement (Connell, Spencer, & Aber, 1994).

As mentioned, many teachers simply neglect to connect. That is, they pay little attention to connecting with students through the creation of emotional or intellectual bonds. They don't do enough to entice students to buy into what they have to offer. Their purview lies only with designing lessons and delivering the curriculum. They deliver the curriculum as is, with no extras or upgrades.

Reexamining what teachers actually do also sheds light on part of the challenge. You would probably agree that the main duty of teachers is to facilitate the process of learning, but does any of that involve selling? Would you say that teachers are in the business of sales? Is it not true that teachers have an inventory of solutions, strategies, skills, ideas, competencies, and knowledge that they continuously try to get the curricular consumers (i.e., students) to buy? Ms. Klein tries different strategies to get her fourth graders to *buy* her ideas about quantity and patterns during math class. Mrs. Jones strives to sell her seventh graders skills for them to become competent readers and writers. Mr. King works to get his sophomores to *purchase* ideas about the production of goods and services and laws of supply and demand. If you would agree with the notion that teachers *are* salespeople, why is it often difficult to get curricular consumers to become repeat buyers?

Imagine going into a newly opened store that you knew nothing about and that you were unfamiliar with the store's employees, products, and services as well. What are the chances that you would swipe your debit card before leaving that day? Thinking of the last big-ticket item (e.g., large screen LCD television set) you purchased, what were all of the things that happened before you actually completed the sale? Chances are you didn't just make a blind purchase without knowing something about the reputation of the store, salesperson, or product. Someone probably referred you to them, you saw an ad lending credibility, or you dug up some information about them. At some point before making the payment, you probably had a strong *feeling* that you *needed* to purchase the product. It's highly likely that in the places where you are a repeat customer, your customer loyalty springs from the presence of people you know, like, and trust.

The classroom is the marketplace where teachers work to meet their sales quotas. Teaching is composed of a series of sales situations that are sometimes successfully closed. However, many classrooms are full of reluctant customers who are mandated by state law to be there. While there, many disgruntled customers do everything possible to make the job of the curricular salesperson very difficult. In high-poverty classrooms with a preponderance of underprepared students, this is often the case.

When students are introduced to teachers for the first time, their reluctance to buy may stem from questioning who the salesperson (teacher) is and whether or not that person is reputable. Resistance to buy may lie in the fact that the salesperson has yet to earn their trust. Hesitancy may also stem from past poor experience (e.g., lack of success) with the product itself (curricular content) or a related product. For instance, a high school freshman may have repeatedly been teased and embarrassed about being a poor reader for the last five school years. The chance that his ninth-grade English instructor will sell him on reading fluency ideas is small. Additionally, the sale may be nullified because the instructional salesperson hasn't demonstrated adequate knowledge of the product. The confluence of these issues in the sales process precludes high sales volumes and promotes the frustrations of teachers.

The currencies used to transact buying and selling in the classroom are attention and emotion, which help procure interest, trust, and desire. They happen to be one of the most short-lived yet highly valuable classroom commodities. If you want students to pay you with their attention, impart their interest, and dole out desire, you've got to first give them compelling reasons to buy. Trying to grab and keep them before emotionally connecting is like the televangelist asking you to write the big check before hearing him or her preach the first sermon. You would be naïve to believe they will lend you their attention on credit before they know who you are, develop rapport with you, and know what the product will do for them. You have to first make deposits into their bank of trust. Everyone knows how important interest, trust, and desire are, but not as many strategically prepare and meticulously plan to pull out all stops to capture them. Other important considerations need be factored in to complete the sale.

When the challenge of engaging students is framed from the position of continuous buying and selling propositions, you are able to ferret out underlying reasons that help you close the sale. Reasons for refusal to buy are unearthed as well as ways to overcome sales objections and to negotiate student buy-in. Addressing engagement from this framework helps you build a wealth of achievement from the accumulation of attention, emotion, interest, trust, and desire.

Chapter Summary

The provision of an engaging educational experience, particularly in HUMS, is most powerful when it is spawned by an engaging practice. The foundation of an engaging educational practice consists of embedded structures that continuously facilitate the creation of emotional bonds between teacher and student and among students. Furthermore, engaging practices have a greater chance of developing when the teacher approaches teaching as if it were a buying and selling proposition. Your success at getting curricular consumers to buy into you and your educational offerings, and to become repeat buyers, stems from how well you are able to sell them on your reputability and trustworthiness as well as the extent to which they believe your product will benefit them. Ideas for getting loyal customers are explored throughout the rest of this book.

ACTIONABLE PROFESSIONAL LEARNING

Please respond individually initially, and then discuss with your collaborative learning team.

1. If you had to choose, which component of engagement—emotional, cognitive, or behavioral—would you say is the greatest challenge for you?

2. Part of the resolution of any issue begins with accurately identifying the issue at the outset. Think of your typical daily interactions with your students. What are a few of the specific barriers that prevent you from consistently engaging them?

   Barriers to emotional engagement

   Barriers to cognitive engagement

   Barriers to behavioral engagement

3. Though it may require a bit more planning and preparation, how might the development of an engaging educational practice benefit you and your students? Explain.

4. What strategies or methods have been most effective in helping you get students to buy into you and what you have to offer? How might you more effectively be able to garner more buy-in and increase sales in your practice?

5. Thinking of a few of your more engaging lessons, what are some common elements that were present in all?

   Teacher commonalities (e.g., great energy during delivery, emotionally expressive delivery, theatrical presentation of content)

   Student commonalities (e.g., actions, words they expressed about the lesson)

   Content commonalities (e.g., highly relevant to them, framed in their world)

   Lesson structure commonalities (e.g., interaction with peers, students moved, shorter periods of direct instruction)

Exploratory Observations

Arrange an observation of a lesson of each one of the members of your teaching team to be conducted by another team member. The purpose of the observation is to explore elements of engagement for your team. Elements to be examined are the following:

1. General student engagement in the classroom.

2. Component(s) of engagement (emotional, cognitive, or behavioral) that appear to be either significant strengths or significant challenges

3. Any other elements that may impact engagement in the room

During the next team meeting, have each member share two strengths and two challenges and any other interesting findings gleaned from observation of each teacher. Teachers can use the observations and shared feedback to identify areas of challenge to focus on.

2

Inspect to Inspire

Become a Scholar of Your Students

Preparing Student-Centered Pedagogy

What do Hollywood movie producers Martin Scorsese, Steven Spielberg, and Spike Lee all have in common? As you may know, they have enjoyed a level of success in engaging audiences with their production of movies. Though a great deal of their success can be attributed to their expertise in various production aspects of theatre, a significant portion lies in their

> Know me to reach me; then you can teach me!

relentless quest to design cinematic productions around the targeted moviegoers. That is, they work to uniquely design content around the targeted audience by continuously seeking as much information as they can about them.

Conversely, practices in teaching that sow the seeds of disengagement are (a) delivering content "as is" out of the textbook or curriculum guide, (b) not seeking to become more knowledgeable about their personal and academic sides of their students, and (c) not customizing the content itself and delivery thereof around their unique students. That's like Scorsese projecting, word for word, the subtitles of the script of his newly released movie on the screen at a randomly chosen theater in a randomly chosen country in the world. Chances are, moviegoers would not understand the language of the script, would dislike the genre of the movie, and would be profoundly bored by such a bland presentation. Of course Hollywood uses drama, music, and a host of theatrical elements to produce compellingly engaging movies. Their success rests on their producers' ability to obtain as much information as they can about their targeted demographic so they can create the perfect blend of art imitating life. They're able to create an enjoyable theatrical *experience.*

Make it an "experience".

Perhaps you'll agree that one of the most incredibly boring and seemingly meaningless situations you can be in is to sit through a class, program, or lecture where the content is remotely relevant and infinitesimally interesting, and provides little, if any, benefit to you. The most engaging deliverers of information are amply able to take *any* content and center it in the middle of the audience's world. They're relentless in their quest to continuously become more knowledgeable about all aspects of their students. It's the use of information-gathering techniques that enables them to make such engaging experiences possible. Simply put, the extent to which you enliven content and present it in engaging ways is inextricably tied to the techniques and tools that consistently assist you in gathering highly useful information about your students.

The core of an engaging educational practice is customized student-centered content. The hallmark of such a practice is that uninspiring content becomes inspirational—packaged in ways that draw students in and presented in ways that make them learn best. As stated throughout the book, irrespective of the program, lesson, activity, or event, everyone wants the WIFM question answered satisfactorily: What's in it for me? When you make the content about them, and develop and design instruction around their interests, issues, and preferences, you not only answer the WIFM question but also address the issue of how to consistently get them to buy in. You might ask the question, "What resources will help me consistently answer WIFM questions to their satisfaction?"

Content centered around experiences of the learner = deeper investment

Studying While Teaching: Creating a Pipeline of Continuously Flowing Information

Do you know where your students' personal and academic interests lie, the ways of learning they like most, and most important, the ways they learn best? One of the most frequent laments I hear from

professional learning session participants is that "my students just
don't care." All students have things that they care deeply about.
However, the challenge is identifying those things and artfully weav-
ing some of those elements into your instructional process. Uncovering
such information may be easier than you think.

Inspecting to inspire: Becoming a scholar of your students is
simply a method for consistently gathering information about students that can be utilized to make deeper emotional connections,
customizing content and then delivering it in ways that appeal to
your students.

When you study your students in such a way, the core content of
the learning involves in-depth case studies of both their personal and
academic sides. You're consciously cognizant of their preferred learning structures (e.g. individually, in pairs, or in small group), learning
styles (e.g., interpersonal, intrapersonal), and favorite modes of presenting what they've learned. You casually yet deliberately elicit
information about students' private lives, such as what their interests
are and how they spend recreational time. In essence, it is a technique
that helps you develop mastery of all facets of your students, such
that you become an expert, or a scholar of students. Tools that aid in
enhancing student scholarship are listed below.

Techniques for Becoming a Scholar of Your Students

The first five practical techniques for inspecting to inspire are not
earth shattering and don't require inordinate amounts of time to prepare but help you stay abreast of the kinds of things that make your
students tick. The techniques are as follows:

- Listen—then list
- The 5/3 rule
- Mining student writing
- Utilizing interest inventories
- Administering a learning profile

They all can be formally or informally conducted and modified to suit
your needs. Informal means of inspecting to inspire include having
casual conversations with students and collecting anecdotal pieces of
information about them as they interact with you and others throughout the day.

A sixth strategy, formally surveying your students, calls for a bit more planning and preparation, but it can be a tremendous asset in shaping pedagogy and practice in ways that get the buy-in and highly sought engagement.

Listen—Then List

[handwritten margin note: Convert idle chatter into recon.]

Students in high-poverty, urban, largely minority schools (HUMS) often talk openly and honestly about what they love to do, how their time is spent, and the things that mean the most to them. Informative looks into their world are opened by the windows of their words. Deliberately listening to them either quietly intimate or boisterously declare such thoughts is a pipeline for keeping your finger on the pulse of your pupils. They'll share *all* that you need to know about themselves, their personal affairs, and then some. At times, I have had to ask students politely to stop divulging so much personal information after the room was drowning in TMI (too much information). One class I had was so garrulous that I nicknamed them CNN— Classroom News Network!

[handwritten margin note: "Being aware" eavesdropping]

However, not only did I just listen to but also noted the critical nuggets they shared when speaking of their personal lives, such as where they liked to hang out, what they did with their families, how they *chose* to spend their free time, and those things that were near and dear to their hearts. Whether it was through engaging them in small talk with me, overhearing their formal and informal conversations with each other (either inside or outside the classroom), or through classroom discussions and dialogue, listening to the students and then listing critical points of their discussions afforded me access to a previously inaccessible world.

As implied, listen—then list involves listening to their words and listing or documenting what aids you in student scholarship. It provides a wealth of information about them, where they come from, and the kinds of things they can relate to. Consistently collecting such information equips you to customize both the content itself and the presentation thereof and to make the highly critical emotional connections. It goes a long way toward endearing them to you, garnering greater levels of trust and supportive actions on their part, and it simply places you in a more favorable light. Such instruction helps you turn disgruntled consumers of content into devoutly loyal classroom customers.

[handwritten margin note: Customization based on input from your consumer]

In a word, the shortest path to engagement is smoothly paved with content wrapped inside the interests and experiences of your

students. The key element in shaping such content in engaging ways lies in purposefully listening to versus hollowly hearing them. Their words are guides to the ever elusive destination of engagement. There are several ways to uncover information that can be used to create student-centered lessons, but I have found that one of the most valuable techniques is keenly listening and then noting what I've heard. The use of the information gleaned to customize instruction in engaging ways is detailed in Chapter 6.

The 5/3 Rule

The 5/3 rule is another tool I used to mine precious nuggets of information from the minds of my students. It entails simply asking the students about five ways they most frequently spend their free time and three things that mean the most to them. When I have asked these questions in the past, engaging in gaming, hanging with friends, spending time with family, and participating in a sport were common responses they provided about how they spent free time. Family, friends, and electronic gadgets (e.g., cell phones, iPods) were frequently cited as elements of great meaning to them. A few ways I then used their responses were as entrées or lead-ins to new content, examples to illustrate concepts, guides to restructure lessons, and ways to demonstrate mastery.

For example, I used family and friends as examples to contextualize content such as genetics, health and hygiene, and how viruses and bacteria are spread. Additionally, family and friends can be used to give meaning to social studies content (e.g., economic principles, impact of government legislation), as a literature focus, and in the application of some mathematical content. Asking thought-provoking questions and then having them investigate the underlying principles of how one of their favorite gadgets works (e.g., electromagnetic waves in cellular communication) is yet another illustration of how to wed their world with content. The 5/3 Rule simply unearths the mystery of what motivates your students and can be immensely helpful in customizing content and presenting it in enjoyable ways. It aids you in enhancing relevance and strategically bridging learning with their world.

Mining Student Writing

Have you ever had a student whose writing prowess and behavior were polar opposites? Erica, a young lady who often giggled at *everything*

A STRUGGLE TO JUGGLE

When Mrs. Jones was a first-year teacher, she felt a great deal of pressure to juggle all of the responsibilities heaped upon teachers, such as keeping pace with the pacing guide; checking and returning papers; and planning, preparing, and presenting quality instruction. However, one of the greatest classroom challenges she struggled to meet was sparking and holding the interest of her seventh graders. Three seventh graders who were personally responsible for early hair graying were Julio, Hector, and Martez. They acted as if her class time equated to nap time or music time and seized every free moment to lay their heads on their desks, or they put their hoodies on to conceal their headphones. Even worse, Tables 4 and 6 always engaged in idle off-task chatter whenever she turned her back to them.

Already anxious about the district's new teacher evaluation rubric, she knew from reading the weekly notes as well as information from staff meetings that 5-minute walk-throughs were beginning this week. However, she had no idea that one would occur on that rainy day. While she was busy assisting one student at her desk with the "Do-Now" (short task assigned at the beginning of each class), the assistant principal, Mr. Upshaw, slipped into the back of the room and sat quietly with his clipboard in one of the unoccupied desks. When she noticed Mr. Upshaw, she quickly finished with the student and then went to the front of the room and began the lesson.

Shortly after Mrs. Jones began her presentation, Ramona—a student who had otherwise been consistently cooperative, compliant, and on task—stood up and blurted out in a funny-sounding voice, "This stuff is boooooring!" Ramona then went to the front of the class, fell to the floor, and pretended to sleep and loudly snore. The class erupted in laughter. During the same lesson, Mrs. Jones had to gently nudge Julio's, Hector's, and Martez's heads off of the table on three separate occasions. She didn't realize that they had been listening to their headphones until Mr. Upshaw went to ask them to put them away. As she continued to try to get the lesson going, students were busily entertaining themselves. She sternly said, "I'll wait, I'll wait!" in an attempt to get them to quiet down. After 5 minutes of no success with that, she began attempting to speak over students' voices about how to identify the antagonist in a text. What was supposed to be a 5-minute walk-through ended up being an unnerving 30-minute observation, with Mr. Upshaw meticulously documenting the events of the day.

Later that day, Mrs. Jones found a sealed envelope on school stationery in her mailbox in the main office, and she knew what was in it. Most of the ratings on the observation sheet were "unsatisfactory." She met with Mr. Upshaw during her prep period; he began the meeting by asking, "How do you think the visit went?" She promised herself she would stay strong and not get emotional during the debriefing conference, but her eyes welled with tears before she could get the first word out. "It was *awful!*" Mr. Upshaw gave her a box of tissues, consoled her a bit, and allowed her to finish sobbing. "Mr. Upshaw, I know I could do better, but I am really struggling with how to reach them, how to keep them interested and engaged in my class. I know I blew it, but I am giving my *all* to that class!"

Mr. Upshaw said, "Just remember this one piece of advice. You can't control what you teach, but can *change* how it's delivered. Start by being more aware of what you hear them say about how they choose to spend free time and what means the most to them, and contextualize learning in ways they can relate to. That will help you begin to plan lessons that place content in their world. That's where you start. I'll send the building substitute to free you for a few periods to observe some of your colleagues who have mastered ways of studying students and using that to frame learning around them."

The colleagues Mrs. Jones observed suggested she not try to change too much at once but instead take a technique or two and work on them for about eight weeks or so, until she could use them perfectly. Using the 5/3 rule, she began meticulously documenting information that she overheard in conversations between students and that was shared in dialogue with her. With at least two assignments each week, she added one question about some personal information, such as how the students liked to spend free time, what they valued most in life, and the types of experiences they'd had. The first few lessons she delivered with content framed around such personalized information didn't go exactly as planned. Her headphone listeners still attempted their usual, and Julio and Hector tried to doze off to sleep. However, Martez and Tables 4 and 5 were much more attentive (for most of the lesson), as they appeared to appreciate the tailoring of the learning for them.

As the weeks passed, the off-task behaviors continued to occur, but with far less frequency. Students more readily responded to that one question or prompt that elicited a bit of personal information about them, as they seemed to begin to realize the benefit of sharing such information. Mrs. Jones still struggled to juggle all of the other responsibilities but developed a more discernibly interesting and engaging delivery of content. During the last academic quarter of school, she even developed a short seven-item survey that elicited more information about how they liked to learn and ways their learning experience could be improved.

during class, was the perfect example. She would often do things that broke classroom rules, stayed on task only intermittently, and was *quite* the classroom social butterfly. However, Erica had a keen ability to produce impeccably composed, voluminous writing. She had an eloquent way of expressing her innermost thoughts in a very compelling way, particularly when writing in her journal. She was quiet when asked to explain her playful behavior but constructed well-developed paragraphs and essays when committing words to paper.

Similarly, some students are introverted or, for other reasons, are highly resistant to expressing inner thoughts aloud or even giving surface-level information about themselves. A second method I have used for investigating while teaching is mining students' journal entries for their RIMs, (things relevant, interesting, and meaningful to them). The particular RIMs I noted were these:

- How leisure time was voluntarily spent
- Elements of popular culture most frequently mentioned or fondly referenced
- Personal things, people, or places they greatly valued
- Any other thing(s) that were of interest to them

How Can Mining Student Writing Be Used to Glean Information About My Students?

A few ways I collected information via journal mining were these:

1. Having students write about some aspect of content experienced in or related to daily activities (e.g., observing the pooling of water around a glass of ice water in the room).
2. Having students respond to contextualized writing prompts involving information you've collected about them.
3. Affording choice in writing—allowing students to write about content in their own unique way.

Utilizing Interest Inventories

Chances are you've used this data-gathering instrument at some point in the school year, in one form or another, perhaps at the beginning of the school year. Interest inventories (see appendix on page 177) are questionnaires that aim to uncover students' tastes, interests, and preferences. They cover areas such as favorite genre of music and preferred modes of electronic communication, and several other preferred elements of both academic and personal life are assessed. How to best utilize this tool depends on your students and whether other members of your teaching team are using it as well.

I often administered this inventory at the beginning of the school year and subsequently selected questions to ask students in an informal way throughout the school year. Continuously posing a few questions from this instrument helped me stay up to date with students' fluidly changing interests. If other members of my teaching team were planning to utilize such an inventory, I found it best to select just a few questions to ask myself as a means of avoiding redundancy.

Administering a Learning Profile

You know that learning modalities vary from student to student, but how much do you really know about the differences in learning preferences that exist among your learners? Learning profiles assist you with gaining more insight into the intricacies of the preferred ways students learn. Learning about where, under what conditions, and how tasks are preferred to be completed are a few of the insights yielded by such instruments. I have found the Learning Profile Questionnaire: How Do You Like to Learn? developed by Denise Murphy and Beth Ann Potter (Tomlinson, 2001, p. 70) to be highly useful.

Utilizing Student Surveys to Inform and Improve Instruction

From your experience as a preservice teacher to your time teaching in the classroom, you have probably received enough feedback from supervisors and administrators to compile a technical educational manual. At most schools, an administrator visits each classroom for either formal or informal observations at least four times a year, and some visit as frequently as two or three times a week. Consultants, coaches, and colleagues routinely sit in, observe your teaching, and provide feedback about various aspects, such as how effectively you use questioning techniques. After the administrative observations, you sometimes receive narrative summaries of observations that total three or four pages and detail aspects of instructional design, delivery of content, and management practices.

Have you considered soliciting the feedback of those who witness you *in action* more than 9,000 instructional minutes per academic year—your students? Indeed, they know more about facets of your teaching than anyone else.

Students are very candid if given a voice (needed)

Kindergarten through twelfth-grade classrooms are one of the few places where a service is delivered and the opinions of the direct recipients of the service are, by and large, ignored. Perhaps this is because the law in most states mandates that students *have* to show up, whether instruction is characterized by powerful practices or is pedagogically porous. Their thoughts about quality of service may be ignored because of the discomfort that comes with the candor that attaches itself to *student talk*. That is, opening yourself up to student critique is the public exposure of your professional practice.

If students' opinions were valued, student feedback would be an essential element in the process of continuous improvement. In asking many teachers why they don't elicit feedback from their students, many publicly lament they don't have time while privately intimating that they fear being scorned by scathing critiques and the brutal honesty of students' words. They avoid being run over by the reality of open honesty and unadulterated candor. Teachers expect students to show up on time, stay seated, and summarize or share information when summoned. Irrespective of their reasons for ignoring students' evaluation of instructional quality, they have to ask themselves who is better positioned to provide critical feedback than the primary recipients of service?

Why consistently survey your students? Surveys can yield a wealth of information, which can be utilized to better craft instruction around them.

Evaluate for improvement

- Exemplary professional practices, which improve over time, have embedded structures that continuously evaluate effectiveness and yield insight for improvement.

invest/buy in

- When information from surveys is used to make improvements, it helps students become vested and sells them on buying in.

becomes student centered

- When the process of improving educational practices is driven by student survey data, it more effectively centers the learning experience around the students, leading to higher levels of engagement.

student empowerment

continuous customization

- Utilizing surveys empowers students, giving them a sense that they have voice.
- Surveys can assist in continuously customizing the learning in more engaging ways and developing deeper emotional bonds with students.

Student surveys allow you to examine your own teaching and overall learning environment from *their* vantage point. It's the ticket to courtside seats at the exhibition of your instructional prowess.

Basics of Designing Your Student Survey

It goes without saying that the type of items (e.g., questions) you include in your survey are dictated by the information you are seeking. If you administer the survey regularly, such as biweekly, you'll want to parse the number of items to address only the most critical issues. If you're looking to develop a more engaging practice, design your survey in such a way that it elicits students' thoughts about such topics as pacing, ease of understanding of content, and the degree to which topics themselves and their presentation holds their interest.

Open-Ended Versus Closed-Ended Questions

When designing your survey, one of the strongest considerations should be to create something that doesn't overwhelm you—that is, you want to be able to create, administer, review, and summarize the responses relatively quickly. If you're planning to administer the survey on a regular basis (e.g., biweekly or monthly), I would suggest you include mostly closed-ended questions with an open-ended question or two at the end. As you probably recall from a college course, open-ended questions widen the parameters for providing a response. They can't be answered with a simple "yes" or "no" response.

Closed-ended questions can be answered with a "yes" or "no" or a selection from a predetermined set of responses. You may want to provide closed-ended, Likert-like choices—for example, providing students with statements and asking them to respond with a 1 if they disagree, a 2 if they somewhat disagree, a 3 if they agree, and a 4 if they strongly agree. Figure 1 gives some examples of questions you could include in your survey.

Addressing the Issue of Time

You may be thinking, "Jelani, that sounds wonderful in theory, but I simply don't have time or room to add one more thing to my plate." Invariably, many of the teachers who vehemently oppose administering such surveys are the ones I've seen struggle with issues of engagement. Indeed, teachers are asked routinely to get results without resources (e.g., time, materials), hit constantly moving achievement targets, and make miracles out of muck.

Consider dedicating 10 minutes of a specific period every other week for students to complete the feedback survey, and continue to strongly encourage honest thoughts about what you have provided. Figure 2 provides some additional considerations for administering

Figure 1   Items That Could Be Included in Your Survey

- What type of teaching helps you learn best?
- Which method of teaching is most engaging/boring?
- Do you think that I go too fast/slow when I teach?
- Have I adjusted/changed my teaching in ways that help you learn better?
- Are there chances for you to be successful during each lesson?
- Which grouping arrangement (e.g., groups, pairs) helps you learn best?
- Would you say that the information taught is something you can relate to?
- Do the examples I provide when teaching help make the content clearer?
- Do I use enough examples from the real world in lessons?
- Do I apply the ideas of the lesson to the real world?
- Thinking of the times I use colorful pictures, diagrams, and words, would you say colors help you remember information?
- What would you like to have more of in the classroom?
- Are there times where you can make a personal connection to the lesson or have personal thoughts about it?
- Would you say I provide equal chances for all students to contribute to class discussions?
- Are directions for classroom assignments usually clear?
- Would you say that you or other students are treated fairly after you break rules?
- Do you think that different consequences unfairly apply to different students?
- What types of things can I do more of to help you be successful?
- Do I acknowledge and value of your ideas, perspectives, and opinions?
- Am I a good listener when you are talking?
- Do I use students' opinions to make the classroom a better place?
- Do you feel you are an important member of this classroom community?
- Are there other types of things I should change to improve your classroom experience? (please be specific)

Figure 2   Additional Considerations for Designing Your Survey

- *Overemphasize the notion that the survey is a tool designed to improve the overall learning experience for* them. State this in the directions on the survey itself and verbally highlight it as well. Students with an ax to grind may feel that noncompliance will be a preemptive strike against you. Keeping the focus on student benefits removes that ammunition from their arsenal. Indicating that it is something that will benefit them answers the WIFM question and provides a greater incentive for them to complete the survey.
- *Keep the survey short and concise.* Avoid creating so many items that their number serves as a disincentive to forthrightly respond to questions. I have found that 10 or fewer questions usually works best for middle and high school. Though surveys developed by psychometricians may include multiple items to measure a given construct, using one or, at most, two items should suffice for your purposes. Students will tell you that if they feel that a task is too cumbersome or monotonous, they are likely to randomly mark answers to speed toward completion.

- *Avoid questions lacking the needed substance to achieve survey objectives.* For example, questions such as whether you are their favorite teacher are inconsequential. Comparisons such as these invite personal attacks and do little to improve the overall quality of the learning experience.
- *Be careful not to make the survey an additional item on your already overfilled plate of things to do.* I thought that administering the survey monthly enabled me to get the desired information without being overwhelmed by having to analyze responses. Start small with perhaps a couple of closed-ended questions and one open-ended one.
- *Maintain their anonymity.* This point is fairly self-explanatory, as you know that students are much less likely to open up to provide candid responses that could benefit you if they feel they can be identified.

your survey that will help you encourage students to fill it out honestly and make the best use of your time and theirs.

Analyzing and Using Your Survey Results

Wear your emotional Teflon while reading! Even as I review participants' evaluations of my professional learning sessions, I have to don my emotional armor to keep from interpreting such responses as a personal attack. A few responses in any survey often emanate from issues that have nothing to do with you! On the other hand, some are brutally honest yet brazenly accurate. Whichever is the case, don't take them personally, and of course, be careful not to respond to such responses punitively.

Make a concerted effort to substantively address concerns indicated by your synthesized data. Although it is logistically impossible to address every issue indicated by each student, there will certainly be some commonalities across survey responses. These are the ones you want to focus on and address. Several students, for instance, may indicate that you are moving too fast or that you don't provide enough explanation when introducing concepts. I thought it was always good to verbally acknowledge such responses after analyzing my surveys by saying something like,

> I see that several of you are concerned with the pacing of the lesson. I really appreciate your candor and you taking the time to complete the surveys. After doing a little thinking this weekend about this issue, this week I will definitely slow the pace and provide more examples to ensure you all are getting it before we move on.

Students will quickly become resistant to completing the survey if they rarely, if ever, see any evidence that their suggestions are put into practice.

How Else Can Feedback Be Elicited?

There are many other ways to get these important pieces of information, and it is a good idea to provide other avenues for students to provide feedback in between the times that surveys are administered. You could provide a feedback or issue box or just reemphasize the fact that you're there for them to approach if there is a pressing issue that needs to be addressed before the next survey is administered. Begin with posing one or two survey items that get to the heart of the essential elements you intend to assess. If you want to improve your practice, make the learning more engaging, and unlock the keys for connecting with them, make survey use a staple of what you do. You'll actually save time in the end by making what you do more efficient, making the learning more powerful by using what you learned from the survey results, and having to address fewer discipline issues because of your more student-centered practice. Administering surveys and then adjusting accordingly gives rise to student voice and often procures the buy-in. They'll give more to you after realizing your willingness to flexibly mold practice around them.

Chapter Summary

Thoroughly inspecting various facets of your learners certifies you as a scholar of your students. There is no secret to discovering how to craft the engaging experience, as it is it is packaged in their spoken words and present in their penned thoughts. Techniques that continuously inform you of both academic and personal aspects of learners are invaluable elements of becoming a student scholar. Listen—then list, the 5/3 rule, mining student writing, interest inventories, learning profiles, and student surveys are the foundation on which engaging practices are erected. Such tools enhance your ability to make the complex more comprehensible and the foreign more familiar and to turn dry content into dynamic learning.

ACTIONABLE PROFESSIONAL LEARNING

Please respond individually initially, and then discuss with your collaborative learning team.

1. In what ways (name specific techniques) are you are able to continuously gather information about the personal lives and experiences of your students?

2. How have you been able to incorporate the information gleaned into your teaching?

3. Using the findings from the informal observations of teaching conducted by your team, engage in dialogue about how becoming a scholar of your students might assist with the main areas of improvement identified by colleagues in the Actionable Professional Learning section in Chapter 1.

Collaborative Inquiry

Using the framework provided in this chapter and sample survey items provided as a guide, collaborate on the development of a short survey to be completed by the students taught by your teaching team. The aim of the survey is to elicit insight into their world (e.g., preferences, interests, meaningful phenomena) and their thoughts about the extent to which the content and delivery they receive at school engage them. Review the findings during your next meeting with an emphasis on using the implications of the results as a way to make your practice more engaging.

1. What are a couple of significant questions relating to becoming a better scholar of students need further investigation?

2. Have each team member select one of the first five techniques for studying students mentioned in this chapter and put it into practice. Use the following to frame dialogue about the technique's effectiveness during an upcoming meeting: What were a few of your major findings (For example, in what ways do your students like to learn? How are they spending free time? What are some common threads among the things of great meaning to students?) What remaining challenges are there for continually collecting information about your students?

3

Nurture Their Attributes

Turn Commonly Perceived
Deficits Into Classroom Deposits

Imagine, for a moment, that you took a trip to Las Vegas. On the day you are to return home, you check out of the hotel and then stop to get lunch on the way to the airport. To your surprise, when you get ready to pay the bill, you realize your return airline ticket is gone, as are your wallet and cellular telephone. All you have left is four dollars. To add insult to injury, your flight leaves in 3 hours. What would you do, in such a high-pressure situation, to get home?

> Building on what they bring is the bridge for them to buy.

Perhaps you would miss your flight, but with some innovation and the assistance of family and friends, you would *find* a way to make it home. Is the challenge of teaching in a K–12 classroom at times similar to being stranded in Vegas without a way to get home? Districts, schools, and administrators mandate that teachers *raise* test scores in short order. There's also a daily push to get the lesson *off the ground* and safely help students arrive at the desired instructional outcomes. However, are there times when you look into the eyes of your students and there seems to be nothing there to get the lesson off the ground? Would it be possible that some of the most important resources you need sit squarely in those 30 desks in front of you?

> *Make it about them; move them to your tune.*

In many high-poverty, urban, largely minority schools (HUMS), affinities for social interaction, expressive movement, and other nontraditional attributes of students are often perceived as deficits that drain the forward movement of the lesson. For example, an element ubiquitously present in every class I taught was students' insatiable desire to socialize with one another. "Why can't they just shut their mouths, stay seated, and get to work?" I often wondered to myself. When they did not comply with classroom rules, I could respond only with the execution of strokes of ink across discipline referrals. I often wished there were some way I could eliminate the constant *chatter*. Indeed, the ways to teach highlighted in the district-mandated curriculum guide and teacher's manual stood in stark contrast to what the students were used to outside of school. It was as if there was a definitive disconnect between the way lessons were structured, the content itself, and how it was presented. Such differences often lead to achievement gap–widening disparities.

Deficit theory attempts to account for the achievement gap of Latino/a Americans, African Americans and other children in HUMS. An assumption of deficit-based theory is that these students and parents need to be resocialized through the process of education because of existing deficiencies in upbringing, knowledge, and skills. Deficit thinking asserts that the families of nonwhite students are behind their poor academic performance, for two reasons: The students come to school lacking normal skills and knowledge, and the parents assign little value to and are not supportive of the education of their children (Yosso, 2005). The patterns of such culture are frequently considered at best deviant and at worst pathological. The impact of such perceived deficits may have more grave consequences. Hilliard (1992) put it best:

> Unfortunately, educationalists tend to treat the stylistic mismatch between some students and schools as a student deficiency, that is, as a problem that requires students to change. As a result, we fail to see the potential for enriching the school experience for all children. Moreover, we fail to see that the traditional school style has severe limitations. (p. 373)

I argue that many of the attributes that are thought of as deficiencies and deficits can be accentuated and utilized as powerful tools which enhance learning. These attributes, such as students' affinity for rhythm and interpersonal interactions, are implicitly dismissed if learning in school rarely incorporates them.

Students bring with them a plethora of strengths, talents, and attributes into classrooms each day. Critically looking back through the windows of reflection during my first years of teaching, I realized I needed to rethink some of the ways things were done. The delivery methods I leaned on most allowed very little student interaction. Like an almighty ruler of the classroom kingdom, I had to control every element of what went on. I was guilty of violating one of Vygotsky's (1978) theories of learning, which is that true learning happens best when it involves a series of social interactions. I became frustrated and then fed up with having discipline issues greedily *gobble* chunks of instructional time. Understanding that I couldn't place the most challenging students on long-term suspension, I knew if I didn't find a different way, I would quickly find myself out of a job and into to another career.

As a result of reflecting on my practice, strategies gleaned from workshops, reading, and advice from competent educators, I asked myself some critical questions: "What are the strengths and other attributes my students bring into the classroom? How could I harness those attributes in ways that are assets to the process of learning?" Subtle nuances and other invaluable information about them were revealed through an ongoing study of students. Additionally, after surveying hundreds of HUMS teachers during workshops over the years, I have compiled a list of the student attributes most often cited as deficits in the classroom; this list is shown in Figure 3.

Figure 3   Frequently Perceived Deficits of HUMS Students

- Incessantly desiring to socialize with others
- Lacking skills and knowledge possessed by dominant culture
- Being very communicative
- Wanting to constantly move around the classroom
- Wanting to be the center of attention
- Being easily distractible
- Showing defiance/strong-willed
- Being unmotivated
- Not caring about learning
- Loving rhythm/music/tapping
- Consistently doodling
- Displaying linguistic creativity
- Having poor literacy skills
- Consistently desiring to debate authority figures
- Using nonstandard English
- Having a love for verve and highly stimulating learning

You can't control who enrolls, but you can uniquely craft their enrichment.

The theoretical framework below describes how building on students' strengths could be effective.

THEORETICAL FRAMEWORK: UNDERLYING REASONS FOR BUILDING ON STRENGTHS

- To assist all students in being successful, teachers must not only be knowledgeable and appreciative of differences in student's experiences; it is essential that they build on cultural strengths as well (Horowitz, Darling-Hammond, & Bransford, 2005).
- When teachers capitalize on assets children bring to the classroom, the children's cognitive and academic performance is enhanced (Boutte, 1999).
- Knowledge of students' culture and community can be used as a vehicle that enhances learning (Ladson-Billings, 2001).
- Latino/a and other nonwhite students enter school with an abundance of untapped and unrecognized abilities, skills, and knowledge evincing the rich cultural wealth of their communities. Marginalized student populations bring with them six types of cultural wealth (Yosso, 2005).
- Building on English language learners' (ELLs') linguistic resources enhances not only content mastery but also proficiency in English (Lucas & Katz, 1994).
- As Latino/as and African Americans speak, they expect the person who is listening to actively engage them through both vocal responses and body movement (Gay, 2010).
- Both African American and Latino/a students achieve more when learning is structured in cooperative groups (Johnson & Johnson, 1985; Webb & Farivar, 1994).
- When certain cultural attributes are integrated into the learning and performance environments of African American children, they learn at high levels (Boykin, 1994).
- African American students' experiences in the community and at home are characterized by the formation of group identity, interpersonal relationships, and shared responsibility. Communal learning methods, which include such elements, can be utilized to enhance the motivation and learning of African American learners (Hurley, Boykin, & Allen, 2005). Learning is enhanced for low-income African American children when contextualized with music and the opportunity for movement expression (Allen & Boykin, 1991; Allen & Butler, 1996). Students are more effectively able to problem-solve when working cooperatively versus competitively (Qin, Johnson, & Johnson, 1995).

- Students perform better when they learn in peer tutoring groups (McDuffie, Mastropieri, & Scruggs, 2009)
- Latina/o students have been found to be more engaged when working with groups and taking part in academic conversations (Yair, 2000).
- The social interactions of peers are characterized by invaluable exchanges of skills and information in which students make cognitive adjustments by relating to others at their same developmental level (Vygotsky, 1978).
- Relationships among peers promote social and academic motivation for students to learn (Wentzel, 1999).
- When teachers affirm, legitimate, and invite students' out-of-school literacies into the classroom, they are able to leverage their affinity for out-of-school literacies, increase school literacy success and engagement, and dispel deficit perspectives on HUMS students (Skerrett & Bomer, 2011).
- Students participate in higher level, complex literacy practices at home, during afterschool activities, in unofficial worlds, and via the World Wide Web (Black & Steinkuhler, 2009; Vadeboncoeur & Stevens, 2005).

Turning Commonly Perceived Deficits Into Classroom Deposits

Once the list was compiled, the next challenge was figuring out how I could turn those attributes into academic assets or deposits. I knew I couldn't change who enrolled but could control how I enriched them once they were there. That is, one of the most powerful changes I made was to focus on those elements that were well within my grasp and to continually think of ways I could use them as tools to aid instruction. Hurley, Boykin, and Allen (2005) highlight the centrality of implementing pedagogy that turns perceived deficits into deposits:

> More broadly, these findings support the notion that the configuration of the environment in which learning takes place is critical in determining how well and how much children learn. These data support the assertion that the incorporation of culturally familiar themes into learning contexts may facilitate students' acquisition of new competencies by allowing them to function in familiar cognitive modes and by allowing them to build on existing competencies, in this case, their familiarity and facility with group interaction. (p. 523)

Strong Penchant for Interacting With Others

I absolutely loved to have the classroom noise level so low that the only sounds you heard were the strokes of pens across papers. However, I often struggled to maintain this tranquility while teaching. I thought that if I was the only one who spoke during lecture and periodically gave students permission to respond to a question or ask me questions, it would minimize the chance of chaotic events occurring. Instead, there was a revolving door of students going in and out of my classroom as they almost refused to stay quiet when asked to do so.

While working on research for a graduate paper, I stumbled across an article espousing the notion that it's a best practice to embrace what children bring to the party as assets of instruction. Investigating a bit further, I found out that there were methods to take the unique yet negatively perceived qualities students bring into the learning environment and harness them as assets. Such qualities, like a strong desire to have social interactions and being rhythmically oriented, had the potential to positively transform the classroom climate and enhance the overall learning process.

I gradually began using more peer-interactive strategies, which gave my students an opportunity to engage in social interactions and simultaneously learn. As I did before introducing any major change to them, I shared with them the benefit-laden *why*. I said,

> You all have this strong desire to talk to each other during class. Many of you have gotten in trouble, and in the past you have been sent out of the room. I am going to teach in a bit different way and allow you all to communicate more with each other while learning. I really believe it will be more effective in helping you learn and make learning more enjoyable as well.

Experience has taught me never to explore more than one or two new teaching techniques at a time, so I started with think-pair-share (Lyman, 1981) and similar strategies where they discussed content with a partner and then shared with the larger group. Think-pair-share (TPS) seemed to be a perfect fit for them, and I was amazed at how it aided elements of the learning process. It motivated them to discuss more than before. When I posed questions for pairs to ponder, discuss, and share, the quality and volume of responses contributed to richer classroom discussions. Students seemed to enjoy talking about the content versus thinking and responding in isolation. It was somewhat of a conversational spark, as students relished the support given by the pairing process.

Though this technique successfully enhanced cognitive and behavioral engagement, students seemed to grow tired of doing this almost every day. Additionally, I was in need of other ways to group more students who could engage in more in-depth learning.

Though I remembered it from my methods courses, I rarely used the technique of cooperative learning. Afraid to loosen my tightly gripped hands, which were clenched around all learning processes in my room, I never gave serious thought to it. In my mind, giving my students some autonomy to learn by themselves was a prescription for classroom chaos and confusion. But I was inspired by the success of the interactivity stimulated by TPS, and so I gave cooperative learning a try.

Of course I heard the usual student complaints, like "I don't want to work with him," "I want to work with the smart group," and "Why is it that only two of us did all of the work but all four got credit?" After using it approximately once per week for five weeks, the biggest challenge that remained was helping to develop the necessary interpersonal skills to successfully get the things done.

Lucas & Katz (1994) explored nine exemplary K–12 settings for ELLs. Among the effective instructional techniques, they described how teachers of ELLs engaged students in activities whereby they could use their native languages with each other.

Table 1 features ways other perceived deficits can be turned into deposits.

Paroling Students From Seat Incarceration: Using Movement as a Tool

One of the best ways to invite boredom, apathy, and disinterest into your lesson is by sentencing your students to seat incarceration. We inadvertently incarcerate students in seats if there are few opportunities to move out of the seat during the lesson. The benefits of movement while learning, such as greater levels of blood and oxygen going to the brain, have been well documented, and I won't devote any attention to them. There are several ways to free students from seats and use movement as a learning tool, but I have found a few to be highly engaging:

- With processes such as mitosis, algorithms for division, the order of events in a story, or how a bill becomes law, type (or place a picture of) each major step, event, or idea on a separate page in a word processing document. Print out each page on

Table 1   Changing Perceived Deficits Into Deposits

Attribute Often Perceived as Deficit	Process(es) to Change Into Deposit	Resources

Strong penchant for interacting/ socializing with others	• Utilize more peer-interactive strategies
	   o Communal learning
	   o Think-pair-share
	   o Peer tutoring
	   o Cooperative grouping
	   o Collaborative writing
		• Hurley, Boykin, & Allen (2005)
		 • Lyman (1981)
		 • McDuffie, Mastropieri, & Scruggs (2009)
		 • Webb & Farivar (1994)
		 • Yarrow & Topping (2001)

Nontraditional communicative discourse/ Emergent English language learning	• Include more participatory-interactive classroom discourse
	   o Call-and-response
	   o Signifying
	 • Providing literature that features native dialect
	 • Teach elements of code switching
	 • Engage in activities that build on students' linguistic capital or various communication and language skills (e.g., communicating using poetry, music, art, social tools of vocabulary, storytelling)
	 • Enlist the support of parents as expert partners in students' biliteracy development
		• Gay (2010)
		 • Hecht, Jackson, & Ribeau (2003)
		 • Wheeler & Swords (2006)
		 • Garza & Nava (2005)
		 • Yosso (2005)
		 • Lucas & Katz (1994)
		 • www.cultureforkids.com
		 • Taylor, Bernhard, Garg, & Cummins (2008)

Emotionally expressive	• Provide avenues to express emotion in nondisruptive, respectful ways o Frequently celebrate classroom wins • Offer times where students can discuss emotional concerns with you	• Nangle, Erdley, Carpenter, & Newman (2002) • Prinz, Blechman, & Dumas (1994)
Defiant posture/ strong-willed/ argumentative	• Provide opportunities to debate positions on topics • Elicit student voice and input • Give chance to earn leadership roles in classroom • Charge with responsibility to lead discussion/teach small chunks of information • During presentations, intentionally include and explicitly express student benefits from the learning	• Shuster & Meany (2005)

Attribute Often Perceived as Deficit	Process(es) to Change Into Deposit	Resources
Wanting to constantly move around the classroom	• Assess mastery by having students respond to true/false or multiple choice questions by actually moving to designated areas of room • Give groups copies of stages of processes, cycles, order of events, timelines, etc. Have group members properly arrange selves in correct order/sequence	• Gurian & Stevens (2010) • See Paroling Students From Seat Incarceration
Wanting to be the center of attention	• Provide multiple opportunities for students to demonstrate mastery in their uniquely designed ways in front of peers	• Silver, Strong, & Perini (2007)
Easily distractible	• Limit direct instruction to 10 minutes • Provide more upbeat pacing of lesson	• Lemov (2010)
Unmotivated/ chronically bored/uncaring attitude toward learning	• Wed instruction with RIMs (relevant, interesting, meaningful things) • Integrate information gleaned from student study • Provide instruction addressing favored learning modalities • Create situations of success	• Techniques for becoming a scholar of students (Chapter 2)
Relish rhythm, music/tapping/ dancing	• Provide opportunity to create presentations with music • Play various kinds of background music to set tone	• See Chapter 6, Intersecting Their Interests and Experience With Instruction • www.live365.com
Love doodling	• Afford students latitude to sketch or draw to show understanding	• Walker-Tileston (2010)
Linguistically creative	• Assign classroom tasks that give latitude to use linguistic creativity to *show what they know* • Poem, rap, song lyrics	• www.educationalrap.com • www.flocabulary.com
Embrace verve	• Facilitate and produce high-impact delivery techniques with stimulating phenomena	• See Chapter 6

card stock, and give each student a card. Direct students to arrange themselves so that the cards show the correct order of the process. Then ask them to justify why they believe their positions to be correct. In math, print variables, symbols, and numbers on the cards, and have the students arrange themselves in such a way as to make an equation true. Endless variations of this can be used in all content areas.

- As opposed to having students simply give a verbal reply indicating which answer they believe to be true or whether they agree or disagree with a statement, post letters (A and D, or agree and disagree) in different sections of the classroom. As you pose questions or make statements, have students physically go to the area near the letter that represents their response. Ask them to collaborate to tell you why they selected that response.
- Have groups physically demonstrate various types of motion (e.g., atoms in science) or other phenomena.

Students' desire to move around the room, and the fact that they do not have enough self-discipline to stay seated, is a concern for teachers in most K–8 classrooms. Utilizing movement as a tool to aid learning effectively turns this oft-perceived deficit into a classroom deposit. As is shown in the vignette that follows, there are several additional ways to use movement as a tool (see also Chapter 6).

THE TURNAROUND QUEEN

Mrs. Jones was known by her colleagues as the turnaround queen, as she had a keen ability to turn irritating student actions into things that positively aided the classroom. One of her students, Caleb, a lanky seventh grader who towered over his classmates, was always getting sent out of his classes for disciplinary reasons. You could count on Caleb to do either one of two things: (1) create an irritating sound and then scan the room with a smirk on his face in anticipation of approving laughter from his classmates, or (2) create rhythmic beats or sounds with his mouth, hands, feet, or pencil on a desk or any object he could use. As a result, Mrs. Jones's colleagues consistently sent him to the school's dean of discipline.

The teaching team expressed their concern about Caleb during a weekly team meeting and pleaded for Mrs. Jones to share her strategies that worked with Caleb. She said,

> I pulled Caleb aside after class and told him that I admired the talent he had for creatively producing sounds. I asked him if he had ever thought about a career in sound production, because that seems to be his *calling*. I even told him that I thought some of his beats rocked! You should have

seen his eyes light up. I went on to say, I am going to give you the oppor-tunity to be our resident sound engineer. You can assist me with working the AV equipment, provide drum rolls to generate anticipation, and take on a few other special assignments from time to time. And to lighten the mood on Mondays, I'll give you 30 seconds before the lesson begins to showcase one of your new sounds or rhythmic beats.

But do you know what I need from you in return? As artistically creative as they are, we need you to make those sounds only during the appropriate times. I had him tell me specific times that weren't appropriate.

Now, he *beams* with pride from being entrusted to have such an esteemed role. At times, he still makes inappropriate noises, but it happens much less frequently. I've even brought in biographies of exemplars in the sound pro-duction industry, and he realizes he's similar to them in some ways.

She went on to tell her colleagues that many of the annoying behaviors that students exhibit in class are really hidden talents that need to be redirected in different ways. It is key not to be dismissive of the attribute but instead to find the talent in it and ways to feature and use it as part of the learning.

What Other Assets Do Students in HUMS Bring to the Table?

Can you answer the following questions?

- How do you do the *Dougie* or *Big Girl Hustle* dances?
- What do you do to defuse a situation when being threatened by gang members?
- What are *zillions* and *kinky twists?*
- How are smoked greens prepared?
- How can Goya best be described?
- To *ear hustle* is do what?

Patricia Fripp says it best, "You are the expert of your own experi-ence." In that vein, life's experiences have honed a level of expertise in many of the areas above for HUMS students. Their everyday lives relate to aspects of urban popular culture. Many are so profoundly knowledgeable in these areas that they could teach a minicourse about them. What does being a pundit on pop culture and other cultural aspects of urban students have to do with engagement and teaching?

The greatest comedians deliver highly engaging performances because of their ability to wed elements of popular culture with the content of their routine. Televangelists skillfully use pop culture referents to illustrate what some consider otherwise dry biblical principles, or as lead-ins to draw the audience in at the beginning of a broadcast. Similarly, HUMS teachers who have developed an engaging practice do not ignore or render irrelevant the cultural capital students bring to the table. They artfully utilize it as an integral element of engaging their students. Giroux and Simon (1989) best illustrate the point: "Educators who refuse to acknowledge popular culture as a significant basis of knowledge often devalue students by refusing to work with the knowledge that students already have" (p. 3).

Such funds of knowledge brought into the classroom are often dismissed as at best illegitimate or at worst irrelevant. However, the integration of such elements into teaching provides foundation on which teachers can execute empirically based best teaching practices. That is, students' expertise in everyday life can be used to activate their prior knowledge, facilitate connections between curricular content and their everyday lives, and enhance the application of content principles, and it will likely give them a more positive outlook on you! Additionally, everyday life expertise can be used as a beginning point to teach ideas and as a wonderful way to bring ideas to life.

For example, when teaching about the culinary traditions of various world cultures, you can lead in by activating students' prior knowledge of dishes from their own culture. There are a limitless number of ways you can contextualize the learning in math, such as calculating costs, understanding percent increases and decreases, or creating and interpreting scatter plots associated with zillions and kinky twists. Chapter 6 delves into greater detail about how it's done.

Customizing Lessons With Student Personas

The planning and preparation of your lesson should rest on the findings from your study of students. After a few weeks with them, you should have demystified what their topics of interest are, what consumes their attention outside of school, and which things mean the most to them. Your tools for learning about them will help you in designing a blueprint for customizing instruction that is the right fit for them, what I call their *student persona*.

A student persona embodies the typical characteristics of all of your students wrapped into one. It's like an abbreviated biography and descriptive representation of your students. Student personas inform you about the preferences of the atypical student as they relate to the following: multimedia and images, goals and aspirations, common phrases and expressions, common life issues and challenges, top challenges with instruction, daily activities, common interests, and learning preferences.

To begin to customize learning during instructional planning, I created separate personas for males and females and gave each a name. My student personas were Nyisha and Nathan. Nathan loved interactive lessons involving movement; high-energy, peer-interactive strategies; and opportunities to demonstrate what he learned in front of the class in his own unique way. He spent long hours engaged in competitive video gaming, and loved both playing and watching basketball and football. Creating and reciting clever rap lyrics and watching rap videos also consumed his time out of school. In school, his pronounced challenges included reading comprehension and expressing thoughts in a written form, while making better decisions before acting and being strong enough to think for himself challenged him both in and out of school. He had to uphold his *tough guy* image and struggled to back down when challenged. Common expressions were *holla' at ya, get at me, on a paper chase, always ballin,' what up doe,* and *this is lame.* Nathan aspired to be a famous entertainer or professional athlete and rich beyond his wildest imagination.

Nyisha also liked interactive learning that involved peer-interactive strategies, particularly working with others in a group. Group presentations were a favorite of hers, and she felt they helped her learn best. She loved to dance (and was quite good at it), love to sing, and relished *anything* dealing with music. Rhythm and blues (R&B) icons Beyonce and Rihanna were her favorites. She never saw a reflection in a mirror she didn't *love* and was constantly concerned about her appearance. Spending time with friends both in and out of school was important to her, as were connecting with friends via social media sites such as Facebook. Taking and posting pictures on social media sites was almost as essential as breathing to her. She aspired to be a highly successful model or a well-paid corporate lawyer. Her immediate goals were to make the honor roll and be known by others to be the best dressed girl in school. She, too, struggled with being easily provoked and not being mature enough to back down. Personal challenges included how to maintain healthy relationships without compromising the morals and values she was raised with.

Student personas are effectively used in the following way. Identify the content you will teach. As you plan and look at how to structure the presentation of such content, let the persona guide you in how it should be delivered. For example, suppose you were going to teach an English language arts lesson on using syntactic and semantic analysis to recognize unfamiliar words in context. Using your student persona as a guide, you might include a few verses from an R&B song and teach students how to recognize some unfamiliar word within the context of the lyrics. Additionally, you may have students bring a few verses from one of their favorite songs to analyze during class.

Your student persona could help you design a mathematics lesson involving solving and understanding problems involving rate. Knowing that your Nathan loves to work with others and be actively moving while learning, you could engage students in an activity in which they worked with a partner or in a small group and used stopwatches to calculate various walking speeds (e.g., fast, slow).

Suppose you were going to have your students explain changes in population and their causes over the last 60 years for social science. Your student persona informs you that they love to work in groups, explore digital multimedia elements, and have a chance to put their own *unique touch* on products. You can organize students into groups to research the causes and effects of population shifts in an assigned region. You could then provide an option for groups to create their own multimedia presentations to present the content in their own unique ways. Such a project may include their preferred background music, a video clip from YouTube or a similar site, or another unique way to show what they know.

A Sample Chemistry Lesson

From your student scholarship, you know that your juniors love multimedia presentations, sugary candies, fireworks, novelty, and interacting with peers. After you teach your 11th graders about decomposition, composition, chemical change, and exothermic chemical reactions, you can have groups observe the following experiment, which involves these concepts, and then synthesize a group presentation. In the lab demonstration, a small amount of potassium chlorate is added to a test tube and liquefied by the heat from a Bunsen burner, and then a gummy bear is added to it. (Of course this should be done in a fume hood because a small amount of chlorine gas is produced.) The two reactions that occur are as follows:

Potassium chlorate decomposes in the presence of heat:

$$2\ KClO_3\ (s) \rightarrow KCl\ (s) + 3\ O_2\ (g)$$

and the sugar (gummy bear) added to the products of the decomposition produces both carbon dioxide and water

$$C_{12}H_{22}O_{11} \text{ (s)} + 12\ O_2 \text{ (g)} \rightarrow 12\ CO_2 \text{ (g)} + 11\ H_2O \text{ (g)}$$

After the presentation, have pairs of students describe the reactions that occurred, write down their observations, write equations that describe both reactions, and provide evidence that the reactions were either exothermic or endothermic. They can then use a PowerPoint presentation with music or similar presentation software to demonstrate their findings.

There is an abundant supply of videos (e.g., on YouTube) that show interesting chemical reactions; this provides you with many other options to satiate their desire for multimedia content. Additional ways to use multimedia content are found in Chapter 6.

The Value of Personalized Presentations

Teachers often lament that they don't have time for such tools, that their job is to be a deliverer of content versus a designer of entertainment. "My students have to make a choice as to whether or not they want to learn. I'm not paid to make learning fun and interesting for them," some have lamented during past professional learning sessions. However, it is not by accident that these are the very ones who struggle with keeping students on task as a result of presenting highly boring yet irrelevant content in vanilla ways. They hate to come to work because of the never-ending struggles with boredom and battles in classroom management. They enviously wonder how their colleagues are able to connect and consistently engage the same group of students they teach. Investing a bit of time in customizing their presentations for their student personas pays high returns in the form of having students who love to come to class and show higher levels of enthusiasm and engagement. Utilizing personas is one of the most effective ways to design engaging lessons for the oft-challenging classrooms in HUMS.

Overextended teachers who work in underresourced HUMS need every instructional advantage to establish and maintain educational climates that are conducive to learning. When you build on the innate ingredients students bring to your classroom, you create the bridge to get them to buy into you and your academic offerings. Turning perceived deficits into deposits provides instructional financing for the construction of such bridges.

The MOVE Checklist

The MOVE checklist works for all students but is particularly geared to check for engagement with African American students. MOVE stands for *movement, one-of-a-kindness, verve,* and *exchange of ideas.* The MOVE checklist was developed around cultural attributes commonly ascribed to African Americans:

- *Movement*—Of course, most students (and adults) do not care to be confined to one place for long hours during instruction. As mentioned, the benefits of movement during instruction have been well documented and are discussed throughout this book.
- *One-of-a-kindness* simply refers to opportunities within the lesson to let Nathan or Nyisha have the stage or be the center of attention and showcase their talents.
- *Verve* is an affinity for a stimulating, lively, or constantly changing environment.
- *Exchange of ideas* refers to peer-interactive strategies, which are highly effective ways for all students to learn.

The Focus on HUMS Students

Am I suggesting that *all* content be contextualized, situated, or otherwise focused on the lives and experiences of HUMS students? In the entire field of education, teaching in HUMS is by and large one of the most difficult challenges. Life challenges for some students in these schools, such as abuse, abject poverty, and conflict resolution, have been well documented. Moreover, by the time many HUMS students have reached the middle grades, their love for learning has dissipated. Utilizing students' experiences and pop culture can serve as a restorative practice to reignite a lost love for learning.

In no way am I suggesting that all content in every portion of each lesson should be enveloped in the popular experiences of students. However, my experiences have taught me that using popular culture as a starting point, referring to it when introducing or illustrating an idea, situating content in real-life contexts, and answering the "Why do I have to learn this stuff?" question are the cogs that turn the wheels of engagement in HUMS. When students see that you are willing to legitimize and value who they are by making their experiences a part of at least some of their instruction, they, in turn, are more likely to give more attention and effort on the days when such elements are missing. They know that you are partnering with them, and they will return the favor.

PLANNING TO HIGHLIGHT IT, NOT FIGHT IT

Mr. King was pretty consistent in engaging his sophomores in small talk conversation and noting how they liked to learn and learned most effectively. The students in his seventh- and eighth-hour classes had a passion for conversing with each other and bickering and arguing about anything and everything while he was teaching. About half of the class periods, he struggled to complete his lesson.

He decided to use student personas as a blueprint for designing more effective lessons for them. The typical student in his persona was very talkative, loved to engage in verbal contests with others, and at times was uninterested in the class. Additionally, he decided to make other major changes to the way he taught.

From experience, he had learned to preface any major change to his teaching by showing students how the changes would give them some immediate benefits. So he explained to them that he intended to use peer-interactive strategies as a part of everyday learning. These included giving them ideas to discuss with each other and then share with the larger group, and using cooperative learning groups to discuss how to apply the laws of supply and demand and other principles of economics to aspects of their lives. He also allowed them to use techniques that built on their strengths *to show what they knew* (demonstrate mastery).

To demonstrate how well they mastered major learning objectives, he gave them several options from which to choose. For example, they could create a newscast in which anchorpersons expressed their ideas or news reporters gave an account of a real-world event demonstrating the economic principles. Groups loved being able to create unique musical openings and closings to the newscasts using instrumentals of their favorite songs. They also liked the creativity of creating a brief commercial advertising the newscast. Though they complained initially, many also liked being able to wear their *Sunday best* to broadcast the news.

After exploring the basic principles of *how to* debate, once a week Mr. King allowed teams to debate application of ideas from content. Most students actively sought to be the moderator, who was at times the center of attention and controlled the flow of the discussion. All newscasts and debates were recorded and critiqued for accuracy of the application of ideas the day after.

Although there were still challenging days in Mr. King's class, they happened far less frequently as student engagement greatly improved.

Chapter Summary

HUMS students bring a wealth of attributes, cultural capital, and underutilized knowledge to the learning environment. Many characteristics that are perceived as deficits can be harnessed into deposits into the learning community. There are a multitude of effective peer-interactive strategies that harness one of the most commonly perceived negative attributes: students' desire to socially interact with others. The harnessing of such attributes helps you make stronger connections with your students, customize the learning, and create a more highly engaging learning experience. Paroling students from seats breathes life into lifeless lessons. Student personas help you to intersect their interests and experiences with instruction and craft unique lessons around them.

ACTIONABLE PROFESSIONAL LEARNING

Please respond individually initially, and then discuss with your collaborative learning team.

1. What are three attributes your students bring to the learning environment that most negatively impact the learning process?

2. Using the framework provided in the chapter, what are some techniques that will assist you in turning these perceived deficits into deposits?

3. To what extent do your students collaborate during learning in your room? Reflecting on the strategies shared, how could your collaborative learning processes become more powerful?

4. Select one of the strategies for using movement as an instructional tool. Utilize it in an upcoming lesson you will teach. Jot down what worked well and how it could be improved.

5. Reflect on the characteristics of your students, create a male and a female persona, and use them to guide your upcoming lesson planning. Check the engagement of the lesson using the MOVE checklist. Describe how effective this tool was in making your lessons more engaging.

Collective Inquiry

1. With colleagues, collectively identify a few perceived student deficits. Use the framework provided in the chapter to discuss how to utilize such attributes as assets of instruction.

2. Are there a couple of significant questions relating to nurturing such attributes needing further investigation?

3. Collectively research how one such attribute can be utilized in instruction, and then try this out in the classroom. During the next team meeting, discuss how things went, using specific evidence.

4

Sew Success Into Your Instructional Fabric

Thinking back in time, what is one task that you've tried and failed repeatedly? Among my *many* challenges, the one thing I have never been good at is dancing. I was the *wallflower* at the high school dances who tried to look *cool while holding up the wall* by attempting to hide the fact that I was allergic—to rhythmic movement. In my young-single-partying days, I had ladies abruptly leave me on the dance floor after my foot landed on their shoes *one too many* times. As if it couldn't get any worse, if you could've been a guest at my wedding shower, you would've seen how a couple of my wife's friends snapped their fingers to the beat to help me stay in time. The only type of dance that I felt comfortable doing was the slow dance where you move from side to side. Because I'm a terrible dancer, I have little interest in it and try to avoid it all costs. The same truth holds for other tasks in life, in that people shy away from those things they're not good at.

Far too often, when students aren't *good* at being *good*, they seek other avenues for finding success. You've probably seen or read more than your share of news stories where young gang members proudly wave their red or blue flag and are willing to do almost anything for it. If you've taught for any length of time, you've invariably been blinded by a sea of metaphorical white flags vigorously waved in your room by students who have simply *given up* on the process of learning. Some have waved their flags since the first day they enrolled, while others gradually raised and waved their flags as the year went on.

I'm not sure if it has happened in your room, but a few of my white flag wavers wreaked havoc during my lessons. They came to class like the uninvited outcast who crashed the party. They tried to hide their inability with machismo and defiance. They refused to even attempt to do the work, even when they were capable of completing at least part of the assignment. As a result, they found counterproductive things to become proficient in. The mastery they achieved was a keen ability to create chaos and disorder. A few even became quite skillful in intentionally committing an act that would get them *kicked out* of class so they could go on a quest of consequence exploration in the hallways or the community. Unaware of their rich reservoirs of potential and capacity for greatness, some appear to have just given up on their academic lives like wounded wildebeests lying down in the Serengeti.

Why Should Placing Students in Positions of Success Be a Priority?

Don't all schools, classrooms, and curricula aim for students to be successful, you may ask? Though it is an assumption in most learning environments that students will be successful, it's not necessarily a priority. Conversely, the principal priority is to cover the curriculum, which often results in content mastery taking a back seat. Educators who focus on covering the curriculum utilize what I call the *Three T Method of Teaching: Tell* them the information; *test* them on the information; *transfer* the information into the gradebook. In other words, these teachers don't continuously seek and then utilize the most effective techniques for enhancing content mastery, nor do they routinely modify instruction based on misunderstandings or misconceptions. Additionally, the learning environment is not structured in the most optimal way for student success.

Placing students in positions of success is important in all schools, but there is a *dire* need for it in high-poverty, urban, largely minority schools (HUMS), where failure and giving up are too frequently routine. Too many students choose either inaction or disruptive reactions. Repeated failure in school is a major cause of both apathy and misbehavior. When students chronically perform poorly, they develop a negative self-perception and then oppose the entity they feel has caused it (Finn, 1989). What are the chances that they give effort to complete tasks if they don't believe they can win? They'll invest little thinking energy (cognitive engagement) and won't become behaviorally engaged if they don't believe mastery is attainable.

Additionally, situating students in situations of success should be a priority because when they have little interest in doing or great difficulty in completing an assigned task, it is unlikely they will use both cognitive and metacognitive strategies to attempt it, nor will they persist if they believe success at completing the task is unattainable (Pintrich & De Groot, 1990). Said simply, neither cognitive nor behavioral engagement will exist.

> *The first success sells the second step.*

Every learner has an innate drive to be successful at *something*. They want to be able to point to that one thing that is a *nuisance* to others but comes naturally to them. Those who meet failure at every endeavor often cower and turn away from any obstacle in their path. Enjoying the feeling of success in some academic subject is no different, as this experience will encourage both cognitive and behavioral engagement. If students have struck out after taking swings at your content *pitches*, they'll seek other places to hit home runs. Additional reasons to make a deliberate effort to place them in a position of success are listed in the theoretical framework below.

THEORETICAL FRAMEWORK: UNDERLYING REASONS FOR CREATING CLASSROOM WINS

- The process of student disengagement can begin early if students experience little success (Marks, 2000). If students are not involved in the learning or experience little success in the first few grades, chances are that they will not become involved in later grades when they look at ability as an added barrier to learning (Finn, 1993).
- When children have a low self-perception in early childhood, there is a greater chance they will become withdrawn in solitary and passive ways and display more reticence (Nelson, Hart, Evans, Coplan, Roper, & Robinson, 2009).
- When students don't believe they have a realistic chance of getting a good grade, they often give up to make it seem that failure is the culprit, rather than lack of ability (Covington & Omelich, 1984).
- When students start the school year doubting their abilities, they experience more anxiety and withdraw behaviorally as the school year goes on (Skinner, Furrer, Marchand, & Kindermann, 2008).

(Continued)

(Continued)

- What students believe about how well they can do and how adept they are in school can directly impact their engagement (Klem & Connell, 2004).
- How students react to success and failure is robustly related to the perception of their academic competence, ability, self-efficacy, and control (Bandura, 1997; Elliot & Dweck, 2005; Wigfield, Eccles, Schiefele, Roeser, & Davis-Kean, 2006).
- The decision people make about the degree to which they persist in a given activity is affected by what they believe about their own abilities (Bandura, 1986; Eccles, 1993).
- When students believe they have the capacity to complete a task, there is a greater chance they will use cognitive and metacognitive strategies and persist at it, even if they find little interest in it or find that it is difficult (Pintrich & De Groot, 1990).
- When students' need for competence is satisfied, they believe that they can control whether they succeed and know what steps need to be implemented to succeed (Connell & Wellborn, 1991).
- Perceived competence and beliefs about control have been linked to emotional and behavioral engagement in both elementary and middle school (Rudolph, Lambert, Clark, & Kurlakowsky, 2001).
- If students perceive that they are in an environment with chances to be successful, are motivated to engage in those chances, and have the requisite skills, there exists little difference among races, genders, and ethnicity on achievement tests (Byrnes, 2003).
- Students who show the greatest academic engagement in school are those who embrace the belief that their success or failure hinges on their effort (Patrick, Skinner, & Connell, 1993).
- When students believe they hold the power of school success in their hands, they fare better on cognitive tasks (Skinner, Wellborn, & Connell, 1990).

How Can Success Be Sewn Into Your Instructional Fabric?

Students in HUMS cite the need to feel supported as one of the most essential elements of their success. With the well-documented challenges facing many of the students, this comes as no surprise. Given that greater percentages of students are not where the curriculum guides or other district-supplied instructional materials indicate they should be, supportive structures are of the essence. Furthermore, short of cloning yourself to effectively provide sorely needed individual or small-group support, it's virtually impossible for you alone to shoulder all content delivery in such rooms. Key aspects that lead to the sewing of success in engaging classroom practices lie in three areas:

1. Support from you

2. Embedding supportive structures throughout the learning environment

3. Delivery of supportive pedagogy that facilitates student success

Get them started with your words; sustain them with support. State and show how they'll benefit early and often.

Begun by Spoken Words, Believed by Sustained Support

How might you characterize your introductory speech, lecture, or direct address to students when they enter your room for the first time each fall? Is it a description of rules that address every conceivable inappropriate action? Do your words paint chilling consequences for breaking each one of your rules? Or do they sincerely communicate your positive expectations of them complemented with your belief that they can continuously improve and become smarter if they are willing to partner with you in the learning process?

In classrooms filled with students who are cynical about you and your content and are consumed with self-doubt, the foundation for beginning the journey toward success can be propelled by your first words. Such words do more than simply set the tone; they serve to shape the trajectory toward success. Begin by building the belief that success is possible by explicitly stating ways in which your students will benefit from your class. Sow seeds for successful mind-sets through describing how you will customize content in ways that are not only relevant and interesting but are also the ways that they learn best. Lay the foundation for buy-in by sharing how they'll have choice in some of what they learn as well as how they learn it along the way. Finally, acknowledge that they may have not been so successful in the past, but propose that if they will lend you their trust up front, they'll be handsomely rewarded with returns of their successful growth.

Though skepticism may prevail as you deliver your first words, doubt is progressively eroded by the revelation of successful results over time. Lessons from learning theory teach that words alone don't effectively change beliefs. Conversely the birthplace of beliefs is the experiences that precede them. Alternately stated, you'll begin to change their beliefs (i.e. perceived competence) in the possibilities of their success once they see evidence of its effectiveness. The foundation for them to have a successful year is best laid by detailing the specific things they will receive from your course.

Words that explicitly express how students will benefit from the support and other aspects of your class help answer the WIFM (what's in it for me?) question and begin the process of sowing seeds of success. Showing that you will provide such support throughout the year helps sustain the successes. Such consistency helps create connections with your students. Highly successful HUMS classrooms are characterized by such strong student–teacher rapport. Chapter 5 highlights processes for creating and sustaining such supportive connections with your students, an essential component of success.

Position Supportive Structures Throughout the Learning Environment

Develop a Classroom Culture of Collaboration Versus Competition

In classrooms that rely heavily on collaboration, feelings of loneliness and isolation stemming from *going it alone* are rooted out. HUMS students often embrace working with others; they value the support of family and feelings of togetherness. Hence, having the opportunity to collaborate with peers to complete classroom tasks in a supportive instructional structure is an important step toward success. Students trust that the teacher and peers will collaborate with them on tasks and in creating collaborative structures of learning. They most often learn in pairs, small groups, or whole groups. Success is collectively defined in such rooms, as learners frequently and freely assist each other in understanding the content. Students find solace in the fact that there is always someone within the community of learners who will take the time to help them overcome academic and social hurdles.

Negotiating Failure: Mold Missteps Into Learning Modules

You would probably agree that phrases such as "everyone makes mistakes" and "no one's perfect" are used ad nauseam, but have you considered using the spirit of them as tools to place students in situations of success? Most teachers talk about missteps and mistakes being "teachable moments" but are either unwilling or unable to teach *in the moment.* How would you describe the perception and treatment of missteps committed by you or your students? What happens when students provide incorrect responses during classroom discussions, inaccurate written answers to questions, or wrongly applied principles or formulae? When students make such errors in your room, are they frowned upon like society sometimes frowns upon a homeless person? Or do you have discussions around the strategies and methods that were used, which thinking processes took place, and what effort was employed?

When you show your students how to mold missteps into learning modules or lessons to be learned, you provide an invaluable paradigm for success in the classroom and life as well. What start out as baby steps become bountiful strides as you teach that the birthplace of learning is missteps and mistakes.

Dweck (2006) makes a compelling case for teaching students that the more effortful mistakes they learn from, the smarter they become. Creating a classroom culture where missteps and effortful mistakes are embraced and used as tools of learning is powerful pedagogy. It makes the environment intellectually safe and sends the message that "it's okay to be wrong because I have learned and become smarter along the way." Not only are students less pressured to always be "right," but they are placed in a better position to be successful. With classroom cultures that promote such thinking, the focus is on the process and understanding the lessons learned from the missteps. In essence, such cultures help create the environment for the win.

Positioning Them to Get the Wins: Creating Instructional SOFAs

When it comes to the instruction you deliver to your well-deserving students, what do you have in place to maximize the likelihood that they will experience success? An oft overlooked barrier to engagement in HUMS classrooms is the design and delivery of instruction in ways that ignore the varied entry points of learners. Given the well-documented achievement gap of HUMS students coupled with learning styles incongruent with traditional school curricula, lags in achievement and engagement challenges persist. Pedagogy that ignores such factors leaves learner mastery to the randomized whims of chance. A way of removing chance from the equation of learning success is to create SOFAs, or Success Opportunities For All.

SOFAs are simply elements of the learning experience that position students to do well. They are not only the heart of engaging lessons but also the hook leading students in. There are a wealth of techniques that facilitate such classroom successes; however, I am listing just a few that I have found to be highly effective. The SOFAs described below are hardly novel but wholly effective in positioning students in HUMS for success.

Me Versus Me: Use Self-Growth as a Barometer of Progress

Creating the win for students sometimes calls for a radical change in the thinking of what a *win* is, that is, taking a closer look at how success is defined in your learning community. Take, for instance, the statistical category of rebounding in basketball. Would it be fair to compare the number of rebounds the shortest NBA player has compiled to that of the tallest? You would probably agree that generally taller players have an advantage in peak jumping height over smaller players and would be able to grab more rebounds. A more fair comparison would be comparing how a given player's rebounding has fared over the course of season or career. Stated differently, it would be measuring progress relative to the player's own baseline (starting point) data. Similarly, given the countless differences among students—such as starting points in the learning, rates at which they learn, and a host of other factors—using students as their own measuring stick is more useful than comparing them to other students. Regularly comparing students' grades to those of their peers may enhance the self-confidence of the higher performing students while eroding the self-perception of the ones whose grades are lower.

The starting points of some of your students may lag so far behind those of their peers that it is highly unlikely that the gap can be closed within an academic year. That's like comparing a slower marathon runner at the starting line to the current position of faster runners who had an hour-and-fifty-minute head start. It is much more prudent to compare that runner's performance relative to his or her unique starting point rather than to the performance of speedier runners who had an earlier start. Making self-comparisons creates a SOFA insofar as it provides a greater chance of showing evidence that individual students are successfully learning. It also helps you stimulate their desire to move forward and more effectively helps you create the classroom win. How can you measure self-growth?

Use Baseline Data to Clearly Define Students' Starting Points

What's the first thing a weight loss program does for a new enrollee? As you already know, it weighs in the new participant to establish a baseline as a comparison against which to measure progress. Over the course of the program, enrollees regularly weigh in to assess how things are going. Excellent teachers not only in HUMS but in all schools find the initial "weight" or starting point of students relative to major learning goals and objectives. No matter what you are teaching, use a pretest to locate each student's starting point. It gives you something against which to measure how much growth has happened over time. I've seen too many teachers just jump into chapter after chapter without first finding out where the students are starting relative to the larger learning goals. Not only does establishing clear baselines help you more prescriptively plan and lay fertile ground for SOFAs, but in this age of accountability, it also provides sound evidence of *your* instructional effectiveness. Though it extends beyond the scope of this writing, using pretests as a part of formative assessment processes exemplifies sound pedagogy for achieving this purpose.

Establish Incremental Targets Along the Road to Goal Mastery

Rome wasn't built in a day, and broader learning objectives aren't met in an hour. One surefire way to stymie behavioral engagement is to heap unreasonably large learning goals on your students. Many students in HUMS experience undue pressure, as they have adult responsibilities mounted on their adolescent shoulders. The entry point of many is below grade level, and being asked to make gargantuan achievement gains in short periods of time adds to their feelings of the being overwhelmed. Conversely, smaller, incremental goals that lead to larger goals help make the learning easier to swallow. They give students a greater chance to be successful by breaking the learning down into bite-sized chunks. Accomplishing the smaller goals is often easier, enables students to see the win, and provides needed intellectual and emotional fuel to move forward. Frameworks for intervening early, such as Response to Intervention (RtI) (Fuchs & Fuchs, 2006), show promise in establishing a clear baseline, measuring student growth from said baseline, and establishing incremental goals along the way. Teachers using similar pedagogical practices have had some success in avoiding the outdated and ineffective methods for ascertaining learning disabilities in a "wait to fail" fashion.

Essential Pedagogical Approaches That Position Students to Succeed

Ineffective instructional practices target one learner entry point (e.g., reading level), interest, and learning style. Furthermore, other ineffective instruction solely relies on summative assessments to gauge mastery, and understanding of students' needs and learning styles is rarely utilized to adjust either the teaching strategies or the ways students learn. A third challenge not addressed by conventional instruction is that many nonwhite HUMS students disidentify with the content being taught, the style of delivery of such content, and the overall learning environment in many schools. Thus, pedagogical frameworks that address such challenges are called for. Of the many pedagogical approaches that exist, three that I have found to have the greatest impact on success in HUMS classrooms are:

1. Differentiated instruction

2. Formative assessment

3. Culturally responsive pedagogy

Effective differentiation addresses learners' varied entry points, interests, and styles of learning. Making appropriate adjustments to teaching strategies, which is made possible by teachers' continuous assessing of understanding of their students, drives formative assessment. Culturally responsive pedagogy provides a blueprint for modifying content, delivery, and the overall learning experience in positively affirming ways. The degree to which the frameworks are utilized may vary among HUMS classrooms; however, schools are in dire need of such pedagogical approaches, which modify instruction in ways for students to best be successful. Comprehensive exploration of such approaches is beyond the scope of this text, but several are briefly described along with suggested readings in Table 2.

Table 2   Essential Pedagogical Frameworks That Position HUMS Students for Success

Framework	Description	Resources
Differentiated Instruction	An instructional framework for adjusting what students learn (content), how they learn it (process), and how mastery is demonstrated (product) according to where students are in the learning (entry point), their interests, and learning modalities.	• Tomlinson (1999, 2001)
Formative Assessment	A preplanned process by which students or teachers use assessment-based evidence to appropriately adjust how teachers teach or how students learn content	• Brookhart (2010) • Black, Harrison, Lee, Marshall, & Wiliam (2003)
Culturally Responsive Pedagogy	A culturally affirming pedagogical approach that not only enhances achievement but also aids in the development of critical perspectives that challenge the perpetuation of inequities	• Gay (2010) • Young (2010) • Brown (2007) • Ladson-Billings (1995)

The Need to Support Teachers in Positioning Their Students for Success

The support of administrators within the school as well as those at the central office level is essential in the process of positioning students to be successful. Inordinate numbers of HUMS students have entry points below grade level, and the pressure on classroom teachers to raise them to grade level by standardized testing time is counterproductive. I am not making an argument that teachers should not be held accountable, but the standards they're held to should be realistically achievable. Measuring student progress using baseline measures is a start. Moreover, effective pedagogy leading to academic success, such as differentiation and formative assessment, calls for pacing that may not align with the pacing chart. A pacing guide should be used as a blueprint in planning rather than as an inflexible referent that guides the pace of instruction for all classrooms and all learners.

Practices That Create Barriers to Success in HUMS

- Learner entry points are not explored (i.e., no preassessments) prior to beginning instructional cycle (e.g., new chapter).
- Ineffective and infrequent use is made of techniques to find out whether true mastery has occurred; few modifications are made to teaching or learning in lieu of student understanding.
- Summative measures are the principal means of assessing mastery.
- Instruction inadequately addresses diversity of learning styles, interests, and entry points.
- Anticipatory techniques and strategies for addressing misunderstandings, misconceptions, or failure are not present.
- Few supportive structures are embedded in the learning environment.
- Consistent comparison is made of learner progress to that of peers.
- Students are condemned for making missteps versus being taught to use missteps as tools for growth.
- Instructional emphasis is on end result (i.e., correct answer) versus on the processes used to arrive there.
- Zero tolerance discipline policies are the order of the day. Preponderant emphasis is on *controlling* students versus connecting with them. There exist few school supports (e.g., mentoring, effective intervention strategies) to address misbehavior. Once a behavior threshold has been crossed (e.g., three strikes), students are banished from the learning process, beginning the perpetual spinning of the revolving door often leading to later school dropout.
- Students are not challenged to stretch.
- Classroom culture breeds mediocrity.
- Expectations of future student success are indelibly etched in stone.

Chapter Summary

In classrooms where chronic failure and underachievement are commonplace, placing students in successful positions is of critical importance. The roots of disruptive behavior in HUMS are grounded in the chronic failure. When experiences with failure are routine, students often seek success in counterproductive ways. Remember, the experience of a successful first step best sells the decision to take a second one.

HUMS students cite support as a precursor for success in schools. The foundation for successful experiences lies in support from you, embedding supportive structures in the learning environment, and delivering supportive pedagogy that facilitates student success. Students' beliefs loom large in achieving success in schools, in that helping students to believe in their capacity to succeed increases the likelihood they will persist, even when facing difficult or uninteresting tasks. Beliefs are more likely to change after students experience positive successes. If they believe they are in an environment that nourishes such success, there's a greater chance engagement will occur.

Supportive structures embedded in the learning environment that lead to success include emphases on providing collaborative academic and social support, and developing a classroom culture that embraces effortful missteps as opportunities for growth. Embedding collaboration into the fabric of the learning community supports the success of all in HUMS.

When you facilitate small victories as students travel the *course* of academics, you create initial successes and second steps toward winning. One powerful way to facilitate such victories comes from measuring how students have progressed from the place they entered. Additionally, establishing smaller, incremental goals keeps the fire of participatory desire kindled. Moreover, molding missteps into learning modules powerfully turns *trip ups* into *triumphs*. Three essential pedagogical approaches that foster student success in HUMS are differentiated instruction, formative assessment, and culturally responsive pedagogy.

ACTIONABLE PROFESSIONAL LEARNING

Please respond individually initially, and then discuss with your collaborative learning team.

1. Identify a couple of your students who consistently struggle with mastery of your content. Where exactly does their struggle lie (e.g., conceptual understanding, retention of content)?

2. What are your SOFAs that already work well?

3. What measures (if any) do you take that help establish a baseline starting point for overall growth for the year/semester?

4. Providing evidence of growth to students is a powerful motivator. How might you provide such evidence to your students? Please be specific.

Action Research

How are effortful missteps perceived and utilized (if at all) in your practice? Is the emphasis on getting it right, or is the emphasis on the process underlying completing tasks? The section presented in this chapter (Mold Missteps Into Learning Modules) based on the work of Dweck (2006) makes a cogent argument for using effortful mistakes as powerful tools of learning. Engage your colleagues in dialogue surrounding how missteps (by teacher or students) are handled in practice. Challenge each other to identify one way effortful missteps could be more effectively utilized as opportunities to learn. I have provided a suggested way for this to occur below.

1. At the conclusion of a lesson or two per week for the next four weeks, have students reflect on the following questions: What misstep or two did I make today that made me smarter? What specifically did I learn? Model the reflection the first few times to give students an idea of the type of thinking you are looking for. For example, "I became a smarter teacher today because I learned from the mistake of not providing enough feedback for you."

2. Anecdotally or formally record your students' responses as well as other indicators of effectiveness of this strategy. Worth noting are elements such as these:

   a. unanticipated student questions, statements, or actions

   b. successful breakthroughs, such as participation from student(s) who are generally withdrawn
   c. remaining challenges or frustrations relating to the strategy

Keep a few samples of student responses (e.g. surprises and remaining challenges) to examine and discuss with colleagues during the next team meeting.

3. During the team meeting (after the four-week period), share data, and engage each other in reflective dialogue surrounding how to make the strategy more effective.

4. Utilize the information gleaned to repeat for approximately four more weeks, and reflectively discuss this second period during the subsequent meeting.

5

Partner to Make Emotional Connections

Emotions are intimately involved in virtually every aspect of the teaching and learning process and, therefore, an understanding of the nature of emotions within the school context is essential.

(Schutz & Lanehart, 2002, p. 67)

No research paper, graduate school group project, or student–teacher practicum could have prepared Mr. King for the battle that lay ahead. The first few days of teaching were eaten up by trying to figure out which students were actually enrolled versus those playing *hooky*, keeping students from freely walking out of the room, and getting through half of an explanation of a concept without having to address a discipline issue. After a few weeks, he was able to *shoo* away the truant students, but he was bewildered by the fact that only 10% of the students in each of his six classes consistently were both present on time and consistently on task. He ran into Manuel, who had not been in attendance since the first day of school, and asked, "Where have you been and why don't you come to class?" Manuel replied,

We really don't need this, like, elective class and we're tired of being mad bored [*sic*] with teachers who just come in here with this same ole' boring way of teaching. 'Sides, you ain't from 'round here. You don' know how hard it is just to *survive!*

Offended by Manuel's comment about him not relating to some of their struggles, Mr. King figured he'd try a new approach to help him better connect and relate to his students. Now, before opening a textbook, he opens up the book on his life. He tells students about the rough times he had growing up, the activities he enjoys with his family, and even the video games he loves to play on his Xbox 360. He talks about the issues and interests of his children, his favorite types of foods and restaurants, his favorite sports teams, and the recreational things he loves to do. Most important, he shows a human element of himself by telling students about some of the mistakes he's made in life and how he didn't let those mistakes defeat him.

Mr. King tells the story about his lower middle class upbringing in Iowa. His family had most of their needs met, but sometimes things were a little thin. For instance, he and his older brother had to do things like share each other's clothes. There were days when his mom was off work because of furlough where the only meal he ate was school lunch. He opens up about one of the biggest obstacles he struggled to overcome: an abusive alcoholic father. He shares some of the coping strategies his brothers, sisters, and mom used when their dad tipped the bottle one too many times.

The point Mr. King reemphasizes with his students is that circumstances may have captured you, but you don't have to allow them to control you. He uses shared experiences to help make a connection with his students and encourages them to buy in to school. His students are better able to identify with him after he shares about his personal struggles and how he overcame them. He endears himself to his students when he chronicles a few of the mistakes he has made in life and the strategies he used to overcome them. He asserts that everyone makes mistakes but mistakes are embraced as opportunities to move upward by people moving forward in life.

Aiming to Connect Versus Control

Have you ever been around someone who took what you said with a grain of salt, questioned your every move, and just never really seemed to trust you? Many students hold little trust in and have high suspicion of schools (Voekl, 1996). Some have developed a calloused shell because of bad experiences with significant adults in their lives. They may be distrustful because of past instances of becoming attached to a teacher only to be torn away by a teacher transfer. Some are suspicious and less trusting because of having been hurt in the past by broken parental promises.

For them, beginning the school year is like going into a new section of a store with a new salesperson and sales pitch. When students are paired with you for the first time, there invariably is a "getting to know you" stage where *they* give the first exams, as they test the water to see how much you will allow them to get away with. They want to know how knowledgeable you are about your product (content) and want their questions answered before they seriously consider buying in. Students also want to know why the product or service should be bought from *you*. Thus they spend much of the time trying to figure out who you really are; learning your preferences, interests, and mannerisms; identifying what you will and will not accept; and figuring out what the chances are you will want to build an emotional bond or relationship with them. Until you have made the sale or established a level of rapport, many students in HUMS are likely to react with suspicion to your every move.

If you fail to connect with students, teaching is like the airing of a radio show, where you broadcast content using the call letters WHCM, or We Have to Cover Material. However, your students are far down the dial at WIFM, or What's In it For Me. As with any sales situation in life, students want the WIFM question fully answered. I am sure you've been asked the "why do we have to learn this *stuff?*" question more often than you care to admit. It goes without saying that they want to have an enjoyable buying experience. Before they are willing to devote the needed emotional and intellectual resources to purchase from you, the cost to them also factors into the equation.

A common course of action in HUMS is for teachers first to establish strong control over the students in the classroom. I have witnessed administrators in many of these schools embrace teachers who are able to consistently negotiate control in such environments. There were instances where teachers delivered at best marginal instruction but were excellent in creating totalitarian environments of absolute control. They received glowing instructional evaluations and were celebrated as being among the best teachers in the school. However, when teachers aim to connect with students, versus control every aspect of learning, behavioral difficulties dwindle, and engaging opportunities for growth spring forth.

The Power of Emotional Appeal

Psychologists tell us that when it comes to buying, the decision to either purchase or pass on a product is pushed by a person's emotions versus logical reasoning. Furthermore, it's said that subconscious emotions account for almost 90% of the decision to buy. That basic truth is extended to other aspects of

> *Logic moves the mind; emotion moves the body.*

life, as people are more likely to engage in a particular course of action after something has emotionally resonated with them. Logical appeal gets them thinking; emotional resonance gets them moving. Reasons compelling youth to act often follow suit.

A student is more likely to volunteer for a leukemia charity after watching a friend endure the disease. Teenagers are less likely to engage in recreational drug use after witnessing someone close to them die from a drug overdose. When you tap students' emotion, you tip the scales of learning in your favor. This is especially true for students in HUMS. Kindling the emotional spark first is one of the most effective ways to close the sale with students. However, consistently closing the sale in the classroom is a bit of a different situation.

Ms. Klein was so excited about delivering what she believed was one of her best science lessons yet that she had trouble sleeping. It was the beginning of her second week of school with her new group of fourth graders. The lesson she was going to teach her students was on how to create and test predictions. She had her materials neatly organized in the middle of each lab table: an assortment of M&M candies. As she took attendance, a red M&M zipped past her face. Before she knew it, the room was overcome with a barrage of flying chocolate-covered candy, which made the classroom look like a colorful candy blizzard. It took her nearly half of the period to restore order, and she spent the other half having students complete sketches of molecules.

She had just *known* that the lesson she'd created with the M&Ms would have had all students on task, interested, and working well together. When the bell finally rang at the end of the day, she took a few moments to reflect on the day's events, searching for the answer to what went wrong.

Creating the Emotional Connections: Getting Critical Buy-In

If you've been in the classroom for at least a few years, you would probably agree that the first few interactions with students are similar to the first few dates after meeting someone new. However, the exploration period is often longer when the teacher and students possess entirely different experiences, are generations apart, and have ostensibly fewer common interests. Furthermore, if the teacher is of a different ethnicity or race than the students, emotionally

Control may get you compliance; creating connections gets you the commitment.

connecting is often more of a challenge, especially if the teacher knows little of the students' shared interests, beliefs, and values and that which means the most to them.

Getting the desired sales and creating an engaging classroom practice becomes easiest when you first engage them emotionally. It is brought about by first creating emotional connections between you and students, and among students as well. This particularly holds true when teaching students who are at risk of poor student outcomes because their trust accounts are often overdrawn.

Supportive emotional connections are developed when you place emphasis on the emotional and academic success of all students, and these connections are the building blocks of emotional engagement. Such connections are most effectively facilitated within the supportive framework of a classroom community (discussed below). They come from the teacher initially modeling acts of care.

This caring environment springs forth when you place students, who are rarely entrusted with classroom responsibilities, in positions where they can earn your trust. It's established when you take the time to sincerely, warmly, and personally greet each student in the morning. It's built when you are as highly attentive to their emotional needs as to their intellectual or academic needs. Structuring your lessons to include supportive peer-interactive elements can facilitate the establishment of supportive emotional bonds between peers as well. The emphasis on creating and sustaining emotional connections among members of the community is an important step in creating the emotionally engaging experience. There are several ways to create emotional connections with students; a few of the most effective ones are listed below.

How Can I Emotionally Connect With My Students?

One of the most powerful things I did to get through to students who were difficult to connect with was to use positive, affirming statements as tools for connecting. When things weren't going well with students, I would look for areas where they had improved, verbally express how I noticed that they've improved, an—adding power to the interaction—make a phone call home to affirm this. When I called the parents of students who chronically misbehaved, the typical initial parental response was, "Yes, what did he do *NOW*?" I'd usually respond by saying something like, "I am actually calling to thank you and your spouse for what you all have done at home to help your child improve. We have to continue to help each other support the positive steps of your child." The majority of the time, I would see positive results from taking a few moments to make such a call. Some of these families rarely if ever have received positive feedback in the form of a phone call.

For students with significant behavioral challenges, you might have to look for a subtle change that you wouldn't think twice about with other students. Tywan, one of Mrs. Jones's most challenging students, refused to work more often than not and did everything he could to disruptively entertain others. However, one week Mrs. Jones felt a telephone call home was warranted because he didn't impulsively bolt out of the room. The day after the call, Tywan promised Mrs. Jones that he was going to "try real hard to act better."

During a recent professional learning workshop, a participant lamented that he made such a positive call but the results backfired. "The young man," he said, "came back to class the next day even worse. He thought that he could get over on me because I said something positive or maybe he thought I was his friend." I stressed the importance of adding as many effective tools to the pedagogical toolbox as possible, so that when the screwdriver doesn't work, you can use a power tool to get the job done. You want to shift odds in your favor, so that when disruptions occur (as they invariably will), they are minimally effective in stopping the flow of your lesson. When you have an engaging practice, you have a wealth of techniques and strategies to pull from the pedagogical toolbox to use to address the issue.

Students enjoy being in the presence of teachers who make it a priority to emotionally connect, because these teachers are warm but demanding, caring, yet convinced of their students' capabilities. These teachers are staunch supporters of their students, and they sensitively attend to their students' social needs. They use self-deprecating humor to better connect with students. Not only are they are quick to admit when they make mistakes, but they embrace the mistakes as opportunities for learning and growth. They're flexible in leading the classroom and utilize student voice to negotiate student buy-in. There are various ways to create emotional connections with students, but a few I have found to be consistently effective; these are shown in Figure 4.

I am not sure what made sharing my four Ws an effective technique for connecting, but I used it quite effectively throughout the years. It simply involves sharing with student(s) an area in which I wasn't so strong (weaknesses), a desire (want), an unfortunate situation (wreck), or a situation or circumstance that I conquered (win). For example, I'd often share my weakness for sweets, my childhood

Figure 4   Effective Ways to Create Emotional Connections With Students

- Make complimentary, positive statements about their appearance, achievement, an attribute, or an action they took.
- Affirm who they are and value where they come from.
- Maintain eye contact while empathetically listening to them.
- Share your four Ws—weaknesses, wants, wrecks, and wins.
- Value students' opinions even if you are not in agreement with them.
- Deliberately engage in any act that shows you care about them personally (not just academically).
- Provide supportive task feedback that is aimed to help them improve.
- Build a belief in their capability to improve.
- Maintain and communicate high expectations.
- Demonstrate a willingness to be flexible.
- Embrace humor as an integral part of the learning experience.
- Uphold standards of fairness in the classroom.
- Warmly acknowledge them when you see them outside of the classroom.
- Attend students' special events outside of school.

desire (want) to be a professional athlete, how I overcame the embarrassment of having an unsightly scalp infection leading to hair loss (wreck), and the strategies I used to resolve being bullied (win). Perhaps it's the aura of ordinariness projected, the empathy shown, or the strategies shared, but utilizing the four Ws helps you develop deeper connections with your students.

Connecting When Your Background, Experiences, and Culture Are Completely Different From Theirs

You may have grown up with a family income vastly different from that of your students, in a community that is demographically dissimilar, or in a household that shared few values with your students' households. However, there are always some basic commonalities that most children experience during childhood and adolescence. It may be how it felt to spend time with your friends, not making a sports team, coping with the loss of a loved one, or the pressure put on you by parents to either do chores or do well in school. Connect with them by describing a commonly experienced emotion, such as joy, happiness, boredom, or loneliness. There are some pervasively shared experiences, like those previously mentioned, which transcend socioeconomic status, ethnic, and racial background. Mr. King skillfully used such shared experiences in the vignette at the beginning of this chapter. If you want to create a larger gap between you and your students, put on the perception that you had a perfect childhood and/ or have a perfect adult life. If you want to bridge the cultural divide, share the stories of past similar emotions and experiences with them to create deeper connections.

Emotional connections are the catalysts that drive students to react in engaging ways in your classroom. Within the context of an emotionally engaging practice, emotional engagement won't come via overnight delivery and isn't made via microwavable teaching strategies. It starts slowly and develops over time from well-formed emotional connections between individuals in the classroom. Though they may not be immediately evident and indeed form at a glacial pace, emotional connections are key elements in the process of emotionally engaging your students. Implementing techniques that engage students emotionally is an important part in creating an engaging educational practice. Emotional engagement comes from first establishing emotional connections or bonds with students. What are characteristics of HUMS teachers who establish such bonds?

Attributes of Teachers Who Successfully Establish Emotional Connections

- Warm demanders
- Empathetic listeners
- Flexible facilitators of learning
- Demonstrators of personal and academic caring for students
- Skillful in garnering the trust of students
- Love to laugh with learners
- Staunch student advocates
- Fighters for what's fair and equitable for students
- Encouragers of student voice

Using Connections to Create Emotional Engagement

Emotional engagement is commonly conceptualized as a dimension of academic engagement. Terms such as *attitude, interest, excitement, stress,* and *identification* are often associated with the concept. The emotional component of academic engagement is also measured by how bored, anxious, happy, or sad students are in the classroom. It's traditionally thought of as the extent to which students feel they belong as members of the classroom or school community. In that vein, it is the degree to which students react to the teacher in either negative or positive ways. I conceptualize emotional engagement a bit differently.

Emotional engagement in an engaging educational practice is a bit more encompassing. Emotional engagement lies at the core of an engaging educational practice. It is not an afterthought or fleeting occurrence that may or may not be a big deal in terms of whether or not it actually happens. When students are emotionally engaged, levels of trust, care, and concern are developed among members of the classroom community. Emotional engagement refers to how students feel about classroom policies, peers, and practices in the classroom. It's about saying to them, "If you invest your attendance, attention, and interest, I'll repay you with rewarding, meaningful, and engaging learning.

> Emotional engagement appears to be the active ingredient in sustaining motivation: It is the strongest contributor to the feedforward internal dynamics of engagement, bolstering behavioral engagement and staving off behavioral disaffection. (Skinner, Furrer, Marchand, & Kindermann, 2008, p. 778)

Why Emotional Engagement Should Be a First Priority in the Process

In my seventh year of teaching, a colleague was having a difficult time connecting with students and getting them to adhere to her rules. One day after dismissal she remarked, "Jelani, the only reason some teachers can connect with students so well is because they share the same African American heritage." After pausing to collect my thoughts I said,

> It may be true that African American teachers have an easier time connecting with African American students, because they often share similar experiences and have firsthand knowledge of cultural norms, mores, et cetera. But I have found that the race of the teacher is of little consequence to students. The thing they really care about is whether the teacher is worthy of their trust, cares about them, has their best interest at heart, and that the teacher has engaging content that benefits them.

Dockter and Lewis (2009) provide an illustrative example of a Caucasian HUMS teacher who developed strong connections with her students, delivered engaging pedagogy, and created a highly engaging practice. One of the mistakes most frequently made in HUMS classrooms is that teachers try to engage students in an activity or lesson before first establishing an emotional connection. Misbehavior is an inevitable occurrence, arising in every classroom. Creating connections helps minimize the chances that small challenges create catastrophic classroom situations. Connections help you get the buy-in and ultimately make the sale. Building key classroom alliances helps negate the potentially disruptive impact of such occurrences.

During the break of a workshop I led few weeks ago, a teacher told me, "My only job responsibilities are to keep pace with the pacing guide, teach the curriculum, and deliver the content. That's the only thing my supervisor is looking for." I have seen far too many teachers with that mind-set who ignore connecting with students, and in turn, miss invaluable ways to get even the most difficult learners to buy in to the program. Additional reasons emphasizing the centrality of emotional engagement are listed below.

THEORETICAL FRAMEWORK: UNDERLYING REASONS FOR CREATING EMOTIONAL ENGAGEMENT

- When children do not adjust well to the classroom environment, having teachers who meet their social and emotional needs may be of equal or greater importance than the delivery of certain instructional strategies (Hamre & Pianta, 2005; Wentzel, 2002).
- Positive emotions experienced by students in school are associated with expanded cognitive and behavioral coping strategies (Reschly, Huebner, Appleton, & Antaramian, 2008).
- When students give positive emotional responses to current contextual situations, they engage in deeper talking and listening (Do & Shallert, 2004).
- Establishing teaching conditions that make emotional understanding possible and developing close student–teacher bonds are essential for successful learning and teaching (Hargreaves, 2001).
- Emotionally engaged students have a higher chance of success in school (Goodenow, 1993; Osterman, 2000) and typically do well academically (Steele, 1992).
- Emotional withdrawal from school is one of the most pervasive issues plaguing today's schools (Voekl, 1996).

- Positive emotional energy can play an effective role in engaging inner-city students (Seiler & Elmesky, 2007).
- An emotional connection to school has a strong relationship to academic success with both African American and White students (Voekl, 1996).
- Latino/a students are more likely to have a positive attitude toward school when they perceive teachers to be socially supportive (Valenzuela, 1999).
- A lack of emotional engagement has been cited as the reason both African American and Latino/a students drop out of school (Fine, 1991).
- The emotional well-being of students can be influential in how they perform academically and how interested they are in classroom tasks (Wentzel, 1998).
- When comparing first-grade classrooms with students who were at high risk for poor academic outcomes, academic achievement was highest in rooms with higher levels of emotional support (Hamre & Pianta, 2005).
- Teachers who provide relatively low emotional support for their students, feel depressed themselves, and believe they can do little to impact their students are more likely to report conflict between themselves and their students (Hamre, Pianta, Downer, & Mashburn, 2008).
- Achievement is highest in first-grade classrooms with high-risk students when teachers create positive emotional climates that are supportive of students' individual needs. Sound student–teacher relationships with primary-grade at-risk students are beneficial to teachers (Hamre & Pianta, 2005).

To consistently make emotional engagement an important part of practice, the establishment of an embedded framework is needed. Such a framework provides many opportunities for emotional bonds to be created through supportive relationships, social interaction coupled with learning, and an atmosphere laden with trust, care, and concern for each other. This is an environment where the aim is not for individual success but for collective achievement. Developing a classroom community fulfills this need.

Building the Classroom Community: Cultivating the Culture for Emotional Engagement to Grow

What factors did you consider when you chose your current place of residence? The structure, spaciousness it affords you, or the closeness in proximity to your job may come to mind. I would bet that the amenities of the community in which you live and the people who compose it weighed heavily in making your choice. Most of us enjoy our communities because of the serenity, security, and comfort they provide. We enjoy the variety of community-sponsored activities where members collaborate on projects, socialize with each other, and have a great time in the process. We enjoy the respect and watchful eye reciprocated among neighbors. We are appreciative of the collective power of the community to have our voices heard in the political process. Simply put, we *love* the climate of the community.

Classroom communities are a lot like the communities that make up the cities in which we live. The teacher and students are all members who reside in the community. In classroom communities that effectively grow emotional engagement, the teacher is the leader who is a staunch advocate for the residents (students) at the town hall meetings (staff/professional development meetings). Community members collectively decide on the ordinances (classroom rules) and consequences for violations. Residents have a voice through community forums (class meetings), meetings with the neighborly leaders (teacher), neighborly discussions (classroom discussions), or classroom feedback forms.

Students and school personnel appreciate the comfort, serenity, and security. They embrace the warm, positive climate present in the classroom. They appreciate the opportunities for social interaction that come with opportunities to collaborate on classroom projects. True classroom communities empower students to have a voice in shaping the instructional path and other important parts of learning. Yet a few new neighbors or community members who don't embrace the core values of the community can wreak havoc on the fiber of the community. Like members of communities that make up cities, they can trigger a mass exodus of those who seek other classroom places to stake their claim.

In caring classroom communities, students care for one another like family. They are collaborative assistants versus competitive associates. Learning processes, such as peer-interactive strategies, are implemented to help develop a sense of camaraderie and unity. Whenever feasible, teachers engage students in team-building activities to help guide the learning process. Concerted efforts such as these make student members feel they actually belong within the community. The best chances for successful learning occur when students feel intellectually safe to express ideas, physically safe from harm, respected by other members, and perceived to be valuable contributors to the community. When they perceive their school as a community that is personally supportive, it is more likely not only that students will be satisfied with their classes but also that they will not drop out. Successful learning is more likely when emotional engagement is aimed for within such a framework. Developing caring classroom communities lays fertile ground for such a framework to blossom.

Essential Elements of the Classroom Community

- Students feel intellectually, emotionally, and physically secure.
- Every member of the community makes important contributions.
- Regular ritualistic practices, such as class meetings, occur.

The role of the teacher in the caring community is often defined as "other mother," "other father," or a surrogate type of role. The teacher relates to students in nurturing ways that help grow bonds. Students know that if they are grappling with an issue, they can always turn to the teacher for support. Mr. King, for instance, carries a few extra dollars and change as his students come to him for bus fare home or money for a hot meal. Mrs. Jones shares her Tuesday and Thursday lunch periods with students; she helps them grapple with various issues, lets them pick her brain, and talks about life, all of which help sustain and deepen relationships. Mrs. Klein keeps a surplus of clean uniform shirts and trousers for students who need them.

Classroom communities that are highly conducive to engaging African American students are communalistic in nature. The individuals in these environments are committed to engaging students in activities that facilitate social connectedness and to emphasizing that responsibilities and social connections supersede privileges of the individual. Learning in these rooms is oriented toward success of the group versus success of the individual. It is characterized by interdependence and sharing. Communalism has been found to produce positive emotional energy in classrooms.

How Are Caring Classroom Communities Built?

Though this is quite a different way to structure teaching and learning processes in the classroom, the foundation for building a caring classroom community begins with a commitment by the teacher to the erection of such a structure. The teacher commits to the belief that success is defined collectively and interdependence lies at the heart of most of what happens in the classroom. Spirited competition and comparisons among students give way to the spirit of cooperation and compassionate provisions of assistance. The focus is not on grades but goal mastery. Progress is indicated by measuring self-improvement over time. Peer-interactive strategies, such as peer questioning and cooperative grouping, are the central vehicles through which content is mastered. The pillars of the community, however, are strong student–teacher relationships.

Anchors of the Academic Experience: Creating and Sustaining Student–Teacher Relationships

Efforts to raise standardized test scores receive the lion's share of attention in today's classrooms. However, efforts to encourage more students to raise their hands or to complete simple classroom tasks are often challenged when teaching students who are underprepared or disengaged. One of the most powerful ways to build the classroom community is through the establishment of strong student–teacher relationships.

As mentioned, people are more likely to do business with those they like and trust than with those they don't know or dislike. In the business of education, you're more likely to get repeat classroom customers through the development of relationships based on trust. Students are also more likely to take action for people they both trust and like (Noddings, 1992).

Strong student–teacher relationships are marked by mutual exchanges of trust, respect, and admiration, while poor ones are marred by distrust, disrespect, and antagonism. Students are more likely to buy into you and what you have to offer if you have first developed a trusting relationship. Teachers play a big role in shaping social interactions and overall climate. Not only do relationships help teachers discover what's relevant, interesting, and meaningful to students, but they also can assist students in embracing rigorous learning (Washor & Mojkowski, 2007).

A FAMILY-LIKE CLASSROOM COMMUNITY

Ms. Klein couldn't wait to meet and greet her new homeroom students for the first time this year. Knowing how first words leave a lasting impression, she highly anticipated giving a warm delivery about the type of experiences her students should expect in her class this school year.

She started out by saying, "I want us to be more than a class of students. I want us to be a family-like community of learners." She had pairs brainstorm lists of the types of things families do. As the groups reported out, some family activities mentioned were as follows: share with each other, have fun together, *watch each other's backs,* eat family dinners together, argue with each other, and care for one another. Ms. Klein went on to say,

> Many of the things you mentioned families do with each other will be done as we build our classroom community this year. You all are the brothers and sisters of all students in school, but we will develop a closer bond in this classroom than we have with those outside of this room.

She went on to ask, "Do brothers and sisters disagree and argue sometimes?" The students said a loud "Yeeeeeeeeeeeeessssss" in unison. Ms. Klein responded, "When we disagree we will work through it to try to find a solution each time it happens." Then she continued,

> Every community has a leader. I will be the leader of our community. You all may want to think of me as like your school mom and dad wrapped into one person. [A few students snickered.] I expect you all to come to me if there is an issue inside or outside of school that you just can't solve. You may always anonymously write a message and place it in the *issue island* box. I will be relentless in looking out for you and will ALWAYS have your back, though I will surely let you know when you are wrong. Most decisions made by adults in schools are in your best interest, but when they're not, I will always stand up for you.
>
> I also expect you all to care, help, and look out for all students, especially those in our homeroom. Each of you all will have important roles in this community. If everyone does not take his or her role seriously, the community will not run as well as it could. I don't expect each of you to be perfect and never make mistakes, as no one on this earth is perfect. In our communities, we embrace mistakes as opportunities to learn and become smarter. I do not expect that you will repeat the mistakes you make. As you move about the school and go home each day, you are representing me and my name. I have worked hard to build a good reputation, care a lot about my name, and expect you to act in a way to uphold the name in the highest regard.
>
> Remember, as we work to build the community, it's about "we," not "me," as together we will be able to overcome any obstacle and support each other in becoming better learners and, more important, better people.

Strong student–teacher relationships are characterized by supportive academic and emotional interactions and open communication between student and teacher (Pianta & Stuhlman, 2004). They are the anchors of academic experiences. They form the foundation for forward movement in the classroom.

In engaging educational practices, teachers relentlessly work to not only build but *sustain* relationships with students. Among the many mistakes I made in the classroom was enacting a zero-tolerance, total control stance. I strove to let them know that I was in control and they were to do *as I said* each minute of the day. As you can imagine, I was met with a lot of resistance to cooperate and refusal to comply. I'll never forget the words of one young lady in my fourth hour science class, Tanisha, who told me during my first year of teaching, "Mr. Jabari, the reason we give you such a hard time is because you are always so hard on us and we're just not *used* to that. Last year *we* ran the class, ran the first two substitute teachers off, and the third one didn't return this year." Back then, each day of work was rife with chaos and conflict in my classroom.

An experienced teacher finally sat me down and said, "Look Jabari, students won't care about what you know until they know you care about them. You've got to get to their *heart* before you get to their head." The next morning I began fourth hour by saying, "Let's not look back at what has happened so far. You all are a great group of young people and I really *care* a great deal about ALL of you!" Unfortunately, that period ended up being no different from the days past. I spent most of the hour pausing to wait for idle conversation to stop, attempting to redirect behavior, and writing discipline referrals.

A breakthrough came when I left work one afternoon. I saw Johnny, a class leader who was also one of most mischievous students, standing at the bus stop and looking a bit distraught. I pulled up, asked him what was going on, and offered him a ride home. As we drove home, he told me how his family's electrical and gas service had been recently shut off for nonpayment and that the family would soon be evicted from the home. I assured him that there were certain things that he would not be able to change and that the best thing he could do for his family was to make sure he gave 110% effort each day in school. I also let him know that I would make myself available if he ever needed to talk to me about life, academics, or anything he needed to get off of his chest.

Over the next few weeks, I noticed a change in Johnny. He still misbehaved, but his misbehavior was far more infrequent. He began to put forth more effort in class and completing assignments, and the biggest surprise came from him becoming an ally in keeping the other students in class in line. I underestimated the impact of reaching out to him through simply offering a ride home, the extension of a listening ear, and wise advice for a young man who was going through some challenges. I figured out that one of the most effective ways to build relationships begins with establishing connections with key classroom stakeholders—classroom leaders. I learned an important lesson in understanding the power structures that exist among students and their potential impact in assisting with the smooth flow of the classroom.

Why Student–Teacher Relationships?

What's one of the main reasons people engage in activities that are of little interest to them? One main reason they do is the value placed on such activities by significant others in their lives with whom they have a relationship or connectedness to (Lee, 2012). The reason that the last incredibly uninteresting assignment you gave was completed by them was most likely related to the emotional ties you have established with them. Moreover, student–teacher relationships are vehicles that help narrow the gap between school and home norms for students (Baker, 1999). They are essential in helping minimize the factors that place underprepared students in HUMS at risk. Emotional and academic support provided through relationships helps students adjust better (Hamre & Pianta, 2005). Student–teacher relationships can also reduce the sense of being alone often experienced by at-risk students. Moreover, positive student–teacher relationships have been found to incentivize students to attend school even when they are facing challenging schoolwork and expectations in the classroom (LeCompte & Dworkin, 1991). There is a strong research basis underlying the importance of creating and sustaining student–teacher relationships.

> ### THEORETICAL FRAMEWORK: UNDERLYING REASONS FOR BUILDING STUDENT–TEACHER RELATIONSHIPS
>
> - Students who have supportive teacher relationships report higher behavioral and psychological engagement (Woolley & Bowen, 2009).
> - Student engagement in school can be enhanced by supportive relationships (Furrer & Skinner, 2003; Hughes, Gleason, & Zhang, 2005).
> - Support by teachers is essential for the school engagement of middle and high school Latino/a at-risk youth (Brewster & Bowen, 2004).
>
> *(Continued)*

(Continued)

- Student–teacher relationships play a pivotal role in school outcomes for Latino/a students (Woolley, Kol, & Bowen, 2009).
- Teachers who show an interest in and are involved with the lives of low-income African American students reported that their students are more engaged in learning (Tucker et al., 2002).
- Early school experiences with teachers impact whether students in HUMS like or dislike school. Teacher support is important in determining school outcomes, particularly for African American students (Baker, 1999; Decker, Dona, & Christenson, 2007).
- When students are aided by positive relationships with teachers, they are more likely to be motivated, to be engaged in school, and to pursue academic goals (Furrer & Skinner, 2003; Wentzel, 2002).
- People have an innate drive to create and keep a minimum number of significant, positive interpersonal relationships with others. Patterns of emotion and cognitive processes are strongly affected by the need to belong. When people create or make stronger social relationships, positive emotions usually result (Baumeister & Leary, 1995).
- At-risk students who have warm, trusting, low-conflict relationships with teachers have a greater chance of attaining positive school outcomes (Baker, Grant, & Morlock, 2008).
- Student–teacher relationships are one of the strongest predictors of levels of motivation of middle school students (Goodenow, 1993).
- Relationships with adults significantly impact student engagement in elementary, middle, and high school (Marks, 2000).
- Student alienation from school is linked to the extent to which student–teacher relationships are characterized by respect and fairness (Murdock, Anderman, & Hodge, 2000).
- Students are more satisfied with school and embrace more positive academic values when there are caring and interpersonal relationships present (Klem & Connell, 2004).
- Students with developmental vulnerabilities and a close relationship with their teacher have a significant advantage in school over similar peers who have no such relationship (Baker, 2006).
- Behavioral outcomes are more strongly predicted than academic outcomes by the quality of student–teacher relationships (Hamre & Pianta, 2001).
- Positive and supportive student–teacher relationships can assist with compensating for student self-regulatory challenges through creating low-conflict learning, which grows future academic achievement (Liew, Chen, & Hughes, 2010).
- The extent to which teachers demonstrate respect to students is a significant predictor of how students behave toward one another (Matsumara, Slater, & Crosson, 2008).

The Four Cs of Building Student–Teacher Relationships

Harmonious student–teacher relationships are developed through deposits of trust, open dialogue, and the devotion of time to each other. They begin with you planting the seed in their minds that your concern about *them* personally trumps everything else. I often hear teachers say, "My students *know* I care a great deal about *how well* they do in my class." However, it's more than just telling them that you care about how well they progress through your academic course. Unbreakable student–teacher connections are based on demonstrating that your number one concern is about their *personal* lives and well-being. When HUMS students are asked about the qualities they desire in an ideal teacher, the number one factor cited is one who personally cares about them.

As there are for many other social structures in the classroom, there are various techniques to build relationships with students. After enough failed attempts, I have developed an effective process for building relationships that works with either the most the charming or challenging students. This process is called the Four Cs of Relationship Building, and it consists of four critical elements: care, communication, consistency, and commitment.

The First C: Care

> Students need to know someone cares for them as persons. In low moments, even though they can't see the sense in it, they will continue to work on mathematics out of trust and love for their teacher. (Noddings, 1992, p. 68)

With each new group of students comes a unique set of challenges, as each class has its own identity. Showing them that you are committed to caring is more important than showing your capability of teaching, especially in classrooms where students aren't intrinsically motivated to learn. Convincing them that you care takes a bit of time, particularly if you are new to your learning community.

Why Care?

- If teachers want students in HUMS to consistently stay on task, the students' needs of care must first be met (Brown, 2003).
- The perception of students of a caring and supportive learning environment significantly impacts how satisfied they are with school (Baker, 1998).

- Caring and supportive classroom environments are essential prerequisites of academic objectives being met (Noddings, 1992).
- When students perceive teachers as caring, they are more motivated to meet academic objectives (Wentzel, 1997).

How Can You Show You Care?

Seek every possible opportunity to provide a helping hand or provide assistance with a personal issue or challenge.

From the time you enter the building until the time you exit at the end of the day, there will be more opportunities than you know to show that you care and thus build a level of trust. One of the most powerful ways to engage students emotionally is through deliberately committing intentional acts of care. An example of an act of care would be staying in tune or being familiar with your students' usual demeanor. When you observe that a student is not his or her "usual self," you express your concern by attempting to find out the issue of concern. Students are usually very appreciative of the gesture, even if they don't openly share what the concern is. Other opportunities may come in helping with a combination lock that won't seem to open, not letting them give up when they feel like quitting, and believing more in them than they believe in themselves.

Mrs. T., high school biology teacher, kept a box full of breakfast snacks because she knew a few of her students were from struggling families and often came to school without breakfast. They could walk in, no questions asked, and get a snack as long as it didn't interrupt class. The act of providing breakfast, "Mrs. T style," was directly *deposited* into students' bank of trust, and she knew her investment would grow in the form of caring student returns.

I deliberately made a conscious effort to search for entry points with my most challenging students. I knew that if I was able to overcome the challenge of establishing a caring connection with them, creating caring bonds with the rest of the class would be a cinch. One of the more consistent characteristics of classes I have observed over the years is that a small portion of students were highly assertive leaders of each class. Often the more assertive ones were also the more disruptive ones. When they spoke, everyone else seemed to echo their words. When I was able to capture the *hearts* of these most challenging classroom leaders, the rest of the class was *hooked* on my line. As mentioned, the ability to discern the pattern of power structure among students and the ability to harness it are powerful tools. When I was finally able to break through and reach Roderick, for example, he, in turn, helped maintain discipline and order by being a field general and assisted with strongly discouraging other students from being disobedient. Monroe (2009) discusses the importance of discerning and understanding the power structure among students:

> I student taught at [school name] in [location] in 1987 and it was an inner-city school, predominately Black, Hispanic, probably 98% minority. . . .
>
> *Researcher:* Did you have experiences during that student teaching that shaped your views on discipline strongly?
>
> *Mr. Holley:* You know . . . I didn't have discipline problems. . . . The day the teacher announced that I was going to take over the next day, a particular class, one of the boys looked at me . . . and said, "You're going to regret it."
>
> *Researcher:* Oh really?
>
> *Mr. Holley:* And it scared me to death because I thought, "Oh my gosh. What have I gotten myself into?" But as soon as he realized that I was there to help him he became my strongest ally. . . . He was like "Don't mess with Mr. Holley. . . ." I don't really recall having a lot of problems that year. (p. 335)

A FAMILY-LIKE CLASSROOM COMMUNITY

Mrs. Klein's fourth graders knew that in Room 127, if they struggled to understand or successfully finish classroom tasks, their study buddy was always someone they could rely on to provide a helping hand. Students never tackled academic or social issues in isolation, as the spirit of collaboration spearheaded success. Before class was dismissed each day, students would voluntarily stand in front of their peers and describe at least one act of caring they either personally received or witnessed another student do. The norm, which was not just accepted but embraced by all in Room 127, was to consciously commit caring acts of kindness without expecting anything in return.

Create a culture where acts of care are modeled,
praised, and valued in your room.

In classrooms where acts of care are modeled, praised, and highly valued, students and teachers jointly embrace them as one of the most important elements of the classroom. The teacher shows the way by consistently showing how to do things for others out of kindness and concern. Mrs. Jones, for example, begins each day with a smile and a warm greeting at the door, and she maintains a genuinely warm posture throughout the day. Students and teachers feel they have each other's backs and are highly supportive of not only the academic but also the social success of all.

Teachers such as Mrs. Jones create instructional routines that facilitate acts of caring through setting up students to help each other with academic tasks. That is, they utilize many peer-interactive learning routines where students lean on each other to learn. For example, they use instructional strategies such as think-pair-share, where students are asked to think about a higher order thinking question, share their response with a partner, clarify misunderstandings, combine responses, and share with the larger class. Other peer-interactive learning strategies include reciprocal questioning, cooperative grouping, and group presentations. The use of such strategies is justified not only because of their research-based foundations but also because they often lead to reciprocal acts of caring. They also enhance the quality of relationships among peers, as the collaboration helps create a bond. It provides an additional layer of support for students.

Demonstrate to students that caring for each other is
as important as covering curricular content.

Demonstrating care is something you should do not only because your students deserve the very best but also because it helps you connect with your students. Creating strong, caring bonds increases the chances your classroom is a place in which students want to voluntarily *hang out.* In turn, you're less likely to be stumped by discipline challenges from students. Students, particularly from challenging circumstances, seek someone in their lives who care about their well-being. Convincing them that you care won't happen overnight, but once they understand your commitment to create a caring classroom community, an emotional connection is cultivated and ultimately created.

Connecting with students by creating caring structures within the classroom also helps shape their perception of you. You will begin to be viewed as someone who they can count on to provide that missing element in the midst of misunderstanding. When students view teachers as supportive and caring, it motivates them to engage in the learning process by reducing the perceived likelihood of becoming swallowed by stress (Wentzel, 1997).

Be sincere when showing care, so that students don't feel you're currying favor.

Have you noticed that all students, from those with significant physical or learning disabilities to the most gifted, are able to perceptively ascertain whether or not the teacher truly cares? Though it's important to intentionally show students you care, your actions shouldn't come off as a contrived performance or feigned presentation. Just let *who you are* naturally come through. As you know, more opportunities than you realize will present themselves to demonstrate your care and concern. Working with students in HUMS will yield ample instances for you to offer a tissue, empathetically listen, or offer some of your sage advice. Allow your actions to be guided by the warm, loving person you truly are.

Be an ardent advocate for students when it comes to raising issues of concern for them.

Being an advocate for students is one of the most powerful ways to show caring. Recently, a resource teacher shared the story of how one of her students was being mistreated by a core content-area teacher. The principal had successfully lobbied human resources to remove the teacher from the building because of his history of mean-spiritedness with students. However, for some odd reason the teacher was reassigned to teach at the building once again that fall. The students complained about how unkindly the teacher spoke to them. The resource teacher even felt that it had gotten so bad that her student didn't want to attend that teacher's classroom ever again. She let this person know in no uncertain terms that his demeanor with students was unacceptable and offered ways to assist him in improving his demeanor. As time went on, the content-area teacher did not become perfect, but he did make some effort to improve his demeanor with students. Her advocacy built a stronger bond with her student.

All people need to know they are cared for, and students are no different. Some teachers have strong instructional methods but don't effectively reach students because of this important missing element. Particularly in HUMS, students must get advance notice that you care before advancing their attention to what you have to share. As Noddings (1992) so eloquently put it: "I want to suggest that caring is the very bedrock of all successful education. . . ." (p. 27). It is not enough to just care about how they fare academically; intentional actions must be made to show you care about them personally. The quality of student–teacher relationships may vary from classroom to classroom, but you don't find strong relationships existing without care.

Although care is highly important in any relationship, communication is yet another central element in relationship building.

The Second C: Communication

Communication is the vehicle through which thoughts and feelings are exchanged. It's the medium through which emotional states are unmasked, interpreted, and understood (or misunderstood) by others. It's the conduit through which ideas, concepts, procedures, and processes flow among teachers and students. Communication lies at the center of the universal exchanges in the classroom. Thus, verbal and nonverbal communication can be used as powerful means of either building or breaking relationships between teacher and student.

A few weeks ago, a middle school social studies teacher asked me the question, "How can I get through to them, Jelani? It seems that every time I teach it's like I'm speaking Latin while trying to teach calculus to French speaking students. Some try to avoid coming to my class, and many nearly run over each other in a rush to get out of here as soon as the bell rings." As her eyes welled and the tears slowly began to trickle down her cheek, she emotionally said, "They just don't seem like they like me. I feel like such a foreigner stranded in a native land!" When I asked her about the kinds of one-on-one interactions she has with them, she intimated that she didn't feel those things were important and her only job was to deliver the curriculum. She also indicated that she rarely had any nonacademic conversations with them. I gave her a few suggestions about connecting through conversations involving everyday experiences and issues. I went on to talk about how the golden informational nuggets she gleaned from such conversations could be used to plan and prepare lessons and, more important, to begin to develop sorely needed relationships. Weeks later, she sent an e-mail expressing her appreciation for the timely suggestions, which worked quite well!

Why Communication?

There is no exchange of information, ideas, or emotional states without it. Students want to know who you really are behind your instructional veil. It's the window through which emotional and intellectual energy radiates. Trust, an important component of any relationship, is partly based on communication processes between people. Students in HUMS often seek interpersonal relationships characterized by warm, communicative exchanges. You are able to build their belief in their ability to improve through your enthusiastic words of encouragement. Expectations of greatness are delivered through clear, concise communication. In short, warm yet stern communication is an invaluable component of strong relationships and helps endear students to you.

Connecting Through Conversations

Did your parents ever end conversations when you asked the "why do I have to" questions by saying, "Because I told you so"? It seemed like I heard that reply more than any other when I questioned a decision or just wanted more information. How open are you with your students as it relates to information pertinent to them or their instructional journey? The following example demonstrates one way Mrs. Jones endears herself to her students:

Mrs. Jones	How was your weekend? Well, what did you do?
Samuel	I spent some time with my family. We went to the beach.
Mrs. Jones	Did you swim?
Samuel	Nah. Just kinda put my feet in the water.
Karen	Ugh! You went to the beach. I went last week. Me and my cousins spent most of Saturday at the skating rink. I love going skating!

[the following Monday]

Mrs. Jones	Hello, Samuel. Did you get back to the beach this weekend?
Samuel	Nah. I just spent most of it playing my Xbox with my brothers and friends.

Mrs. Jones	Which games are your favorites?
Samuel	Madden 2012.
Mrs. Jones	How about your weekend, Karen? Did you spend the weekend skating with Sam (her classmate)?
Karen	Awww, Mrs. Jones. I never said I was going skating with Sam!

KEEPING AN OPEN LINE

Many high school students felt that they were often left in the dark about school issues that directly and indirectly impacted them. To help with this issue, Mr. King scanned the weekly electronic teacher newsletter for pertinent student items on Monday mornings before school began. He copied, pasted, printed, and prominently posted those items on his classroom bulletin board before his first class came in. In addition, he posted pertinent student informational items on his Facebook economics page, which only students of his school had access to. Pressing issues were briefly discussed with students before he began his instructional delivery.

He strongly encouraged students to examine the feedback he and other teachers gave on students' papers. As communication is held in high regard by him, he made it mandatory for each student to meet with him to discuss where they went wrong on major assignments and to jointly uncover learning opportunity in the midst of a misstep. He even had students who fared well on the assignment meet with him to find ways to better their best.

Some colleagues enviously wondered why his students elevated him to *rock star* status. Students constantly stopped to warmly greet him or engage in quick conversation when they saw him outside of class, and always seemed to gravitate to his room. He routinely received a rousing round of applause when called on stage during assemblies. When asked why this happened, he simply said,

It's about empathetically listening to them and being driven by the question, "What would *I* want if I were in their shoes?" It's about investing that up-front time, openly and honestly communicating with 'em, and just being endearingly stern and warmly fair.

It's those kinds of things that sow the seeds of sound student–teacher relationships.

Students really enjoy coming to Mrs. Jones's class because she is personable and down to earth. As she began to talk to Samuel, Karen was eager to join in and share how her weekend was. Mrs. Jones is very skilled in connecting through informal conversations with students. This informal talk gave her some rich information that could be used to deepen the connection between her and the students. Conversations are often about nonacademic issues, are very informal, and are often personal exchanges between teacher and student.

Like Mrs. Jones, I was deliberate in using connecting through conversations to help develop relationships with my students. I strategically made it my business to make positive personal comments every opportunity. Some examples were, "I love what you have done with your hair! How's your brother's leg healing after the surgery? What did you do over the weekend?" I relentlessly went out of my way to positively comment on such elements as students' appearance, work, and performance on tasks. I asked about family members I met at school family events or became familiar with through students' writing. I made a special effort to uplift members of the class who may have recently lost a loved one, lacked self-confidence or self-esteem, or just needed a little boost. I would tell even my most behaviorally challenging students how much they were missed when they were absent. Making such connections through conversation was a mundane yet powerfully effective tool of communication. My commitment was not only to construct the bridge to form the relationship but to conduct regular maintenance, even if the bridge seemed structurally sound.

Though points such as these may seem trivial to some, they contribute tremendously toward laying the foundation for connecting and developing relationships with students. Engaging students in positive conversations around their personal lives sends the powerful message that *this guy's different, he's down to earth and really takes an interest in me!* Remember, people do business with those they like and trust, and 90% of a buying decision is rooted in people's subconscious emotions. Informal conversations help you use such small talk to make the emotional connection.

Communicate through lingo and gestures.

A wise man once said, "If you want to communicate with a person, you have to first speak his or her language." Have you ever wondered how some teachers are able to communicate with students as if they co-authored the dictionary of *studentese* (student lingo) with them? Do you know a few common (appropriate) expressions that are unique to your students and used in their everyday language? What are their expressions for an exciting moment or for doing a good job? Finding the answer to these questions will help you make deeper connections and further the process of relationship building with them.

On several occasions, for instance, Mrs. Jones overheard her students use the term *swag*, connoting the way a person carries him or herself. From time to time, she would interject such terms while teaching and say something like, "Tywan, you really have your *swag on* today because I am really feelin' (enjoying) that effort you're giving. The first time her students heard this they were pleasantly amused, and one student even asked, "Mrs. Jones! How do YOU know what swag is?"

Table 3 shows several ways to communicate effectively through conversations.

Table 3 Effectively Connecting Through Conversations as Communicative Tools of Relationship Building

Type of Statement or Question	Sample Categories	Examples
I noticed. . . .	appearance, academic performance, dress, demeanor, social competence	• I see you've changed your hairstyle. It looks really great on you! • I noticed how much effort you've put into your work lately. I am really proud of you! • You're really rocking that new coat. I bet it really keeps you warm, huh? • Look at how you persisted and kept at it! You didn't give up! • I noticed you don't look like your usual self. Is everything okay? Would you like to talk about it? • You *can't* be the same person who was here yesterday? I am really noticing this new mature way of handling disagreements!
What did you do . . .	over the summer, over the weekend, during the holiday, during lunch, for your birthday	• So, tell me about your summer. What sorts of fun/interesting things did you do? • Did you and Nicole get a chance to hang out together over the weekend? • Did you eat Thanksgiving dinner at your house? What dish did you make? • Was the cafeteria food any better today? • How does it feel to be the big one-four (14 years old)? What did you and your family do to celebrate the occasion?

Type of Statement or Question	Sample Categories	Examples
How is . . .	family member, injury/illness, challenging issue	• How is your darling 7-month-old baby brother? Is he sleeping all night yet? Do you have to watch him often? • I know your grandmother is going through a series of chemotherapy treatments. How is she managing it? • We talked about some strategies for dealing with you being bullied by ____. How are those strategies working?
Tell me about. . . .	gadget, game, anything that means a lot to them	• Is that a new cell phone? Tell me about the cool features. • Did you guys really stand in line for 4 hours to get the new Xbox game? Was the wait worth you standing in line for all of that time? • Did your dad actually let you have the dog you wanted from the Humane Society? Tell me how that's working out. Is he house trained yet? Do you have to clean up after him?

When I taught, I tirelessly worked to become a better scholar of my students as I studied many aspects about them, such how they learned best. An additional element of study was the type of gestures they used to communicate with each other. With the expense of a little embarrassment and a small investment of time to practice, I was able to master a few of these gestures. Trying new gestures and words for the first few times may generate some self-deprecating laughter you'll surely share with students. Nonetheless, they will appreciate the effort you have made to connect with them and love the laugh that comes with it. It gives them a sense of validation and affirmation of who they are and the world they live in.

Do you remember a gesture called *raising the roof*, a gesture where you place both hands shoulder height with palms up, then simultaneously raise them up and down? To celebrate effort, improvement, correct responses or any good occurrence, our classroom community collectively *raised the roof* from time to time. All students actively participated when I used such gestures.

All it requires is some attentive listening, careful observation of communicative processes and style, and mentally or physically documenting what students said. Sometimes I heard a new term or saw unfamiliar gestures and wanted to incorporate them into my instructional practice. To enhance my student *cred* (credibility), I would go to resources such as urbandictionary.com and surprise my students by using a new term or gesture while teaching or during other interactions. As a caveat, be careful to not make it sound canned or like you are making a deliberate attempt to "be cool."

I can't tell you exactly what it was about these, but use of them really strengthened the bonds and empowered me to communicate much more effectively.

CELEBRATORY GESTURES TO BE REMEMBERED

Mrs. Jones was always in search of ways to connect more deeply with her students. One of her seventh graders, Hector, consistently walked around the room, distracted others by talking, and often made a cacophony of sounds during class. Each time she attempted to address this behavior, he belligerently reacted and defiantly refused to comply. After the fourth time within a week of referring him to the dean of discipline, she received a memo instructing her to "refer to the teacher's handbook for effective strategies to handle such trivial issues. Teachers are expected to resolve such matters internally." Exasperated, she resorted to frequently calling in sick and began to quickly deplete her bank of sick days.

One Tuesday when she did return to work, a student, Marcia, said, "You are always on us about our attendance, but why are you absent so much?" Feeling somewhat guilty upon hearing this sobering question, she resolved to try a different approach.

After hearing Hector brag about his shooting acumen on the basketball court, she went to the gym and asked him to show her how well he had been able to master the three point jump shot in basketball. He missed about the first 20 shots, but he finally made one. The way he celebrated the shot with his friends was quite interesting to Mrs. Jones. Hector pretended to shake something from his left hand into his right and then pretended to shake an imaginary substance from the right into the left. Then he pretended to toss the substance into the air. After that, he and Charles ran toward each other, leapt into each other and gave a chest bump.

Mrs. Jones congratulated Hector on making the shot by chanting, "Hector, Hector, Hector!" The look on his face was as if he had just won the national junior spelling bee. Later she asked, "What type of celebration were you doing after you swished that shot?" "You know," he replied, "The LeBron James powder toss. You have seen the Miami Heat player do that? Then, me and Charles ran to each other to finish it with a jumping chest bump."

Later that evening, Mrs. Jones googled "LeBron James powder toss" and pulled up a couple of videos of the basketball superstar doing his ritualistic powder toss.

She also found video on football players doing the chest bump. The next day in class, after her students had engaged in powerful dialogue using techniques such as building on each others' ideas, she had them all stand and do the powder toss. When individual students did well, she bumped shoulders with them in a modified version of the chest bump that she called her shoulder bump: She lightly bumped shoulders as she stood on on tiptoe (or lower for shorter students).

Hector told her one day, "Mrs. Jones, you're not like the other teachers I have had. You're like one of us!" She was always searching for ways to affirm them and lighten things up with them, and she used gestures such as the powder toss and shoulder bump to build stronger relationships with her students.

Including a few common student gestures as a technique in your communicative repertoire will enhance the exchange of ideas and information as well as the emotional connectedness between you and your students. It will help you connect in ways you never thought you could.

Use feedback as a communication tool.

Have you ever been asked for your opinion on how an outfit looked? Some years ago, I was asked by a friend of mine about how a new dress looked on her. I asked her, "Do you want my honest opinion?" to which she responded, "Yes." I said, "It um, it uh, it makes you look a little bigger than you actually are. I would return it to the store if I was you." She ended up ignoring my phone calls and not speaking to me for months afterward. I realized that sometimes people tell you that they want honest feedback but in reality seek only honey-laden feedback.

Feedback is the provision of information about how well a person or entity has either understood or performed. It's a powerful tool used in our personal and professional lives. It is the mother's milk that corporate America utilizes to drive improvement. Retailer JC Penney, for example, values feedback so highly that it offers a 15% discount on the next purchase if you take the time to give feedback via a survey. School administrators use feedback to communicate elements of teaching performance during observations.

Think about an assignment with multiple choice items that you correct and return to your students. The only markings on the paper are Xs on the incorrectly answered questions and a fraction showing the ratio of correct responses to the total number of items at the top of the paper. You have probably returned a paper to your students with this type of feedback at some point in your teaching career. In what way does this returned paper enhance the learning or move students toward mastery? Without any significant guidance on identifying the places where conceptual misunderstanding occurred or other factors led to the incorrect responses, feedback of this kind does not aid mastery for your students. Without appropriate feedback, such an exercise is of little benefit to students.

Effective feedback about academic or social performance has many benefits. It can be utilized as an effective means of communicating with students. An added benefit is that it can help you bond and make connections with your students. Effective feedback can have a powerful impact on academic achievement (Hattie & Timperley, 2007; Kluger & DeNisi, 1996). Its effectiveness depends on the type of feedback and the way it's given.

The process of correcting student papers for accuracy provides an excellent opportunity to provide a personal touch with your students. When given in supportively suggestive ways, it sends the message that you care. There are a litany of effective methods for providing feedback. I have developed one I call the DISC technique that has worked well with students.

The DISC technique of giving communicative feedback is a way of providing feedback that it is Descriptive, Immediate, centered on Strategy use, and highlights only the Critical points. The question that should be focused on by the feedback communicated about tasks is, "How can I move students from where they are to where they have learned what I want them to learn?" The DISC method is briefly described below.

- *Descriptive*—The feedback should describe the specific shortcomings or inadequacies of the student response. Ideally these descriptive comments should (a) be provided without a grade, to help them move from the current state to the goal, and (b) describe the work and provide ways to help scaffold the student to the desired learning outcomes.

- *Immediate*—The feedback should be communicated to the students as quickly as possible after they submit the relevant work, and after they receive the feedback, they should be given an ample amount of time to have a fair shot at mastery of the goal. Too often, assignments are returned long after the given unit of study has been completed. It provides little incentive for students to go back and master learning just for intrinsic knowledge of subject matter.

• *Strategic (coupled with effort)*—Communicated feedback should be laden with emphasis on how to employ strategies and techniques for achieving the intended learning outcomes. It should always build the students' beliefs in their capability to improve if they expend the energy and exert the effort to employ specified strategies. If this feedback is communicated orally, students should be encouraged to explain their thinking during classroom discourse and provide evidence to justify their responses.

• *Critical points*—Have you ever had a college professor or K–12 teacher who had a love affair with red ink? Mrs. Schick, my 12th-grade English instructor, was a teacher with such a love. We often joked that she would use all of the ink from a single pen to check just one of our essays. Many teachers are like Mrs. Schick—they make the mistake of trying to emphasize several different areas or make too many marks and comments on a given assignment. Doing so often overwhelms students and sometimes leads them to learn little. Feedback should be prioritized to highlight only the most essential points for meeting the desired learning goals. Diminishing returns on instruction often ensue when you fall in love with the power of red ink.

Communicating with students via feedback can profoundly impact achievement and learning. The aim when providing feedback is to move students from a current position to goal mastery. Its effectiveness depends on the type of feedback given and the way it is given. Providing feedback that is descriptive, given with a degree of immediacy, pointing to strategy use, and highlighting only essential points can effectively impact learning and achievement. It communicates the message to students that you care.

The Third C: Consistency

Many students who come from precariously risky home situations are challenged with consistently inconsistent and unstable elements in their lives. Mounting inconsistencies may include

> *Teachers by nature are gift givers; the best gift that you give is your presence.*

shelter, caregivers, nourishment, health care, and other important life elements. The pain of repeatedly broken relationships has imprisoned their desire to create future bonds with others. Family instability has been linked to poor student behavior, drug abuse, loneliness, and school failure. Thus, the institution of the school and its staff are the most stable facets of many students' lives.

Why Consistency?

Though it may seem mundane, the fact that you are present on a daily basis to teach and touch their lives is significant. In the midst of episodic chaos and continual life crises, students look forward to seeing your warm smiles and welcoming presence in their classroom community. They know that as certain as the dawn of a new day, they will have a supportive environment to learn and grow in in *your* room.

It always amazed me with how strongly many of my students wanted to come to school on days with several inches of snow, bone-chilling temperatures, or even days immediately preceding a holiday break when many others typically stay home. It took me a while to get it, but I finally came to the realization that for some, we were the *best* thing going, and being with us provided temporary relief from strife and turmoil.

Consistent classroom expectations aid the growth of student–teacher relationships as well. Students appreciate an environment with equitably enforced rules. They know that there are no *favorites* per se who have a different set of rules to comply with. They relish your maintenance of high expectations for them to improve. They value your consistent belief in their ability to become smarter. They welcome your unwavering push for them to relentlessly give the effort and energy to succeed.

How can you provide consistency?

There are no magical methods, secret strategies, or transformational techniques for being consistently, *ahem,* consistent. It simply boils down to you regularly being the warmly demanding yet caring and loving person you truly are. Consistently providing a supportive presence in students' lives helps develop student–teacher relationships. Such relationships grow from them counting on you to take the time to provide sage wisdom, timely advice, and insightful guidance when they need it. They develop from the consistency of having an opportunity to stop by your room to receive extra help or just hang out either during lunch or after school. Relationships blossom from the confidence they have in your supportive student advocacy. Simply put, students' knowledge that they can look forward to a reliable, caring, and loving adult who consistently has their best interests at heart helps student–teacher relationships exponentially grow.

> To the universe, all of us are just one person . . . but to one person, you can be the universe.
>
> —Coach Ken Carter

The Fourth C: Commitment

Commitment is something people love to receive but sometimes loath to reciprocate. Many absolutely love the unwavering loyalty given by the golden retriever yet despise the obligation of cleaning up after it. We love to receive the commitment to customer service excellence by a high-end auto manufacturer yet shy away from committing to make the high monthly payments. Couples love the spousal commitment that comes with the "I do" but soon wonder "do I really want to do" the necessary things to make the marriage work. Commitment in schools is worthy of exploration.

Why Commitment?

- Commitment to students has been found to be a pivotal factor of teacher retention in HUMS (Freedman & Appleman, 2009).
- Teacher commitment has been positively linked to job satisfaction for both White and Black teachers (Culver, Wolfe, & Cross, 1990) and job satisfaction for teachers in general (Fresko, Kfir, & Nasser, 1997).
- Enhancing the commitment of teachers in the workplace has become an integral part of school reform, particularly in HUMS (Kushman, 1992).
- When teachers are committed, it helps them become more innovative and collaborate better, and it breeds a culture of teacher professionalism (Rosenholtz, 1985).

The commitment of teachers to learning is composed of the extent to which they believe they can impact the learning process (efficacy), their belief that students will learn, and the extent to which they are willing to put forth the energy and effort for learning outcomes to be met. Furthermore, Bandura (1997) has shown that the commitment of teachers to work and their performance quality is related to their level of motivation to influence the learning of students. Though teacher commitment encompasses many areas, I will limit the discussion to two components of teacher commitment: commitment to student learning and commitment to assist students in achieving positive social outcomes.

How Is Commitment Evident in Your Teaching?

When a person is committed to someone else, there exists a psychological identification or bond, a deep belief in the value of the other person, a willingness to do more than the minimum for them, and a strong desire to maintain an association with that person (Firestone & Pennell, 1993). Committed teachers are known for strong psychological ties to their students, their school, and the content they teach. They voluntarily give of themselves so that students can emulate them and succeed.

Teacher commitment to students often contributes to endearingly warm classroom climates. It is a necessary component of strong student–teacher relationships. Commitment to students means you will always take principled stances on issues in their best interest. It means that you will believe in their ability to improve and to progress toward levels of excellence. You'll maintain that belief in them until their own belief in themselves takes over. Committing to your students means you won't give up on them after they make mistakes. In short, commitment to students means you will help them realize their hidden talents and the greatness locked within.

Providing the Assist: When You Find the Issue, You Find the Entrance

PROVIDING THE ASSIST BY HELPING WITH ORGANIZATION

Mrs. Jones was at wit's end because her students were the poster children of disorganization. Marquise, for example, would often sit for 10 minutes frantically searching for his homework through a pile of wrinkled papers stuffed into his backpack. When Mrs. Jones asked Marquise about it, he replied, "I know you probably don't believe me, but I did it Mrs. Jones! I *did* do it!" When Mrs. Jones brought it to Marquise's parents' attention, his dad said,

When you find the issue, you find the entrance.

> That boy would lose his legs if he didn't use them to keep his body upright! But we sit down at the kitchen table after dinner each night, help him with his homework, and make sure it's done. . . . each night. Now what happens to it between the time it's done and when you ask for it is an entirely different story.

Tamara was a little bit better, but she kept all of her returned assignments (e.g., homework, tests, quizzes, class work) in the same folder. For various students, Mrs. Jones often found herself frustrated when she found worksheets left underneath desks and when students gave poor presentations because they had lost their rubrics. Her students had a myriad of issues related to poor organizational skills.

As she reflected on the issue over the summer, she came up with the idea that she would make a classroom requirement for each student to have a 2-inch, 3-ring binder with 8 tab dividers for her class. She thought that this would be tremendous in helping students organize work for her class. She purchased a few extra binders for families she knew would have a difficult time shelling out the extra five dollars. As an added measure, she took a letter printed on school letterhead to the local office supply store to request that a few extra binders be donated. They were happy to do so if the school would allow them to set up a table at the upcoming open house night. She also persuaded her principal to purchase planners for each student in grades 3–8.

As an added organizational technique, Mrs. Jones planned to emphasize the DIN (do it now) edict for staying on top of important things. Whenever an important date, assignment, or piece of information was shared, she would sing in her own humorous way, "Gonna win time; it's DIN time!" Students would immediately take out their planners and note what it was and when it was due. It was such a big hit that two of her colleagues made it a requirement for their classes beginning in the second semester. Though students griped about the extra work initially, several thanked her for teaching them how to become more organized, not only in her class but in others as well. Many talked about how they had adopted the DIN slogan in other aspects of life, such as when asked to do chores so they didn't forget. Marquise even made his own thank-you card out of construction paper to express his gratitude for the assistance in becoming better organized.

Have you ever had a student in your room who was so introverted or standoffish that you just couldn't connect—as if the student were surrounded by a shark-filled emotional moat? That is, the type of student who was very difficult to develop a level of trust or openly communicate with? As you are aware, students are affected by issues that you have no control over, but those issues find a way to infect the emotional climate of your classroom. One of the most effective ways to successfully cross the moat is through assisting with the resolution of issues. When you find your students' issues, you find the needed entrances to make the connection. Aiding in resolution will help you get the keys to the castle.

Providing an assist in sports like basketball, hockey, or soccer means one player helps a teammate achieve the goal of scoring a point or points. Classroom assists happen when a team member helps another member of the community hit a goal. The goal can be hit through the resolution of an academic or personal issue, obstacle, or challenge. The strength in this technique lies not just in its potential to help students get through a challenging task you assigned. It becomes a highly powerful technique when you provide an assist that helps students overcome a challenge that extends beyond your four walls.

There are many academic issues, such as the organization skills Mrs. Jones assisted with, that are not necessarily content specific. Other commonly encountered issues are poor study skills, unfamiliarity with how to use context clues, or a lack of knowledge about how to best encode information for later retrieval and recall from memory. Tables 4 and 5 highlight several ways you can provide academic and social assists that will deepen the emotional connection between you and your students.

Table 4   Connecting by Assisting With Academic Issues

Issue	Strategies	Resources
Encoding information into and recalling from memory	Model how instructional interventions such as mnemonic techniques (e.g., keyword, pegword, letter, chunking) have aided you and will work for them.	• Scruggs, Mastropieri, Berkeley, & Marshak (2010) • Terrill, Scruggs, & Mastropieri (2004) • Calder (2006)
Accurately understanding and responding to questions on tasks	Use the question-answer relationship (QAR) strategy.	• Mesmer & Hutchins (2002) • Raphael (1986)
Procrastinating before beginning work	Pinpoint behaviors that lead to procrastination. Teach them how to break large projects into smaller pieces with well-defined goals and dates. Emphasize the DIN approach for accomplishing tasks.	• www.procrastinus.com • http://ub-counseling.buffalo.edu/stressprocrast.php
Limited vocabulary	Build vocabulary by providing ample opportunities to learn words from context. Challenge students to use new words in everyday and classroom conversation.	• Sternberg (1987) • Nagy, Herman, & Anderson (1985)
Being overwhelmed by test anxiety	Comfort students with the notion that when they have adequately prepared for assignments and tests, everything will be fine. Emphasize that no matter what happens, the world will not end. Encourage them to answer easy questions first as confidence builders.	• Hembree (1988) • Wigfield & Eccles (1989)
Summarizing, paraphrasing, and restating author's words	Break summarizing into subskills (e.g., retelling, restating)	• Kissner (2006)

Table 5   Connecting by Assisting With Personal Issues

Issue	Strategies	Resources
Constantly wanting to give up when challenged with adversity	• Provide daily or weekly inspirational quotes. • Provide literature/stories chronicling what someone with shared ethnicity/struggles achieved in the face of adversity. • Share your stories of how you succeeded after being dealt one of life's blows.	• www.quotationspage.com • Association for Library Service to Children • (see Chapter 6)
Not being mindful of future consequences to guide current actions	• Share self-regulatory strategies that minimize impulsive behavior.	• Boekaerts & Corno (2005) • Zimmerman & Schunk (2008)
Impulsively speaking every word that comes to mind	• Teach to pause and think carefully about the impact of each word. • Teach to think of words like a sparrow; once they fly out of the mouth, you can't get them back.	• Boekaerts & Corno (2005) • Zimmerman & Schunk (2008)
Periodically needing a few dollars (e.g., bus fare, lunch money, dance ticket)	• Keep a small stash of currency in the event students need it.	• Paycheck, change from purchases
Managing emotional outbursts	• Teach self-regulatory strategies. • Provide social skills training (SST). • Avoid using directive language about feelings, but have students discuss feelings. • Teach calming strategies (e.g., turtle technique) to use before outbursts occur. • Teach how to respond assertively yet in a controlled manner. • Teach how to become more adept at recognizing the signs that precipitate an outburst.	• Nangle, Erdley, Carpenter, & Newman (2002) • Prinz, Blechman, & Dumas (1994) • Webster-Stratton (2005) • Webster-Stratton & Reid (2003) • www.rootsofempathy.org

(Continued)

(Continued)

Issue	Strategies	Resources
	• Teach positive self-talk using catch phrases such as "no one's perfect." • Create a classroom safe zone for students to relax and regain control. • Remain even keeled in your response.	
Overcoming bullying	• Encourage students to elicit support of a trusted adult. • Teach to calmly but firmly tell bully to "stop because I don't like the behavior."	• School counselor, administrator, parents • www.pacer.org/ bullying/ • bullies2buddies.com • www.stopcyberbullying .org • www.stopbullying.gov

What academic or personal issues can you help resolve using techniques that students can use outside of your subject area?

The suggested resources are by no means an exhaustive listing of available resources for remedying the issues listed in the tables. Clearly there are entire books and semester-long courses designed around topics such as alleviating test anxiety and overcoming procrastination. However, I have given attention to commonly encountered personal and academic issues facing many students. I have been able to get through to some of the toughest students using some of these techniques and strategies. If you are truly serious about emotionally engaging your students, select one assisting strategy, and use it to help your students overcome an issue or two. This attention provides useful starting blocks for addressing commonly encountered student issues, which will lead to the building of a trusting, caring rapport between teacher and student.

How Can I Provide an Assist Given the Overwhelming Number of Other Things I'm Already Asked to Do?

In many cases, the aforementioned assists can be integrated into something you're doing already and won't add layers. For example, I modeled the letter-mnemonic strategy for my students, and it began to take on a life of its own. I shared how it helped me remember the names of the Great Lakes and the planets of the solar system many years after learning them. Practicing these techniques minutes at a time is all it takes. You could also challenge students to paraphrase what others said during class dialogue, use the DIN, or have them paraphrase a few assigned sentences for homework. You don't have to necessarily stop the lesson to teach this skill. The best thing about it is that your students will absolutely hold you in higher regard because you equipped them with tools that empowered them to be successful in your class, other classes, and aspects of life as well. Your students *need* you to create a supportive environment, and providing the assist helps fulfill this need.

ANNOTATING TEXT TO PROVIDE THE ASSIST

Mr. King assigns pages from the economics text for his students to read and take notes periodically throughout the study of each new unit. However, when he engaged students in dialogue about what they read, they often were at a loss for words. Because of their poor responses during class discussions, he questioned, "How many of you actually took time to (a) read and (b) take notes?" Most of the class raised their hands both times. He said, "You guys *couldn't* have read the text with the kind of responses you gave!" He chided them for not taking the assignment seriously and just *blowing it off* as something that wouldn't be graded.

After this happened a second time, he asked all of the students to close the books and called a class meeting during the last 15 minutes of class. He reminded them, "I would do whatever it takes to consistently place you in a position to be successful in this class. But I need you to hold up your end of the bargain. So I need you all to tell me what's really going on that you can't answer many of the questions and contribute little to the discussion." Mr. King's students already knew it was safe and appropriate to freely share opinions during class meetings as long as this was done with appropriate language and addressed issues and actions, not people. Jacinthia, an honor student who usually completed all assigned work, said, "Mr. K, we did take notes. But this material is just really hard to understand." During his department and staff meetings, Mr. King found out that this was an issue with other teachers as well.

He decided that for the next 4 weeks, during the last 10 minutes of each class period on Tuesday, he would teach his sophomores how to annotate text. The goal was to teach them a skill for getting a deeper and longer-lasting understanding of what was read. He began by modeling the process on the overhead projector, and then he put students into pairs and had them annotate small chunks of text. After the first month, he observed a demonstrable difference in classroom dialogue. His colleagues who taught that group of students commended him as well for the job he did with his students.

Chapter Summary

Controlling students may get you classroom *compliance,* but making connections gets the *commitment.* Such strong emotional connections are the lifeblood HUMS classrooms. Flexing disciplinary muscles provides only temporary relief. If you don't allow them to see your human side, don't demonstrate that you care about their personal well-being, and don't work to build connections that lead to relationships with them, you invite unwanted elements to rear their heads in the classroom. Research has documented and practice has confirmed that the number one reason students engage in activities that are of little interest to them is by first creating strong emotional bonds with the teacher. Creating emotional connections makes it much easier to begin the process of emotionally engaging your students. Connections are best made when you are consistently aiming to develop a classroom community.

Emotional engagement is best grown from initially establishing emotional connections with students. You've got to give them something before they give two cents about your content or you. Appealing to students' emotional side versus logical reasoning gives you a better chance of having them take a desired action. Your ability to quickly identify the power structure existing among HUMS students is essential. Initially forming stronger emotional connections with those in the upper echelons of such structures is beneficial for orderly rooms.

When you find the issues of challenge in your students' lives, you find the entrance to make the bonds. Students in HUMS may be underprepared when they show up each day, but they have an overabundant, oft-replenished reservoir of issues just *waiting* to be addressed. If you continue to ignore issues saddling your students, you're missing invaluable opportunities to create critical connections. Commit to an up-front investment of a bit of your time and wisdom, and you'll reap the rich returns of student loyalty, trust, and unyielding support.

ACTIONABLE PROFESSIONAL LEARNING

Please respond individually initially, and then discuss with your collaborative learning team.

1. A case was made for establishing an emotional connection to lay the foundation for creating emotional engagement. Would you say the rapport with your students is accurately characterized by a controlling stance or by strong emotional ties? Using strategies gleaned from this chapter, how might you develop even stronger emotional connections with them?

2. Does your classroom operate as a community of learners or as learners in a classroom? If it is not a classroom community, what steps will you take to begin the process of community building in the classroom?

3. Considering the Four Cs of Relationship Building, which of the Cs do you feel needs the most improvement to enhance your relationships with students? Thinking of the information shared in this chapter, which strategies will you use to improve the C you identified?

4. When you find and help resolve issues that challenge students, you find entrances for establishing stronger connections. Of the many things challenging your students during the course of a day, what specific issue or two can you aid them with that would benefit them outside of your class?

Action Research

During your collaborative team meeting, identify and discuss specific challenges with establishing emotional connections with students. Have each member of your team decide on one strategy for building stronger emotional connections with a couple of the most challenging students. Applying ideas to practice, use that strategy with the aim of developing stronger connections with the identified student(s) for the next four weeks. Have each member of your team either anecdotally or more formally note specific evidence of the strategy's effectiveness. Such evidence may include statements made by the student(s), descriptions of interactions with the student(s), or the extent to which discernible changes in each student's behavior were observed. Be prepared to engage in reflective dialogue during the next meeting (after the four weeks), which should include such elements as the following:

a. your data and other findings (e.g., successes, shortcomings, questions)

b. how the strategy itself may be tweaked to be more effective

c. other elements (e.g., teacher action, more time) that may make the strategy more effective

Using what was gleaned from your reflective dialogue, repeat the process outlined above, and reflectively dialogue about the findings during the subsequent team meetings.

6

Intersect Their Interests and Experiences With Instruction

From the standpoint of the child, the great waste in the school comes from his inability to utilize the experiences he gets outside in the school in any complete and free way within the school itself; while on the other hand, he is unable to apply in daily life what he is learning in school.

(Dewey, 1900, p. 76)

Beginning the Engagement When the Tardy Bell Rings

Would you say that you truly begin to engage your students after they complete *Do-Nows* and the attendance is taken? Or can you honestly say that your engagement begins the moment they set foot in your room? One of the most frequent mistakes teachers make is giving the same dry format of the do-now or introductory task each day and then attempting to begin engaging their students once the lesson has begun.

The problem is that at that point, it's an uphill climb to recapture minds that have gone on rescue missions in search of students' interests. Successfully setting the stage for engagement during the first few minutes of class involves establishing consistent routines to follow as you complete administrative tasks (e.g. taking attendance).

I had a new twist for them as soon as they walked in the door at least three times a week. Such twists included these:

- A new way of grouping them for the activity for the day
- A reorganization of the seating arrangement in the room
- A change to my appearance (e.g., use of wig, costume)
- A provocative or thought-provoking image on the whiteboard or overhead projector
- A unique object/prop displayed in the room.

An additional way that I laid the groundwork for engagement is something you may take for granted because it likely defines your practice: being thoroughly prepared for instruction each day. I believed it helped garner a greater level of respect for me in that it showed I valued them and their precious learning time. Succinctly, whether through use of novelty or some unique element in the learning environment, I aimed to get the engagement as soon as they stepped in the door. If you aren't able to immediately captivate their thinking, corral their interest, or develop a desire to act, they'll quickly *spend* their attention elsewhere.

The uninvited guests that pay at least an occasional visit to every classroom are boredom, apathy, and disinterest. Students too often expect an emotionally sterile classroom with content that is divorced from their reality, remotely interesting, and minimally meaningful to them. You see warm bodies but feel wandering minds moving in search of emotional and intellectual mates. The attractive mate that entices wandering minds to *settle down* is instruction that is intersected with their interests and experiences.

How Are Interests and Experiences Intersected With Instruction?

Traditional academic content and the conventional modes of delivery in schools have been shown to ineffectively engage students, particularly those in high-poverty, urban, largely minority schools (HUMS). Trying to engage them in such ways is like trying to get them to voluntarily eat raw broccoli: They know both may be beneficial to them but are unpleasant to experience. Signs that unpleasant classroom experiences have changed for the better are likely to have appeared if you've implemented a few of the techniques, tools, and strategies shared in the first five chapters. How then do you turn baby steps into bountiful sprints toward the academic finish line of the objectives of your daily lessons? That is, what else can you do to get them to be consistently interested and eagerly willing to complete what's asked of them during your daily lesson?

The most effective method for getting the engagement is to make the first stop along the journey of learning at *123 Student Place,* otherwise known as the outside world of your students. Enveloping a lesson or activity with references to familiar places, experiences, and feelings immediately grabs their attention and pulls their interest close to you. One such method for creating the confluence of content and their world is intersecting their interests and experiences with instruction.

Intersecting their interests and experiences with content is about beginning the journey of learning in the lair of students' minds. It's about framing the lesson around things that mean the most to them. Surrounding teaching topics with familiar settings, emotional states, common student interests, and shared experiences is the way to build such intersections. Additionally, framing topics in such a benefit-driven fashion answers unasked WIFM (what's in it for me) and "why do we have to learn this stuff?" questions. Utilizing information gathered during your study of students is like an instructional GPS (global positioning system) as it directs you to where students' interests and experiences cross the *content* road. Contextualizing learning in the aforementioned familiar ways that students can relate to is an example of how such intersections are made. Theoretical reasons underlying the need for intersecting content in similar ways are worth noting.

First Focus: Intersecting Interests and Experiences With Text

Whether it's decoding, fluency, or reading comprehension, you know that reading is a foundational competency that is essential for success in most other content areas. In addition, enhancing reading ability is a principal focus of the Common Core State Standards. As a result, high-stakes tests challenge students to demonstrate competency in reading and in other content areas where reading ability is an essential precursor of success. Thus, we will turn our initial attention to examining how to intersect students' interests and experiences with the reading of text.

THEORETICAL FRAMEWORK: UNDERLYING REASONS FOR INTERSECTING STUDENTS' INTERESTS AND EXPERIENCES WITH INSTRUCTION

- If HUMS students are afforded learning opportunities that include meaningful collaboration, building of their own understandings, critical and creative thinking, and authentic audiences, they are more likely to participate, passionately complete tasks, and find the content very meaningful (Dockter & Lewis, 2009).
- When students view their academic tasks as interesting, important, and of use to them, they feel a greater sense of belonging (Anderman, 2003).
- Engagement is enhanced when instructional goals are linked to student interests and lives (Ainley, Hidi, & Berndorf, 2002).
- When at-risk Latino/a and African American students perceive instruction to be irrelevant, they are more likely to attend to other things (Yair, 2000).
- The recognition and application of mathematics in outside contexts is essential for all students (NCTM, 2000).
- Mathematical concepts and procedures have a greater chance of being remembered when learned in contextually familiar settings. The problems in math textbooks often reflect the lives of the authors rather than those of the students the book is intended to edify (Romberg, 1992).
- There exists a disconnect between the homes of some racial and ethnic minority students and the mainstream culture prevalent in many schools (Gutstein, Lipman, Hernandez, & de los Reyes, 1997).
- High school students have been found to be engaged when problem-based historical content was intersected with multimedia (e.g., videos, audio clips, and social media). Multimedia tools are effective in creating authentic contexts for student learning (Brush & Saye, 2008).
- Middle school students have been found to be engaged when interactive media were intersected with problem-based learning. As a result, teachers were more motivated to use the interactive media program (Liu, Wivagg, Geurtz, Lee, & Chang, 2012).
- When students can select texts from pop culture and engage in personal reading, it not only leads to the development of engagement and motivation but potentially results in more profound comprehension and analyses (Alvermann, 2001).
- More than 40% of students who considered dropping out of high school cited finding little value in the work they completed (Yazzie-Mintz, 2010).

Characteristics of Texts That Engage Students in HUMS

If your aim is to engage students in your English language arts (ELA) course with text, it is critical that you be highly selective of the first texts you expose them to. Introducing them to text with irrelevant or uninteresting characters, plots, and images is likely to erode their belief in your ability to engage them. Succinctly, I have found that the types of texts that intersect the experience and interests of students in HUMS have a few common elements:

- Realistic, authentic, and accurate depictions of students' lives
- Dialogue and other interactional patterns that reflect what takes place among family and other community members outside of school.

The texts listed in Table 6 and 7 are reflective of such characteristics.

The Bare Essentials: A Realistic Exposure

Three of the greatest challenges for ELA teachers in HUMS are to get students to embrace what is taught (i.e., show that they care about content), to help students develop a love for reading, and to equip them with stronger reading competencies. An effective tool that addresses all three issues is the exposure of students in HUMS to realistic fiction texts that mirror the students' out-of-school lives. Succinctly, teachers need realistic fiction texts that feature protagonists like their students—who face similar issues, hold similar interests, have experiences students can identify with, are cast in similar settings, and have similar cultural attributes. Authors of such realistic fiction texts use dialogue similar to the discourse among students in HUMS.

Use of texts in this genre is one of the most potent techniques for developing a student's love for reading. These texts weave students' everyday experiences into ELA content. One student commented that "it's like going to the movies minus the sound." Such texts have inspired many of them to want to read, develop the reading habit, and become independent readers. One of the most frequent statements heard after exposure to such texts is, "I hated reading before I came to your class, but now I LOVE to read."

One realistic fiction genre that embodies such text is street literature, or *street lit* for short. This genre, which has grown in popularity, features characters who live in urban areas and struggle to overcome commonly encountered social ills. Originally targeting older teens and up, street lit was known for broaching risqué topics involving sex, violence, and other adult-oriented issues. Moreover, early critics of this genre lamented the proliferation of poorly published texts whose writing lacked editorial guidance, which often led to relatively poorly written text. However, a number of traditional publishers are currently producing such text, and this, coupled with better editorial oversight, has led to an enhanced quality of writing and a more polished product. Furthermore, its evolution has given rise to texts that are situated in similar settings but are more appropriate for students in fourth grade and above.

Which Specific Texts Can I Use to Engage My Students?

Tables 6 and 7 provide a listing of realistic fiction texts that are highly engaging to HUMS students. As you are probably aware, incongruence between a book's reading level and a student's reading ability is a central reason for disengagement while reading. Hence, I included the reading grade level equivalent to help you match the text's reading level to your students' readiness. In addition, considering the text's plot, themes, and characters, and the students' interest and grade level, provides assistance for selecting texts that are likely to match the interests of your students at a given grade. It's important, however, that members of your teaching team (e.g., media specialist, administrators) make prudent decisions about appropriateness of content for your students. The tables also list a few issues the books address and provide a brief description of each text.

Providing texts with characters who face circumstances and challenges similar to those of your students can be highly beneficial. The benefits include (a) captivating students' interest, (b) providing substantive strategies for students to use to overcome challenges, and (c) building students' belief in the possibility of prevailing against such odds. The list of texts is by no means an exhaustive listing of resources, but it is reflective of a selected number of texts that have engaged HUMS students in practice.

There are a wealth of forceful life lessons commonly experienced that transcend racial and ethnic barriers. Broadening students' perspectives by introducing them to texts with such lessons is not only edifying but simply good teaching. I suggest you have an eclectic mix of texts that reflect the diverse experiences, unique customs and traditions, and rich cultural mores of all of your students. Given that HUMS are populated with primarily African American and Latino/a students, I have included texts that reflect the experiences of both ethnicities in these tables.

Table 6 Realistic Fiction Texts That Intersect Experiences of African American Students With Content

Author(s)	Title(s)	Reading Grade Level Equivalent		Interest Grade Level(s)	Themes/Issues Explored	Brief Description
Anne Schraff, Paul Langan, John Langan, Peggy Kern, Karyn Langhorne Folan	Bluford High Series				Trust, friendship, family, isolation, violence, peer pressure, learning from mistakes, coming of age, making prudent/well-thought-out decisions	A highly acclaimed collection of 20 stories about students who attend a rough yet nurturing fictional inner-city school, Bluford High. The series features both male and female students and their families who deal with a multitude of social issues and experiences. It features literary genres such as romance, suspense, and mystery.
		Lost and Found	4.7	4–8		
		A Matter of Trust	4.6	4–8		
		Secrets in the Shadows	4.7	4–8		
		Someone to Love Me	4.5	4–8		
		The Bully	4.7	4–8		
		The Gun	4.7	4–8		
		Until We Meet Again	4.8	4–8		
		Blood Is Thicker	4.8	4–8		
		Brothers in Arms	4.1	4–8		
		Summer Secrets	4.6	4–8		
		The Fallen	4.2	4–8		
		Shattered	4.4	4–8		
		Search for Safety	4.2	4–8		
		No Way Out	4.1	4–8		

(Continued)

Author(s)	Title(s)	Reading Grade Level Equivalent	Interest Grade Level(s)	Themes/Issues Explored	Brief Description
Anne Schraff, Paul Langan, John Langan, Peggy Kern, Karyn Langhorne Folan		Schooled — 4.9	4–8		
		Breaking Point — 4.2	4–8		
		The Test — 4.0	4–8		
		Pretty Ugly — 4.4	4–8		
		Promises to Keep — N/A	4–8		
		Survivor — N/A	4–8		
Stephanie Perry Moore	Perry Skyy Jr. Series	Prayed Up — 4.6	9–12	Abstinence, resisting peer pressure, negotiating the choice/consequence paradigm, drug use, faith	The protagonist of this five-book Christianity-based series, Perry, is a high school senior with extraordinary athletic and academic prowess. He struggles to deal with pressure to violate the morals with which he was raised.
		Pressing Hard — 4.2	9–12		
		Prime Choice — 4.3	9–12		
		Problem Solved — 5.1	9–12		
		Promise Kept — 5.0	9–12		
	Payton Skyy Jr. Series	True Friends — 4.9	4–8	Abstinence, resisting peer pressure, male-female relationships, alcohol/drug use	The protagonist of this five book Christianity-based series, Payton, is challenged with the pressures of trying to uphold her morality and the challenges of teenage social and academic life.
		Surrendered Heart — 4.0	9–12		
		Sober Faith — 4.7	9–12		
		Staying Pure — 4.9	9–12		

Author(s)	Title(s)	Reading Grade Level Equivalent	Interest Grade Level(s)	Themes/Issues Explored	Brief Description
Stephanie Perry Moore	Carmen Browne			Common challenges of adolescence, fitting in, cultural differences, domestic violence, gossiping, self-esteem, adoption, longing for birth parents, developing independence	Ten-year-old Carmen Browne tries to balance her spiritual faith with a multitude of social, familial, and academic challenges.
	True Friends	4.9	4–8		
	Sweet Honesty	4.6	4–8		
	Golden Spirit	4.6	4–8		
	Happy Princess	4.3	4–8		
L. Divine	Drama High Series			Male-female relationships, overcoming adversity, trust, surviving the tough streets, overcoming stereotypes, adjusting to a predominantly white school environment, conflict resolution	Jayd Jackson is a 16-year-old student who attends a predominantly white high school in Los Angeles and tackles racial stereotypes.
	The Fight	5.2	9–12		
	Second Chance	5.1	9–12		
	Jayd's Legacy	5.4	9–12		
	Frenemies	5.6	9–12		
	Lady J	5.5	9–12		
Ni-Ni Simone	Ni-Ni Simone Series			Self-esteem, relationships, dating, adjusting to college, peer influence, coming of age, shouldering adult responsibilities prematurely, parental abandonment, drug addiction	The author chronicles many of the twists and turns that challenge teenagers in urban environments.
	If I Was Your Girl	3.7	9–12		
	The Break-Up Diaries	4.3	9–12		
	Shortie Like Mine	4.0	9–12		
	Teenage Love Affair	4.1	9–12		
	A Girl Like Me	4.0	9–12		
	Upgrade U	4.3	9–12		

(Continued)

Author(s)	Title(s)	Reading Grade Level Equivalent	Interest Grade Level(s)	Themes/Issues Explored	Brief Description
Sharon Flake	Bang	3.0	7–12	Forgiveness, coping with grief, violence, choice/consequence paradigm, emotional aftermath of losing a sibling	Mann, a 13-year-old who is a talented artist, grapples with a new set of circumstances his father places him in. In order to move on the right path, he has to make some difficult choices.
	Money Hungry	4.2		Relationships, poverty, mother-daughter relationships, perseverance,	Protagonist Raspberry Hill loves money and has to make hard decisions surrounding it. Raspberry faces unendingly challenging relationship issues both within and outside the home.
	Begging for Change (sequel to Money Hungry)	3.7	4–8	overcoming adversity, longing for the love and protection of a father, learning from making bad decisions	
	The Skin I'm In	4.1	7–10	Poverty, peer pressure, bullying, familial bonds, self-esteem, overcoming teasing about appearance, overcoming the death of a spouse	Seventh grader Maleeka attempts to distance herself from poor peer influences and belittling because of her skin complexion.

Author(s)	Title(s)	Reading Grade Level Equivalent	Interest Grade Level(s)	Themes/Issues Explored	Brief Description
Sharon Flake	*Who Am I Without Him*	4.0	7–10	Friendship, loyalty, identity, self-worth, disrespect, abuse, seeking boyfriend, learning from mistakes	In this collection of short stories, Flake takes readers on a journey through the minds of girls who ponder common teenage issues.
Sharon Draper	*Tears of a Tiger*	4.3	7–12	Drinking and driving, guilt, forgiveness, suicide, poverty, child abuse, drug abuse, perseverance, surmounting life's challenges, loss of bond with close relative	Andy Jackson, protagonist, had an accident while driving after drinking, and his friend was killed as a result. He struggles with feelings of guilt and contemplates suicide.
	Forged by Fire (sequel to *Tears of a Tiger*)	5.1	4–8	Abuse, death, family strife, familial bonds, child abuse, facing persistent challenges, strong friendships	The protagonist, Gerald, is entranced by fire. Gerald struggles to overcome many internal and external issues that come his way.
	Darkness Before Dawn sequel to *Forged by Fire*)	4.8	7–12	Trust, love, friendship, suicide, betrayal, anorexia, adult-oriented issues, overcoming grief	Trying to come to grips with the suicide of her ex-boyfriend, high school senior Keisha abandons those close to her for Jonathan, the principal's son.

(Continued)

(Continued)

Author(s)	Title(s)	Reading Grade Level Equivalent	Interest Grade Level(s)	Themes/Issues Explored	Brief Description
Sharon Draper	Copper Sun	4.8	7–12	Slavery, inhumane treatment, human exploitation, cruelty, perseverance, resilience, rape	While engaged to the most attractive man in her tribe, 15-year-old Amari struggles to cope not only with the massacre of her family and tribe but being sold into slavery as well.
	Romiette and Julio	6.6	7–12	Tolerance, bullying, gang violence, interracial dating	African American Romiette and Latino Julio are threatened by a local gang whose members disapprove of their relationship. They devise a plan to thwart the opposition.
Walter Dean Meyers	Monster	7.1	5–10	Abuse, violence, bullying, learning lessons from making mistakes, searching for true identity, life in jail	16-year-old Steve Harmon is on trial for murdering a drugstore owner and writes a script for a movie that depicts the events of his trial.

Author(s)	Title(s)	Reading Grade Level Equivalent	Interest Grade Level(s)	Themes/Issues Explored	Brief Description
Walter Dean Meyers	Shooter	3.7	8–12	Bullying, gun violence, suicide, death	Len struggles with bullying, a fascination with guns, and the temptation of retaliation. Myer uses multiple narratives to help the story transcend case history.
	Scorpions	3.7	8–12	Negotiating the choice/consequence paradigm, gangs, drug distribution, gun violence, criminal trial proceedings	The protagonist, Jamal, is a troubled teen who is tormented by the allure of joining a drug-selling gang so he can raise money for his brother's appeal.
Brenda Woods	Emako Blue	3.5	7–12	Interpersonal relationships, adjusting to a new school, violence, pursuit of dreams, grief	Talented 15-year-old singer Emako Blue hails from the unrelenting streets of south central Los Angeles. She struggles to cope with common issues plaguing youth in urban areas.

(Continued)

(Continued)

Author(s)	Title(s)	Reading Grade Level Equivalent	Interest Grade Level(s)	Themes/Issues Explored	Brief Description
Jacqueline Woodson	If You Come Softly	4.0	7–12	Fitting in at school, tolerance, conforming to societal norms, male–female relationships	15-year-olds Jeremiah (Miah) and Ellie attend the private high school Percy Academy. They grapple with the societal taboo of interracial dating and face trying to adjust to school.
Dana Davidson	Jason and Kyra	4.7	9–12	Teen romance, loneliness, vengeance, perseverance, preconceived notions	Star athlete Jason and intelligent Kyra work to develop a relationship as they face challenges from his ex-girlfriend and other common teenage issues.

Table 7 Realistic Fiction Texts That Intersect Experiences of Latino/a Students With Content

Author(s)	Title(s)	Reading Grade Level Equivalent	Interest Grade Level(s)	Themes/Issues Explored	Brief Description
Julia Alvarez	*Return to Sender*	5.6	5–8	Familial bonds, cooperation, patriotism, poverty, struggles of illegal immigrants, longing for a missing parent, questioning morality	When 11-year-old Tyler Paquette's father is injured in a tractor accident, the family enlists the assistance of a family of illegal immigrants to help save the farm. The plot progresses with Tyler befriending Mari, a member of the new family, attempts to locate Mari's missing mother, the families developing closer bonds, and the looming threat of Homeland Security (La Migra) raiding the farm.
	Before We Were Free	6.5	5–8	Fighting for a cause, pursuit of freedom, living under a dictatorial regime, broken family bonds, suspense, espionage	The story is set in the early 1960s Dominican Republic, where Trujillo's dictatorial regime rules. Twelve-year-old Anita de la Torre longs to be free of the despotism and endures ever-present suspicion, jailing of her father and uncle, and adjusting to life underground.
	How the Garcia Girls Lost Their Accents	6.8	9–12	Assimilation, maintaining cultural identity, developing individual identity, familial love, overcoming bullying	A well-to-do family is forced to flee their native Dominican Republic and move to the Bronx. The four sisters, Carla, Sandra, Yolanda, and Sofía, struggle to adjust. Through a series of vignettes, the story is told in reverse chronological order.

(Continued)

Author(s)	Title(s)	Reading Grade Level Equivalent	Interest Grade Level(s)	Themes/Issues Explored	Brief Description
Jessica Lee Anderson	Border Crossing	6	9–12	Illegal immigration, mental illness, trusting others, alcoholism	Fifteen-year-old Manz works during summer on a cattle ranch. Along with a constant search for self, he begins to hear voices that tell him to trust no one and that La Migra wants to ship him back to Mexico.
Jen Calonita	Belles	5.4	9–12	Overcoming salacious gossip and rumors, adjusting to new living circumstances, dealing with biases within the family	When her grandmother is unable to continue to care for her, Isabelle, a 15-year-old teen, is sent to live with wealthy relatives. Isabelle struggles to adjust to her new environs as Calonita includes many twists and turns.
Viola Canales	The Tequila Worm	5.4	6	Determination, adjusting to life with privileged students, assimilation, moving away from family / friends, Mexican-American culture, traditions	Sofia, a bright young lady of Mexican-American descent, is from a family that highly embraces cultural practices and traditions. She aims to attend an esteemed boarding school, which would mean having to leave family and friends.
Janet Nichols Lynch	Messed Up	6	6–8	Suddenly having to shoulder adult responsibilities, overcoming adversity, developing independence, abandonment	R.D., a 15-year-old young man, is raised by his grandmother and her live-in boyfriend until she leaves town with another man. The live-in boyfriend, Earl, dies. R.D. decides to conceal the fact that he's living alone to avoid being sent to a group home and struggles with being thrust into adulthood.

Author(s)	Title(s)	Reading Grade Level Equivalent	Interest Grade Level(s)	Themes/Issues Explored	Brief Description
Nancy Osa	*Cuba 15*	5.6	9	Assimilation, quest for knowledge about cultural roots, dating	Protagonist, Violet Paz, recently turned 15 and is preparing for her quinceañera. She reluctantly accepts her abuela's plan for her quinceañera and becomes increasingly more inquisitive about her Cuban cultural roots.
Rene Saldana Jr.	*The Jumping Tree*	5.2	6–8	Love, poverty, grief, cultural pride, loss of friendship, developing attributes of manhood	Vignettes are used to tell the story of Rey Castañeda's middle school experiences. Rey questions central elements in society, enjoys activities with his friends, and begins to develop an understanding of what manhood is about.
Pam Muñoz Ryan	*The Dreamer*	3.7	6–8	Managing familial and social expectations, art, perseverance, identity, embracing imagination	Against his father's wishes for him to become a physician, a frail and shy Chilean boy, Neftali Reyes, enjoys reading, writing, daydreaming, and treasure collecting. Through determination, he becomes an esteemed poet, Pablo Neruda, in this work of historical fiction.
Guadalupe Garcia McCall	*Under the Mesquite*	5.7	6–10	Coping with loss of loved one, family bonds, assimilation, resilience, shouldering adult responsibilities	This novel, written in free verse, is about a family that moves across the border and adjusts to life in a new country. Lupita, an aspiring poet and actress who struggles to overcome the death of a parent, has to shoulder the responsibility of taking care of seven younger brothers and sisters.

(Continued)

Author(s)	Title(s)	Reading Grade Level Equivalent	Interest Grade Level(s)	Themes/Issues Explored	Brief Description
Mike Lupica	*Heat*	5.5	6–8	Loneliness, sportsmanship, coping with absent parents, family bonds, friendship, humor	Michael Arroyo, a 12-year-old who is gifted with a baseball pitching prowess, dreams of playing in the Little League World Series. When he is accused of being older than he actually is, he is deemed ineligible to continue to play. Along with overcoming that challenge, he is faced with the looming possibility of having to enter foster care, as his father is absent and his mother died years earlier.
Matt de la Peña	*We Were Here*	5.0	8–12	Faith, friendship, humor, redemption, rejection, adventure, violence, youth incarceration.	Miguel Casteñeda is sentenced to a juvenile detention facility and has to keep a journal as well. He befriends Rondell and Mong and escapes with them with the intention of going to Mexico. Their adventurous journey on the lam on the California coast is chronicled.
Coert Voorhees	*The Brothers Torres*	4.8	9—12	Resiliency, humor, conflict resolution, vengeance, friendship, family loyalty, stereotypes, profanity, sexual situations	High school sophomore Frankie Torres is pulled into a series of confrontations by his older brother, Steve. In the midst of pursuing a young lady he's attracted to, Rebecca Sanchez, he inadvertently creates more conflict.
Tony Johnston	*Any Small Goodness: A Novel of the Barrios*	5.1	4–7	Assimilation, maintaining cultural identity, gang violence, family celebrations	Eleven-year-old Arturo Rodriguez's family has recently moved to East Los Angeles, where they adjust to life while maintaining their cultural identity.

Author(s)	Title(s)	Reading Grade Level Equivalent	Interest Grade Level(s)	Themes/Issues Explored	Brief Description
Victor Martínez	*Parrot in the Oven: Mi Vida*	7.1	9	Alcoholism, gang violence, family dysfunction, overcoming poverty, discovering identity	Manuel Hernandez struggles to find his place in the world in the midst of family strife, acceptance in a gang, and other peer-related challenges in school.
Alan Sitomer	*The Secret Story of Sonia Rodriguez*	5	8–12	Perseverance, overcoming stereotypes, balancing academic and familial responsibilities	Sonia Rodriguez, a 15-year-old daughter of illegal immigrants, works to overcome life's challenges to be the first high school graduate in her family.
	Homeboyz	5.5	8–12	Gang violence, incarceration, vengeance, need for love and trust	Teddy Anderson's younger sister is gunned down as the victim of a random act of violence. Teddy is subsequently arrested for attempted homicide as he seeks revenge for her death. Mariana Diaz, a smart, no-nonsense probation officer, tries to help him stay on the right track upon his release from prison.
Simone Elkeles	*Rules of Attraction*	4.3	9–12	Teen romance, gang violence, overcoming social differences, adult-oriented content	Carlos Fuentes is shipped off to Colorado to live with an older sibling, Alex, after gang involvement in Mexico. After Carlos gets into more gang-related trouble, Alex's former instructor, Professor Westford, attempts to help him stay on the right track.
	Chain Reaction: A Perfect Chemistry	4.3	9–12	Teen romance, learning from mistakes, gang activity, violence, sexual situations, profanity, adult-oriented content	Luis Fuentes aims to become an aerospace engineer and has his eyes set on a young lady from a higher socioeconomic class. He struggles to rebound after making a series of poor choices.

Some unfortunate realities within HUMS loom large. Unusually high proportions of students are reading at levels significantly below grade. Even if the books students read mirror their experiences and interests, reading challenges will be compounded if the books are not at the appropriate reading level. Thus, I have included many texts in the table that have protagonists who are in high school but that are written at a middle or elementary school reading level.

A second unfortunate truth is that the harsh realities facing many HUMS students prematurely expose them to issues typically tackled by adults. Some texts in Tables 6 and 7 broach topics and adult-oriented situations that have been traditionally reserved for older audiences. Advocates for exposing HUMS students to such texts argue that the socially redeeming value of the lessons taught through such reading far outweigh the cost of exposing students to a few controversial topics.

I can't overstate the importance of reading the entire texts and familiarizing yourself with the issues before introducing these books to your students. The need for some of your students to become familiar with strategies for not only coping but developing resilience may outweigh the angst of exposure to somewhat questionable topics. In any event, I strongly suggest that a well-planned approach, including administrative (school or central office) approval and parental consent, accompany instruction with texts that explore controversial topics (e.g., rape). The texts included in the tables abound with invaluable life lessons. Teachers who have had success in engaging HUMS students with reading consistently provide texts that intersect with the students' reality.

Is This the Only Genre of Text HUMS Students Should Be Exposed To?

It goes without saying that excellent educational experiences entail providing multiple opportunities to learn about topics that transcend students' current experiences. Exposing students to a plethora of texts in a multitude of genres fulfills such an aim. Utilizing realistic fiction texts that reflect the interests and experiences of HUMS students is a tool that seductively draws them in and also sparks an interest in reading. It helps build the belief that reading can be a rewarding, interesting, and fulfilling activity. Once the belief is built, it can be utilized as a pipeline into forays with other traditional genres and literary canons.

The reality is that some students are simply not interested in texts of the realistic fiction genre. Build a classroom library that is composed not only of the rich traditions and customs but is also reflective of diverse student interests. Historical fiction and mysteries are also popular genres in HUMS, as are books of the graphic novel format.

In What Other Ways Can I Engage My Students With Text?

Getting Highly Resistant Readers to Get Started

The process described below has been effective for students who are highly reluctant to read:

1. Provide instructional time where they can choose a text that interests them.

2. Start by giving them a choice of four or five specific texts that have been demonstrated to be of great interest to other students in the past.

3. Have them read the back cover of each and then select one of those texts.

4. Encourage them to read the first few pages or chapter.

5. Tell them they have the option of selecting a different text if they are not interested.

Use an Entrée to Introduce the Lesson

A simple process for engaging students with text is described below. A mistake made far too often is jumping into a lesson without providing a proper setup for or entrée into the lesson. Utilizing an entrée that seductively draws the students in can be the difference that either makes or breaks a lesson. The following simplistic process not only prevents such a misstep and helps sustain the engagement throughout the reading lesson. The process is as follows:

1. Engage students in a prereading exercise such as semantic mapping, prequestioning, or using a cognitive organizer.

2. Read the text aloud.

3. Have students respond to what was read via journal writing.

4. Facilitate a whole-group discussion about what was read.

5. Have students continue reading independently.

Utilize the read-aloud technique to animate the text by giving life to the dialogue between characters through intonation of words and use of other familiar interactional patterns.

Introduce Culturally Relevant and Socially Significant Texts

Introducing students to expository texts that are both culturally relevant and socially significant is essential in helping shape students' identity and instilling an innate sense of worth and pride. However, if an academic aim is to assist students in becoming independent readers, developing a belief that they *can* successfully read and consider reading a pleasurable experience are critical preliminary steps in the process. Remember, the first success sells the second step. Realistic fiction texts that intersect with students' interests and experiences inspire them to take steps down the path toward becoming avid readers. Initial exposure of HUMS students to such texts is of great import. Tatum (2005) makes a significant argument for utilizing culturally relevant and socially significant texts.

Utilize Critical Literacy to Engage Students

It should come as no surprise that HUMS students sometimes question social inequities (e.g., wealth distribution) and other racial or cultural biases existing in the larger society. Critically reading text is an empowering pedagogy that addresses such questions by challenging students to engage in profound textual analyses. With it, readers are active participants in the process. This pedagogy entails having students pose questions about text content, author's craft, other textual elements, and larger society. Additionally, they create interpretations of text and explore the existing relations of power between the author and reader. More than simply reading for pleasure or to gain knowledge, critically reading text is about students engaging in deeper analyses of text, such as unearthing social messages and being in charge of the ways they position themselves with respect to such messages as well. In essence, it involves students meaningfully in juxtaposing text with their world, asking text-related questions they are interested in, and conducting critical analyses germane to them. To that end, including such pedagogy in your literacy repertoire positions you well to engage your learners. Duncan-Andrade and Morrell (2008), Hall and Piazza, (2008) and McLaughlin and DeVoogd (2004) shed great light on how to integrate critical literacy into practice.

Envelop Content in Popular Culture and Media Arts

Taking a peek into the lives of many young people evinces how strongly they embrace various forms of media as essential elements undergirding their social existence. When you're able to cloak their learning in the canvas of such arts, odds have it that your classroom will be a portrait of engagement. Dockter and Lewis (2009) provided a wonderful case study of how such portraits are created (briefly discussed in Chapter 3). In a HUMS high school English classroom, instruction was provided in the areas of reading, writing, media analysis, and media production, and defined by rigor and critical engagement. Students synthesized analyses and produced media texts such as digital stories and podcast memoirs, and collaborative groups even produced a documentary film. State standards were met in English and history, while the amount of reading and writing mirrored that of conventional English classrooms. The study found that curricula in HUMS English language arts classrooms call for students to create knowledge through utilizing complex literary tasks. Sample elements of such curricula include these:

- Production of digital media for authentic audiences (e.g., peers and adults in the community)
- Critical analysis of media tied to the identity of students
- Interaction patterns in the classroom characterized by expectations of excellence and accountability to members of the community of learners
- Provision of specific feedback at appropriate times that serves to place students in the best position to be successful and helps bolster their belief in their own abilities.

A Few Other Suggestions for Engaging Students

- Continuously build your classroom library by staying abreast of (and adding) those *can-I-please-read-a-few-more-pages* texts that have been demonstrated to be a favorite of your students.
- Have them create and prominently post testimonials/recommendations of texts they've read
  - o on web spaces (e.g., wikis).
  - o in areas of the classroom (e.g., bulletin board).
- Demonstrate your interest and enthusiasm for texts by *conversationally* asking questions about specific scenes, themes, characters, and plots.
  - o Have you got to the part where [scene]?
  - o What do you think about how [character] carries herself?
  - o Did you get the feeling that there was some hidden meaning to [theme]?

How Will I Know if My Students Are Engaged With Text?

If students don't want to put their books down, try to sneak and read while in other classes, and seem to *lose track of time* when reading, it's high likely that they are engaged. A few teachers in HUMS have shared that one unintended consequence of students being engaged with text is an increase in the number of texts that permanently *disappear* from the shelves. A participant in one of my workshops told me,

> I know they a love a book series when I find many of them coming up missing. I've had some receive a suspension from school and come find me before going home to ask if they could take the book to read the book while out of school. That's when I know they've got the reading bug.

After a chorus of sighs, moans, and groans, "ugh, I don't read," "I *hate* reading," and "reading is so boring" were complaints Mrs. Jones heard after telling her new class of seventh graders they would be reading that day. After a few minutes of silent reading, Denzel blurted out the obscenity, "——- reading" and forcefully threw the novel against the back wall. After she addressed Denzel's inappropriate actions in the hallway, she returned to the class and said,

> For those of you saying "I hate reading," what you're really saying is "I hate that I haven't really learned to read well yet." Mark my words, by the end of the school year, each and every one of you in this room will be bitten by the reading bug and become a *much* better reader.

For the reading instructional time, *Stop Drop and Read*, students were allowed to choose a book from Mrs. Jones's classroom library, which included various genres. In addition to the genre most popular with her students, realistic fiction, her library included books classified as historical fiction, mysteries, and graphic novels. Though school funds for new book purchases for her library are limited, she has developed a great relationship with the librarian at the local public library, who is thrilled to have demand for underutilized books. Mrs. Jones goes to the local public library to borrow both classroom sets and individual books that have been recommended by the librarian and that she knows are a match for her students' tastes.

For students who highly resist reading or for those who cannot find a book that interests them, she chooses five books she herself has read and has the students read the summary on the back of each book and select one of them. After she showed five books in a similar fashion to Denzel, he still wasn't interested and did not choose any of the five. She then chose a book she knew to be very appealing to her boys, *Tears of a Tiger*, and said, "Denzel, read the first the chapter or two. If you don't like it, you can choose a different one." At the end of the period, Denzel said, "Mrs. Jones, could I take this book home with me? You probably don't trust me, but I'll bring it back tomorrow." She smiled and said, "Sure, just be sure to bring it back tomorrow."

After reluctant readers, such as Denzel, are well under way with reading their books, she pulls them aside and skillfully asks a few questions such as, "Did you get to the part about _____?" or "What is your opinion about [certain characters]?" She does this to give herself greater credibility with her students by letting them know that she indeed has read the text and also enjoyed the experience. They often asked questions like, "Did you *really* read this book, Mrs. Jones?" Hector even excitedly ran up to her one morning and said, "Mrs. Jones, I got to the part about him being sent to Colorado! Can you believe he still thought about joining a gang?"

She frequently engages students in book talk, where they are encouraged to share the events in their book and also recommend readings to peers. She has them type a sentence or two about why they recommend a book and print it out. Then she cuts these printouts into small strips and posts them, along with pictures of each student holding the book she or he recommended, on the bulletin board near her classroom library.

Fridays are teacher read-aloud days, where she reads from her *book of the month*. For this special day, she purchases three jumbo bags of popcorn from the dollar store along with a jumbo container of pop and two packages of 55 Styrofoam cups, all for one dollar each. She tells them, "Instead of going to see a movie, you're creating images of events in your minds." She started the Friday read-alouds to help build students' imagination and also to use it as an entrée into writing.

After finishing *Tears of a Tiger*, Denzel said, "Mrs. Jones, I don't want to choose a book. Can you tell me what would be another good book to read?" As the year went on, he routinely sought her opinion on the selection of a new book. At the end of the year, Mrs. Jones pulled Denzel aside and sarcastically said, "Soooooo, you don't read books, huh, Denzel?" He embarrassedly looked down at the floor, blushed, and said, "Mrs. Jones, I have to give it to you; you were right. I never thought I could learn to love to do something I used to hate with a passion." Mrs. Jones replied, "As I often tell you all, there are many books out there that are a good match for you. You just have to find the *right* ones!"

In an interview with a 16-year-old eighth grade African American male who had been retained three times, Tatum (2008) provides an illustrative example of how one knows students are engaged with text:

> I don't know what made me read it, but I was, like, totally involved in what he's saying. . . . As I was going along I wanted to stop, but I couldn't. I was like, I started it, and I ain't going to sleep 'til about six in the morning. That's how into it I was, and I didn't know I could get into a book like that. To tell you the truth, I forgot I was reading. (Tatum, 2008, pp. 170–171)

Creating Intersections in Mathematics

> *If we see children's informal mathematical knowledge as part of a well-connected network of ideas and concepts, then using that knowledge as a starting point from which to base instruction makes sense.*
>
> (Gutstein et al., 1997, p. 711)

If your students are like many, then they embrace the notion that math is a dry subject full of hard-to-understand ideas and abstract concepts that are exiled from the students' current existence. Furthermore, students view math as several distinctly different topics that bear little relation to one another. Adding to the negative perception are the oft-shared experiences of parents or significant adults in their lives, such as, "I was never good in math *either*," or "some people are just *naturally* good at math." Coupled with poor or uninteresting early school experiences in math, these factors make it an uphill climb to get students excited and eager to learn about math.

> *School mathematics is presented in ways that are divorced from the everyday experiences of most students, not just African American students.*
>
> (Ladson-Billings, 1997, pp. 700–701)

How Is Math Made Engaging by Successful Teachers of Mathematics?

How do you reconcile the estranged relationship between math content and students' everyday experiences? Simply, make math meaningful by packing abstract symbols and numbers in the package of their everyday lives. Successful teachers make the integration of the experiences of their students into instruction a priority. It's not done as an afterthought or ancillary addition, and it's not considered a tip or trick for good teaching; it's essential to their instruction. In contrast, the mathematics conceptual difficulty facing an inordinate number of students in HUMS is compounded by their being presented with math concepts in contexts that reflect the experiences others. Here are a few suggestions for intersecting interests and experiences with math content:

- Situate the problems in their SELF (something they've Seen, Experienced, Like, or Felt)
- Have students log their math experiences outside of school, and have them inform you about these as part of the process of *your* student scholarship. Use those experiences as a crucible for creating authentically contextualized math problems.
- Use common, familiar names and places (e.g., the name of a store in the students' community) in teaching examples.
- Have students create their own math problems for others to solve as a way to develop greater proficiency with concepts.
- Contextualize math within favorite exercise activity (e.g., heart rate after running down the basketball court, skipping rope)
- Take pictures of buildings and other structures in the students' community, and examine these in geometry and other math classes.
- Allow students to write problems reflecting their own experiences.

Intersecting Mathematics, Science, and Social Science Content With Students' Interests and Experiences

Tables 8–10 below list common content expectations/topics in math, science, and social studies and contrast conventional tasks with those that intersect with students' interests and experiences.

Table 8 Engineering Intersections of Interests and Experience With Mathematics

Content Area Strand	Expectation	Conventional Math Task or Problem	Math Learning That Intersects Interests and Experiences With Content
Algebra	Compute various rates	Use the data in the graph on the worksheet and calculate the rates.	Please select two exercise activities from the ones your class listed as their favorites. Predict and then calculate your pulse rate after 30 seconds of engaging in each. Repeat three times for each exercise you select. Calculate the average of three trials for each activity.
	Apply directly proportional relationships	Determine whether or not the ratio of y to x is the same for all values.	When talking about scale, draw or present a picture or model of some object from the students' world, and ask if the model accurately reflects the real dimensions of the object (see Gutstein et al., 1997, p. 723).
Geometry	Recognize basic geometric shapes with components	Match the description of the shape with its correct picture.	Create a collage or diorama using pictures of objects—from your home, community, recreation center, or some activity you engage in outside of school—that represents some of the shapes you have learned about. Use the presentation rubric to prepare a short presentation about the collection of objects you put together, and explain how you know they represent the objects you chose.
	Construct and draw geometric objects	Draw a parallelogram and an isosceles triangle.	Select one of the shapes we have studied this week to sketch an object you choose.
Numbers and Operations	Add/subtract whole numbers	What is the sum of 25, 15, and 10?	Charletta skipped rope 25 times before she got out the first time, 15 times the second, and 10 the third. How many times did she skip rope altogether?
		Find the difference between 112 and 53.	The afternoon train Jose rode home on had 112 passengers. The city bus he next rode had 53 passengers. How many fewer people were on the bus?
	Multiply/divide whole numbers	What is the quotient of 225 and 15?	Using something you see on the way home, at home, or someplace you visit outside of school, create two math problems involving three-digit numbers being divided into equal groups for a classmate to answer. Please use your name and the names of the objects being divided in the problems.

Content Area Strand	Expectation	Conventional Math Task or Problem	Math Learning That Intersects Interests and Experiences With Content
	Understand meaning of percentages, decimals, and fractions	Convert the fraction 90/120 to a decimal and a percentage.	You have the results of the class survey about our favorite foods, television shows, musical artists, and things you like to do for fun. Your group will tally the results of one category of the surveys and then express each choice as a fraction, decimal, or percent.
Measurement	Become proficient with units of weight, length, and time	Express the measurement 10 *centimeters* in millimeters and meters.	Remove your shoe and trace an outline of your foot on the paper provided, and then measure the length of your tracing to the nearest centimeter. With a partner, use your foot outline to measure the following distances: length of the classroom, your height, and distance to the main office. In addition, measure two distances of your choice outside of school. Tomorrow, you and your partner will help each other convert the distances/heights you measured in centimeters to millimeters and meters. You will also share why you selected those things outside of school and your results with the class.
	Convert within basic measurement units	Complete the metric conversion worksheet converting centimeters to millimeters.	
Data and Probability	Using data in bar graphs and tables, solve the problems	Which is the most/least liked movie according to the bar graph on the worksheet? Identify the independent and dependent variables.	Bring in your favorite bouncing ball tomorrow; we will explore whether the height you drop it from affects how high it bounces. With your partner, make a conjecture about the bounce height, and explain the reasoning behind it. What are your independent and dependent variables? Do any variables need to be held constant? Drop the ball from each of three assigned heights, measure the height with a meter stick, record the heights of the bounces in a data table, and then create a bar graph to display the data. Formulate two questions about your graph to be answered by another pair in the class.
	Understand what probability is and solve problems involving it	A container has 4 red, 3 blue and 7 green marbles. What is the probability of selecting each?	Using the handout as a guide, tally the number of *tricked-out* rides you observe on the way home or during a 30-minute period while out of school. Using your data and what you learned about probability, how likely is it that a tricked-out ride will be observed by someone in your community? Using poster board, markers, or your unique, creative way, present your findings to the class.

Table 9 Engineering Intersections of Interests and Experience With Science Content

Content Area Strand	Topic	Conventional Science Task or Problem	Science Learning That Intersects Interests and Experiences with Content
Life Science	How living things are organized	Write three things you know about plant cells.	Choose one of your favorite vegetables from the list provided. Design an experiment that tests whether changes in one variable affect its growth.
		Compare/contrast the sketches of the cheek cell on the handout.	How might your cheek cell be similar to or different from that of a pit bull terrier? Write your predictions. Prepare a slide of your own cheek cell and that of a pit bull terrier. Then make detailed comparisons of the structure and components of each.
		Read the handout and write a short paragraph about how bacteria grow.	It's often said that the human hand and mouth have more bacteria than any other place on the body. Do you agree/disagree? Using what you know about culturing bacteria, design an experiment to test whether your hands or mouth have more bacteria.
Earth Science	Fluid earth	Tell what is happening in the diagram of the water cycle.	On our field trip next week, we will collect water samples from two local parks. We will then test the effect of temperature on rates of evaporation of the samples.
		Describe how water moves across land.	To explore how water moves across land, work with your team to create a stream table using the newspaper, diatomaceous earth, sand, and aluminum pans.
		Discuss what occurs in the concept map describing how water moves across land.	I have included a listing of local officials for you to interview about a local watershed. Ask five of the ten questions from the list along with three questions that address what you want to know about local watersheds. Present the findings by re-creating the interview in front of your peers or in your own unique way.

Content Area Strand	Topic	Conventional Science Task or Problem	Science Learning That Intersects Interests and Experiences with Content
Physical Science	Properties of matter	Classify each object on the demonstration table as a solid, liquid, or gas.	With your parent/guardian's consent, bring any object of your choice from home tomorrow. Classify it according to observable attributes such as hardness, flexibility, texture, weight, et cetera. Then describe your special object and present your classifications to the class.
		Complete the fill-in-the-blank worksheet on density.	Choose your favorite syrup from the list provided. Test whether changes in three different variables affect its density.
		Read the text/article on lead and write an essay on it.	With your group, synthesize a report on the impact of lead poisoning in your community. Each group has been assigned a different zip code. Interview the alderman/councilperson for the zip code you've been assigned, as well as a health department official responsible for that area. Research the public health impact of lead in that zip code. Use the rubric to present your findings via PowerPoint or Keynote. Part of the assessment of your report will be on the creativity (e.g., music, photos, special effects) you put into your presentation. Your findings will be published on the schocl website and will be submitted to the local paper for publishing.

Table 10 Constructing Intersections of Interests and Experience With Social Studies Content

Content Area Strand	Topic	*Conventional Social Studies Task or Problem*	*Social Studies Learning That Intersects Interests and Experiences With Content*
Government/Civics	Government structure/ function	Identify whether each situation on the worksheet is a local, state, or national government function.	Using what we have learned about the role of local government elected officials, select one seat you would be interested in running for. Create a short campaign speech for that position. Your speech must include the criteria on the handout, and you will be assessed according to the rubric. You may choose to record a video, deliver a speech live, or deliver it in your own (approved) way.
		Discuss three reasons for limiting the government's power.	Research an instance in which one branch of the city's government tried to limit the powers of another branch. Present your findings according to the criteria listed, in the form of a news broadcast.
		Explain how a system of checks and balances work in government.	(Teacher shows a video clip of their mayor and city council/aldermen discussing whether to pass an ordinance that bans teens from public malls after 7:00 p.m.) Explain how a system of checks and balances works between the mayor and city council/aldermen. With your team, prepare to debate the merits of such legislation.
History	The Civil War	Use the timeline on the worksheet to answer questions about the Civil War.	(Before learning about the Civil War) Sketch a picture that displays a disagreement between you and a sibling or close friend. On the back, write how it began, what the major issues were, and how it was resolved.
		Read the passage and answer the questions about the Civil War that follow.	We will visit two historical Underground Railroad sites in our city on Friday. Use what you learn on the visit to write a short skit.
		How was the indigenous population of America impacted by the British and French in the 17th century?	Create a social media campaign that highlights the impact of the French on the Indian population in the 17th century. Find a related quote worth tweeting, select an exchange between two prominent individuals from that era that can be displayed as a Facebook interaction, and record a 3- to 5-minute video to be posted on YouTube.

Content Area Strand	Topic	Conventional Social Studies Task or Problem	Social Studies Learning That Intersects Interests and Experiences With Content
Geography	The effect of people on the environment	Explain how pollution from a factory affects the environment.	I have invited Mr. John Smith, from the mayor's task force on contaminated land, to talk about how two old factories have affected your community. Please write two questions you want to ask Mr. Smith about contaminated land.
		How has the Industrial Revolution impacted the people of this country?	With your group, produce a 2- to 3-minute video about the impact of one of the contaminated waste sites on the community. Your video must include the criteria set forth in the assignment. You will be assessed according to the rubric.
		Respond to the questions on the handout regarding impact of the oil spill from the *Exxon Valdez* on the ecosystem.	I have listed several human-made disasters that either directly or indirectly impacted our community. With your team, create an infomercial that chronicles important pertinent information about one of these disasters. Creatively include as many special effects and features as you like.
Economics	Interrelationship of supply, demand, and prices	What are the supplies needed to make a car tire?	Submit a proposal to sell a snack food item at a school store that will be set up in the empty classroom next month. Give a 1-minute presentation describing why you chose it and how its supply, price, and demand are related.
		Explain how supply, price, and demand are related.	Use the criteria in the rubric to create a project that shows the relationship between the price, demand, and supply of your favorite game, DVD movie, or other item you purchased for entertainment.
		Read the news article on price elasticity and respond to the questions that follow.	With your group, create a report about how the price, supply, and demand of the most popular designer jeans are interrelated. Present your findings as a podcast that will ultimately be uploaded to the web.

Additional Strategies for Intersecting Interests and Experiences With Content

Using Their Love for Play as a Tool

Undoubtedly you've seen the movie where a spark instantly grows into a fire that engulfs a room. The spark that fuels the excitement in the lives of not only HUMS students but all children is *play*. Intersecting play, such as playing games, with content is a compellingly engaging way to ignite the learning. The reality is that the likes of Xboxes and Nintendo Wiis are staples in many households. Be it adolescent learners or aging adults, utilizing the tool of games is the spark that always creates the excitement that envelops the room. I have found that games are most useful in instruction to review learned content. Table 11 highlights a few ways to intersect content with games.

Additional benefits of using games include the following:

- Reduction in incidence of off-task behavior
- Greater confidence in your willingness and ability to be flexible and make the learning fun
- Enhancement of student desire to participate in other learning tasks (Because they see that the teacher consistently designs the learning with them in mind, they're more likely to reciprocate their attention and participate in the learning.)
- Aid in the development of principles of collaboration

It always helped to have nominal prizes for student winners, such as multicolored pencils or other cool-looking things they found of value. I often purchased small things like these from the dollar store. Gift certificates for the school store, homework passes, and currency printed in my name ("Jabari bucks") were also helpful in rewarding winners of games.

Using Multimedia Tools

Media technologies are among the most powerful tools for creating intersections of interest with *any* content. Much has been written about how to utilize multimedia tools in practice (Brush & Saye, 2008; Liu et al., 2012; Reich & Daccord, 2008). The intricacies of how to use them extend beyond the scope of this writing. However, I do suggest you obtain software that enables you to harness real-world multimedia elements to make your lessons engaging. Among the many

Table 11 Intersecting Games With Content

Game	Materials	Content Area Uses / How Used	Description
Slam Dunk!	• Index cards or handout, each with a question to be reviewed/retaught written on it and with a number (1, 2, or 3) indicating how many extra points it is worth • three large cylindrical containers or garbage cans (with new trash liners) • a balled-up sheet of paper for each question • short audio clips of various favorite students' songs	• All content areas • To review or reteach content	1. Divide students into two teams. Assign one student to be the referee. 2. Mark the shooting line with masking tape. Place first container (1 pointer) 3 feet away, second container (2 pointer) 6 feet away, third container (3 pointer) 10 feet away. 3. Teams take turns playing. For each turn, the referee reads a question off an index card to the team whose turn it is. 4. The first member of the team to hit his or her desk with a hand and correctly respond will earn one point for the team. That team member then gets to shoot a balled-up piece of paper into a container/garbage can to earn the extra point(s). 5. A 10-second clip of that team's favorite song is played for each made basket. 6. The game continues until questions are answered and each student has had at least one turn to answer a question.
Classbook	• Blank strips of paper (one per student) • Sheet with questions to be reviewed/retaught • Image of thumbs-up printed on card stock (one per group of students)	• All content areas • To review or reteach content	1. Have students write on a slip of paper one positive yet little-known fact about themselves. Collect these and place them in a bag. 2. Divide the class into teams of four. 3. Ask the first team a question, or ask them to demonstrate a process relating to content to be reviewed or retaught. 4. Once their answer is given, other teams indicate their desire to respond by displaying the thumbs-up image. The first team to display the image may either correct the original answer (if it was wrong) or provide more detail/additional information (if it was correct)

(Continued)

(Continued)

Game	Materials	Content Area Uses / How Used	Description
			5. Draw a slip of paper from the bag and read it aloud. Give the team whose turn it is a chance to guess which classmate wrote the fact.
			6. If the team guesses correctly, they add the student who wrote the fact to their *friend* list. After all the questions have been asked, the team with the most *friends* wins.
First Responders	• Worksheet with blanks that need to be filled in with content, one copy of same worksheet per row of student desks. (I suggest having at least two blanks for each student in a row.) Additionally, include one short answer at the end of the worksheet that students in the row will have to collaborate on to complete. • Clock or stopwatch	• All content areas • To review content • Best used with rote facts, short answers	1. Group student desks into rows. 2. Give a worksheet to the first student in the row (facedown). 3. When you give the signal, the first student fills in one blank and then passes the worksheet over the shoulder, without looking, to the person behind. 4. The second student now fills in a blank and passes the worksheet again. This step is repeated until the worksheet reaches the last student in the row, who fills in a blank and then quickly takes the worksheet back to the front to repeat the process. 5. Once all the blanks have been filled in, the group collaborates to formulate a response to the short-answer question. 6. When a group has responded to all the questions, the first person in the row says, "Respond!" Groups are awarded points based on the order in which they respond (If there are four rows, first finished gets 4 extra points, 2nd finished gets 3 extra points, etc.). 7. When you call time, rows exchange papers with each other to check them for accuracy. The short-answer question is assessed according to a short rubric where responses can earn either 3, 2, 1, or 0 points. 8. The group that has earned the most points wins.

Game	Materials	Content Area Uses / How Used	Description
Rolling Until Right	• Number cube or spinners (one per pair) with various colored spaces • Review worksheet, flash cards, or desired content to be retaught/ reviewed	• All content areas • To review or reteach content • Best used with rote information or quickly recalled facts	1. Select or have a student select a number (1–6) or a color (for spinner to land on) for the day. 2. Group students into pairs. 3. One person in each pair rolls the number cube (or spins the spinner), while the partner completes the review task (e.g., write spelling words, fill in the periodic table, write multiplication facts, list presidents) 4. Partners stop and exchange roles when the number for the day is rolled (or the color for the day is landed on). Model the activity with a student volunteer before beginning.
Homerun	• Masking tape/ cones to denote four bases of baseball game • Index cards, each with a question on it and one of these words: single, double, triple, home run	• All content areas • To review or reteach content	1. Divide the class into two teams. Assign one student to be quiz master. 2. Have a coin flip to decide which team which "bats" and which takes the field first. 3. One member of each team goes on opposite sides of a desk in front of the quiz master. 4. The quiz master pulls an index card from the pile and poses the question written on it. For the team members at the desk, the goal is to be the first to hit the desk after the question is asked to have the right to answer the question. If the member of the "at bat" team hits the desk first and answers the question correctly, she or he is considered to have moved to the base indicated by the card (first base for single, second base for double, and so on). If the at-bat person's answer is incorrect, it's considered an out. If a member of the fielding team hits the desk first and answers the question correctly, an out is scored against the other team. If the fielding team hits the desk first and answers incorrectly, an additional out is given to the at-bat team. Once three outs are accumulated, teams switch roles.

(Continued)

Game	Materials	Content Area Uses / How Used	Description
			5. The at-bat team moves around the bases by being the quicker to respond to the questions posed (e.g., if the person at the desk gets a double and there's a person on second base, that person moves forward two bases (to home base), and the answerer goes to second base.
			6. One point is awarded for each person who crosses home plate.
			7. A 10-second musical audio clip selected by each team is played each time a player from that team scores.
			8. The game continues until all questions have been asked and all students have had at least one turn at bat. The team with the higher score wins.
Animated *Jeopardy*	• LCD projector • Computer with Microsoft PowerPoint or *Jeopardy* software • Files with audio and/or video clips • Gray-haired or unique wig for game show host	• All content areas • To review content	1. Create a PowerPoint slide with category headings representing categories of content to be reviewed (e.g., condensation, precipitation) and points (100, 250, 500). This first slide should be similar to the game show board on the television program *Jeopardy*.
			2. Create a corresponding slide with an answer for each point value within a category.
			3. Hyperlink slides to corresponding slides. For instance, on the slide with category headings and points, "100" under "condensation" will be hyperlinked to a slide that has a corresponding answer for which students have to form a question.
			4. Once the question has been phrased and any bonus slides hyperlinked to, the last slide in the series will hyperlink to the original one. Using information from your study of students, insert audio and video clips from favorite shows, music, and movies into the linked slides.
			5. Divide students into groups, and alternate giving each group a chance to provide a question that is appropriate for the answer provided on a slide.
			6. After the group provides the question, click on the embedded audio or video link in the slide.
			7. Groups earn the points associated with the answer if they provide a correct question. The team with the most points wins.

software packages available, I highly recommend you get one that enables you to do the following:

- capture online video
- make digital copies of streaming video and MP3 audio
- convert, create, or burn files
- trim, chop, and split both audio and video files.

Replay Capture Suite, produced by Applian Technologies, is the one I have been most pleased with. It allows you to capture any video content, create video clips, convert media into various formats, et cetera. I have also found Windows Live Movie Maker to be helpful and user friendly in creating and editing video.

Multimedia is the inhaled oxygen of the social life of today's youth. HUMS students follow suit. Among the many ways you can use multimedia to breathe life into your lessons are the following:

- Capture a YouTube or other online video as a way to provide an engaging introduction, illustrate concepts, resuscitate your presentation of content, or just bring pop culture into class.
- Capture content-related audio for similar uses.
- Have your students create personalized compact discs (CDs) or digital video discs (DVDs) with content they have learned. Students will relish the latitude to create their unique CD/DVD cover and label.
- Convert an audio file of you speaking or content you've taught to something they can carry on their iPods.

Given the pervasiveness of multimedia use in the lives of students, you're missing prime opportunities to engage them if you do not intersect multimedia elements with content.

Using Closure as a Tool of Engagement

As you're well aware, lesson closure involves assessment of objective mastery. Have you considered, by any chance, using closure as a time to start the wheels of engagement rolling for the next day? Like airing a glimpse of the next sitcom episode, a subtle yet powerful tool is to whet their intellectual appetites and stimulate their curiosity by ending the lesson with a scintillating sneak peek into the next lesson. It's best to have this be one of the last things you address with them before they leave. You can do this by

1. asking a thought-provoking question about an issue or challenge they have.

2. briefly describing one of the most engaging parts of tomorrow's lesson.

3. sharing a few of the benefits they will receive from tomorrow's lesson.

4. intimating how enjoyable or interesting the lesson was for a prior year's class.

Ending your lesson in such a way enhances the likelihood that they'll show up the next day eagerly awaiting you and your edifying offerings.

Chapter Summary

Situating the start of learning at 123 Student Place effectively makes the learning more appealing and relevant and captures student attention from the get-go. Beginning the process of engagement as soon as they walk into the room or right after closure helps facilitate the process of ongoing student engagement. Whetting students' appetite during closure is a subtle principle that preinitiates the next day's engagement.

Decoding, fluency, and reading comprehension are foundational skills essential to success in most academic content areas. Hence first engaging students with text is a must. Realistic or historical fiction, mysteries, and graphic novels are highly interesting to HUMS students. Moreover, texts that they are likely to love to read are those that pull from their experiences and have protagonists with strengths, struggles, and mores similar to theirs. Such texts also have themes and plots that are relevant to them, appeal to their interests, and have interactional and/or dialogic patterns that are reflective of students' lives outside of school. Carefully provide choices of your *most interesting* texts first to your most resistant readers. Exposing students to culturally relevant and socially significant texts, providing them with critical literacy instruction, and enveloping content in popular culture and media arts are additionally effective at engaging students in reading.

In a similar fashion, intersecting their interests and experiences with mathematics, science, and social studies content involves contextualizing content in out-of-school experiences and placing an emphasis on including student interests as an integral component. Play in the form of games is one of the most engaging tools to add to your pedagogical toolbox. Integrating multimedia and similar tools get the lesson soaring.

ACTIONABLE PROFESSIONAL LEARNING

Please respond individually initially, and then discuss with your collaborative learning team.

1. Considering the suggestions examined in this chapter, in what specific ways might you begin the process of engagement earlier in the lesson (e.g., when the tardy bell rings) and after closure?

2. Developing a classroom library not only extends the learning but also provides a more edifying experience in *all* content areas. To what extent does your classroom library/collection of texts reflect diverse student interests, real-world experiences, and elements that are of meaning to your students? Which genres and formats of text (e.g., graphic novels) are included in your library? How might you make your collection of texts of greater interest to your students?

3. Research a few texts that are culturally relevant or socially significant to your students. Start by exposing your students to one such text as an extension of the learning, to broaden their perspective, or to demonstrate how someone with a shared experience has succeeded. Provide multiple choices to demonstrate what they've learned from the text, such as using presentation software with music/video elements they can add, creating a podcast, creating a collage, writing a script, or sketching a cartoon.

4. Using clips from YouTube (or some other source) and the SELF (Seen, Experienced, Like, Felt) checklist, plan, prepare, and present a lesson that intersects with something from your students' world. Complete the following sentences:

   a. The aim of the activity is . . .
   b. Materials needed to conduct the activity are . . .
   c. Two observations of positive student engagement in the activity are . . .
   d. Two areas where the activity could be improved are . . .

Journal Study

Read *Redefining Academic Rigor: Documentary Film Making in the New English/Language Arts Classroom* (Dockter & Lewis, 2009) or a similar journal article that examines how to integrate students' interests and experiences into your content area; then discuss with colleagues. Explore the specific strategies and techniques described in the article to effectively engage students. Select one or two of them to use with your students.

Action Research

Several suggestions for intersecting students' interests and experiences in core content areas are highlighted in this chapter. Brainstorm ways to envelop content in the world of your students during your team meeting. Identify a particular challenge related to incorporating your students' interests and experiences in the content area you teach. Over the next few weeks, utilize a strategy or two from this chapter that aims to address that issue. Note its (their) effectiveness, citing specific indicators of engagement (or lack thereof) in such areas as participatory behavior, emotional involvement, and interest in completing the task. Engage in reflective dialogue with colleagues about the analysis of your findings with the aim of more effectively using the strategy in upcoming instruction. Repeat the process.

7

Reflect on Practice as a Tool of Improvement

Would you agree that one of the most pressing challenges you struggle with is having so many things to do, yet not enough time to get them done? And that as a result, you feel that the only thing you've mastered is the art of juggling several things at once without ever *dropping the ball?* You may have spent hours planning a lesson on how electrical circuits work, or had students assess the symbolic significance of motifs in narrative text, or had them solve for variables in algebraic equations, only to have the lesson fall flat. As if that weren't enough, you may have also had to cover an absent teacher's class during your prep period, work with a few students after school, contact the parents of a few difficult students, and then dedicate the little time you had left to your *full-time job* of your family. If you're like many teachers, you just don't have enough time to add one more thing to an already full plate!

> The absence of reflection ensures repetition!

Finding the time to get more things done and consistently becoming more effective can happen by adding hours to the day, decreasing hours of sleep, or freeing up time by utilizing reflective practice as a tool of improvement. When used with purpose and deliberation, such a tool can help you improve several aspects of what you do and make more effective use of your time. Said differently, refinement is the reward of reflection. That is, you become more efficient by engaging in processes of examining, polishing, practicing, and improving as a result of continual critical looks in the rearview mirror of your experiences.

You may recall the strong emphasis on reflecting on practice during your preservice training. Have you noticed, however, that it receives comparatively little attention in your inservice trainings, professional development, evaluation criteria, or other methods for improving what you do? The underlying reasons for relatively scant attention given to such processes extend beyond the aim of this text. However, with the incredibly and increasingly challenging circumstances teachers in high-poverty, urban, largely minority schools (HUMS) routinely face, there exists a need for examining what research and practice have shown to be a sound means of improving practice.

Reflecting Versus Reflective Practice

Are the terms *reflecting* and *reflective practice* synonymous? More broad in scope, *reflecting* connotes an act of simply meditating or deliberating on a topic. You might spend a few quiet moments reflecting on why students were not cognitively engaged during your lesson on properties of triangles. However, such serene moments may not necessarily give you the reason behind the issue, create a window for altering your perspective, or open doors leading to improvement. To the point, merely reflecting on an issue does not methodically lead to an understanding of that issue or a change of perspective on that issue, nor does it result in changed actions on the path to improvement.

Though similar, *reflective practice* differs from *reflecting* and is frequently conceived in a variety of ways. As Loughran explains, "For some, it simply means thinking about something, whereas for others, it is a well-defined and crafted practice that carries very specific meaning and associated action" (2002, p. 33). In a similar vein, I use the term *reflective practice* to mean a process of framing and reframing experiences encountered in the performance of duty with the aim of enhancing understanding, developing professional knowledge, and altering perspective, and in turn improving performance. Reflective practice is about repeatedly taking magnified looks at a specimen of experience with the goal of generating improved future specimens.

Of note is that the success of your reflective practice is tied to the extent to which the framing and reframing of experiences both alters perspectives and influences future actions. In a word, processes of effective reflective practice can turn the rich ingredients of experience into masterful learning and measureable improvement.

Why Engage in Reflective Practice?

Investing the time and energy to consistently engage in reflective processes generates greater returns in the form of powerful lessons and more engaging pedagogy for your students. It results in your taking less time to be more effective in enhancing their mastery. You are able to more readily respond to them with a variety of techniques and tools when the lessons *flame out*. You spend far less time suffering from student misbehavior, because you've eliminated elements of your teaching that invite boredom, apathy, and disinterest and replaced them with activities to which your students are cognitively tuned in. Further reasons for engaging in reflective practice are listed below.

THEORETICAL FRAMEWORK: UNDERLYING REASONS FOR ENGAGING IN REFLECTIVE PRACTICE

- Reflecting using authentic representations of practice (e.g., video), has been found to be beneficial to teachers (Brophy, 2004; Sherin & van Es, 2009).
- Using video-recorded lessons to reflect on practice has been found to have a direct impact on pedagogy and what students learn (Finn, 2002).
- Using video annotation tools as a means of reflection can assist teachers in examining whether active student engagement is present (Rich & Hannafin, 2009).
- Engaging in reflective practice is a substantive way for teachers to learn about teaching, become more competent practitioners, and contribute to the profession through the informing of elements of practice (Loughran, 2002).
- Reflective practice enhances the ability to exercise professional judgment and sustain both one's competence and professional well-being (Day, 1999).
- Reflection is an essential element of teacher development (Richards, 1990).

(Continued)

(Continued)

- Reflective practice is a process of professional development that effectively changes behavior (Osterman & Kottkamp, 1993).
- The ability to reflect and learn from experience on a continuous basis is an essential attribute of all effective practitioners in any field (Schön, 1983)
- Reflective journaling can produce effective conditions for learning that lead to meaningful learning (Hubbs & Brand, 2005; Kolb, 1984).
- Preservice teachers have a greater chance of being more sensitive to and better understand issues of diverse cultures when they engage in reflective thinking processes (Farber & Armaline, 1994).
- A characteristic of professionalism is having a keen ability to utilize reflection to solve challenges faced in practice (Clarke, 1995; Kelsay, 1989).
- Reflective teaching has been found to efficiently and effectively effect statistically significant changes in the behavior of teachers in the classroom (Killen, 1989).
- People are frequently unaware that they need to undergo change (Prochaska, Norcross, & DiClemente, 1994). Reflecting on practice helps people become more cognizant of the type of change that is called for.

Suggestions for Engaging in Reflective Practice

Imagine you just found out that you're being honored next month at a large gala for the selfless work you did for the local charity over the past year. Of course, you immediately think about your hair, makeup, attire, and even your acceptance speech. How likely is it that you'll rely solely on your *own* eyes and best judgment to determine whether or not you're looking like a million bucks? Odds are you won't *go it alone* but will be aided by your opinion of what you see in the mirror, as well as an untold number of opinions, critiques, and advice from friends, family, and perhaps a few professionals. That is, you'll most likely use a tool of reflection (e.g., mirror) and collaborate with others to ensure you're *dressed to impress* and have prepared a rousing acceptance speech.

Similar to your preparation for the gala, using self-reflection, collaborative reflection, and tools (i.e., audio recorder) to engage in reflective practice can be greatly beneficial. Reflective practice is most successful when structured collaboratively (Osterman & Kottkamp, 1993). Advantages of structuring it collaboratively are that you and colleagues will be more likely to benefit from varied analyses, where the colleagues may observe elements you may miss. Additionally, you are likely to hold each other accountable, and as a result, have a greater likelihood of implementing ideas. Though extensive guidance for engaging in reflective practice exists in the literature (Loughran, 2002; Osterman & Kottkamp, 1993; Schön, 1983), here are a few basic suggestions for getting started.

Decide whom you will collaborate with to begin the process. Reflecting on practice with colleagues who teach the same content has been found to be the optimal situation. If you are the only one teaching such content in your building, consider collaborating with those who teach the same students you teach (e.g., teaching team). Perhaps it may not be logistically feasible to collaboratively reflect on practice, or you simply strongly prefer to do it individually. Irrespective of whether it happens collaboratively or individually, ensure that reflective practice becomes an essential part of what you do.

Think back on experiences with the basic dimensions of engagement (emotional, cognitive, behavioral) in your classroom(s). Are you or colleagues challenged with coming up with effective ways to find out what things are relevant, interesting, or meaningful to students? Do you feel that there is some unknown element that is inhibiting mastery of content or limiting the emotional connection(s) with them? A suggested next step is to come to an agreement about which facets of student engagement may be most fruitful as a starting point for critical examination.

A third step in the process is to determine what method will be used to gather information (i.e., record evidence) from instructional or other interactional episodes. I strongly suggest you have someone record video to capture the instructional experience. Recording video of you in the classroom is like capturing your animated reflection in a large vanity mirror with a four-dimensional panoramic view. You probably know too well your strengths for teaching in the classroom, but do you really know the specific areas you need to improve in? Video provides a different way of seeing *you* in action.

Why Video?

What tool do the four major professional sports leagues in the United States use to review whether the correct call was made during a game and to sharpen the professional skills of the officials? The National Hockey League (NHL), National Football League (NFL), National Basketball Association (NBA), and recently Major League Baseball (MLB) use recorded video to ensure that the right calls are made, as a reflective tool for game officials' training, and to preserve the integrity of the game. Similarly, in the classroom *field of play*, recorded video can be used to review instructional calls and as a tool of ongoing reflection and improvement. As Borko, Jacobs, Eiteljorg, and Pittman (2008) framed it, "Video records can highlight aspects of classroom life that a teacher might not notice in the midst of carrying out a lesson, and can capture the social fabric of a classroom." Other compelling reasons for including video are the following:

- Teachers often feel the urgent need to improve achievement in the classroom once they see themselves in the video (Knight et al., 2012).
- Teacher video clubs can be an effective means for learning to attend to and critically examine student thinking (Sherin & van Es, 2009).
- Recorded video provides access to teachers' classrooms in ways other media are unable to and potentially can drive change and improvement (LeFevre, 2004).
- Using videotaped lessons to reflect on practice is a means of directly impacting both classroom pedagogy and student learning (Finn, 2002).

In a word, video provides an additional avenue of feedback that will help you improve what you do.

THE TALE OF THE TAPE

To her surprise when she opened the envelope, Mrs. Jones was rated less than satisfactory by the assistant principal, Mr. Handley. He conceded that students were on task, but he wrote that they were cognitively disengaged. Angered by the remarks, she insisted on having a meeting immediately. In the meeting, she said,

> I really feel that you have a personal vendetta against me. My students and I have a great relationship, my room is never out of order, and they are always learning. This is, by far, the worst evaluation I have received in my years of teaching!

After seeking advice on possible recourse with the building union representative, she agreed to have a lesson videotaped. To her surprise, when she viewed the tape, she saw that students indeed were on task, but many students' body language and facial expressions suggested they were begrudgingly completing the assignment, as they appeared highly uninterested. She reviewed the tape several more times and then invited her assistant principal to view it with her.

Though he would not rescind the teaching evaluation, citing fairness to her colleagues, he did agree to support Mrs. Jones in her quest to spearhead having videotaped lessons become part of the teacher evaluation process for the district. She said, "I do believe having another piece of evidence that sheds light on how teachers really fare in the classroom is long overdue."

Mrs. Jones even formed a video study group with her teaching team where they shared and critiqued each other's teaching and implemented more effective pedagogy as a result. She conceded,

> I had no clue. The video uncovered things I was completely unaware of as it opened our eyes to aspects that we would never have seen otherwise and motivated each one of us to go back and change the things that were pointed out.

Using Video as a Tool of Reflective Practice

Here are a few suggestions for using video to reflect on practice:

- Identify the facet you want to improve
- Have a checklist (or clearly delineated elements) of items you will observe before viewing.
- Select a place free of distractions and where you probably won't be disturbed while watching the video.
- View your video alone at least three to four times in order to pick up nuances of the specific teaching challenge or issue of focus.
- After highlighting a few areas you want feedback on, view the video with a coach, colleague, or video study group.
- Engage in dialogue for feedback that identifies areas of strength, challenges, and specific ways to improve.

Of import is that to utilize video as an effective learning tool, clarity of purpose for reviewing the video must lie at the heart of the process (Brophy, 2004). Simply *watching the recorded video* is not sufficient to glean new insight or improve practice. Questions to guide you and your colleagues as you collectively analyze the data (i.e., video) are as follows:

- What was the intended outcome for the activity/instructional episode?
- What challenge or element are we aiming to observe?

- What student actions are we examining?
- What actually occurred that was noteworthy?
- What factors may have led to such an occurrence?

Table 12 summarizes the process that can be used to reflect on your teaching practice and provides some resources for each.

Table 12   Processes Utilized to Engage in Reflective Practice

Type of Process Utilized for Reflective Practice	How It Works	Resources
Engage in reflective practice with instructional coach/ specialist	• Initially, review video by yourself several times. • Review video with coach or specialist.	• Brophy (2004) • Knight et al. (2012)
	• Use PDA or voice recorder to record notes to transcribe later.	• Shuster & Meany (2005)
Form a video study/video club	• Collaboratively reflect on shared practice.	• Brophy (2004) • Finn (2002) • Sherin & van Es (2009)
	• Use video annotation tool for recording, scaffolding, and structuring teacher self-reflection.	• Rich & Hannafin (2009)
Reflective journal writing	• Chronicle classroom experiences.	• Boud (2001) • Moon (1999)

Those who excel in any venue in life are the ones who are consistently seeking ways to improve. The shortest path to improvement in any profession is paved with the informed insight born from reflecting on practice. A highly engaging educational practice is developed from consistent use of such pedagogy, whereby you are enabled to learn about your teaching, become more competent in what you do, and continually improve what you do. Reflective practices assist you in identifying and purging ineffective practices and replacing them with those shown as effective by experience. Reflective tools can be utilized to transform often immensely challenging experiences in HUMS classrooms into productive learning for both teacher and students.

Chapter Summary

More deliberate in aim and process than *reflection,* the process of framing and reframing experiences encountered in the duty to improve practice defines *reflective practice.* It is most effective when it is rooted in collaboration. Reflective practice assists in identifying and resolving issues, informs the profession, and enhances the competency of professionals. Remember, the absence of reflection ensures repetition. When you don't make time to think and debrief about a situation and make no changes in light of the debriefing, you're ensured a trip down repetition road. A fundamental guide for beginning reflective practice is to identify an issue or element of interest and collect data relating to that element. Recorded video provides an effective way to collect such data. Subsequently, conduct an individual review and analysis, and then collectively review and analyze the video with a coach, colleague, or video study group. Act on their suggestions or critique after they have reframed your performance.

ACTIONABLE PROFESSIONAL LEARNING

Please respond individually initially, and then discuss with your collaborative learning team.

1. How, if at all, have you utilized reflective practice in the past? To what extent did it help you improve? (Please provide a detailed response.)

2. What are a few of the barriers that may get in the way of your consistently engaging in reflective practice (e.g., logistics of a video recording process)?

3. Identify one issue or challenge that limits the emotional, cognitive, or behavioral engagement in your classroom that you have yet to reflectively examine. Use the following steps to begin the process of reflectively examining the challenge. (See the section above, Suggestions for Engaging in Reflective Practice, for more detail.)

   a. The challenge/issue I am examining is . . .
   b. Technique(s) I will use to gather data about the challenge is/are . . .
   c. I will review the video where I know I will be neither disturbed nor disrupted in . . .
   d. Based on my observations and notes taken during the video, I would like feedback from my instructional coach/colleague on these particular techniques or tools that lead to engagement . . .

4. Since I've began reflecting on practice, I've noticed/learned . . .

Shared Practice

Building on what you started in 3(c) above, view a video or two of a member or members of your team each meeting and collectively analyze and critique the practice shown in it with your video study group. Assist each other with framing, reframing, and providing analysis, feedback, and insight on issues or challenges identified by each team member.

8

Expect Nothing Short
of Excellence

As if the challenges of teaching in high-poverty, urban, largely minority schools (HUMS) classrooms weren't enough, one of the fiercest battles facing HUMS teachers rages within. The raging internal struggle is about the fight to believe in the possibility that students, often from unthinkably challenging circumstances, are capable of emulating and attaining levels of both academic and social excellence. Too often, visions of great things they can become are imprisoned by beliefs formed from the visible. The formation of such beliefs is molded from viewing daily matinees played out in the classroom that feature overwhelmed teachers and uninspired students. They are cemented by daily scenes depicting boredom, apathy, and disinterest in starring roles. On rare occasions, engagement makes a cameo appearance. When belief in a happy ending begins to give way to despair, scrolling subtitles such as "the rate of prison construction is calculated from the fourth grade reading scores of HUMS students," "more Latino and African American males are in prison than in college," or "African Americans and Latino students are more likely to drop out of school than any other ethnic groups," the fate of the protagonist pupils is sealed in the subconscious mind.

Is it just me, or does it seem that one of the most overused phrases in school vision statements and other statements of belief about children is "We believe all children can learn"? Though such statements are

Trust the vision, not the visible.

plastered on the walls throughout schools, the actual beliefs and resulting expectations of teachers, particularly in HUMS, quite often paint a different portrait. Many believe that all children can excel with, *ahem*, a few caveats: if they had more involved parents, hailed from a different community, or simply had a more enriching home environment. Because of the well-documented challenges besetting such students coupled with bleak images and information disseminated by some media, a struggle to maintain optimistic outlooks and expectancies of excellence ensues.

Teacher Expectations and Their Importance in HUMS

Teacher expectations are simply preconceptions of future student capacity, achievement, and behavior formed from current beliefs. Interest in teacher expectations arose from the work of Robert Rosenthal and Lenore Jacobson (1968), in which expectations of teachers were found to impact student outcomes.

When expectations are lowered by teachers, the commensurate actions that follow have a deleterious impact on several student outcomes. Higher quality instruction is often delivered when teacher expectations are higher. Students perceptively key in to lowered expectations and respond to them with less effort. Teacher expectations are of greater concern in HUMS than in other schools because they are more strongly linked with school outcomes for Latino and African American students than for nonminority students.

How much energy, skill, and planning does it take for you to cross over a two-inch high bar? The obvious answer is not much. However, if the bar is raised to a height of four feet, a successful leap over it requires a considerably greater level of planning, skill, and certainly energy. Similarly, when the *bar is lowered* in the classroom by giving children tasks that have little or no challenge, students are less likely to be cognitively engaged. When expectations of students are heightened to levels of excellence where moderately challenging tasks invite them to intellectually stretch, they often give more skill and effort to do what's necessary to *rise* to the challenge. Students are more likely to be emotionally, cognitively, and behaviorally engaged when you implicitly and explicitly demonstrate that your expectation for them to excel is the norm. Additionally, expectations of excellence held by teachers lie at the heart of academic rigor, an integral component of sound educational pedagogy. Further rationale is listed in the theoretical framework below.

THEORETICAL FRAMEWORK: UNDERLYING REASONS FOR ELEVATED TEACHER EXPECTATIONS

- Teachers characterized as holding high expectations have been found to have created structures for students to learn, asked more questions that elicited higher order thinking skills, given more feedback, and had more positive classroom management (Rubie-Davies, 2007).
- When students are in classrooms with elevated levels of academic press, (when teachers continuously expect students to produce their best work), there is a greater chance they will be behaviorally engaged. When teachers hold high expectations, students are more likely to persevere and give greater effort (Lee, 2012).
- Whether accurate or inaccurate, teachers' perception of children's achievement impacts how well the children fare on standardized tests, their grades, and the scores they receive in the classroom (Jussim & Harber, 2005). Expectations of achievement held by teachers in early grades affect how well students currently and in the future adjust to school (Jussim, Eccles, & Madon, 1996).
- Teachers' expectations of children's reading abilities were linked to future performance of minority boys. When minority boys' abilities were underestimated, they had the lowest performance, and, conversely, they had the greatest improvements when their abilities were overestimated. Expectations were also thought to be impactful on future outcomes of low-income students (Hinnant, O'Brien, & Ghazarian, 2009).
- Teachers in low-SES and low-achieving settings have been found to underestimate the literacy ability of low-SES children (Ready & Wright, 2010).
- Meta-analyses have found that teachers hold higher expectations for European American children than for African American or Latino children (Tenenbaum & Ruck, 2007).
- When students receive higher academic placements, they are likely to elevate their performance to meet such challenges. Teachers have been found to underestimate the capacity of African American and/or low-income students even when their achievement is equal to that of others. Such biased expectations contribute to the Black–White achievement gap (Hughes, Gleason, & Zhang, 2005; Weinstein, Gregory, & Strambler, 2004).
- The expectancy effect of teachers has been found to account for 5% to 10% of achievement variance (Brophy, 1983; Jussim & Harber, 2005) and appears to have the greatest impact on children who are both low-income and minority (Gill & Reynolds, 1999; Jussim et al., 1996).
- Academic predictions made by teachers have been found to be more positive for students who are friendly, attentive, and female (Tournaki & Podell, 2005).
- Where teachers collectively perceive students as less teachable, it is less likely that students will develop supportive relationships with their teachers, and in turn they will be more likely to violate rules in schools. When teachers

(Continued)

(Continued)

hold such lowered expectations about the *teachability* of students, it can create more student misbehavior (Demanet & Van Houtte, 2012).
- Teacher expectations have been found to be stronger than parental expectations in predicting outcomes in both math and reading (Gill & Reynolds, 1999).
- Lower expectations for both the performance and the abilities of African American students are held by teachers across grades. Additionally, teachers tended to provide African American students with less exposure to math and science role models (Thomas & Stevenson, 2009).

Assessing, Elevating, and Maintaining Expectations for Your Students to Excel

Assess Your Expectations While Reflecting on Practice

When you reflect on practice through viewing videos of your teaching, do you seem to give equal wait-time to *all* students, or do you find that you afford your more high-achieving students a bit more time than you give to the ones who often struggle? Engaging in reflective practice (see Chapter 7) is a means of discerning whether you differentially express expectations, either implicitly or explicitly, for your students. The true expectations you hold of your students lie in the stories told by your interactions with them. The following questions will help you assess your level expectations while reflecting on practice:

- Do I equitably pose challenging tasks to engage all learners?
- To what extent do assigned tasks compel all students to stretch one step beyond their current readiness level?
- During classroom dialogue,
  - are all encouraged to and given ample opportunity to participate?
  - do I frequently use revoicing and linking of ideas for all students?
  - are all students afforded ample wait time when prompted to respond?
  - do I give a few moments for each student to rethink initially inaccurate responses and provide a follow-up response?
  - do I provide subtle clues or other scaffolding techniques?
- Do nonverbal emotional cues send the message that I expect less from challenging or struggling learners?

- When interacting with certain students, do I appear to show or actually show less enthusiasm for their success or optimism that they will succeed?
- Does my verbal and written feedback on tasks indicate I hold high expectations for all?

Survey Student Perceptions of Your Expectations

Who is better qualified to provide feedback about your expectations than your students? Whether in HUMS, affluent schools, or somewhere in between, students are very perceptive about what their teachers expect of them. Devise a brief survey to assess your students' perception of your expectations. It goes without saying that your chances of receiving candid feedback increase to the extent that you provide for anonymity in the process. Remember, brevity is king. That is, include only a small number of concisely written items. I provided a few tips and suggestions for creating surveys in Chapter 2 and won't provide much more detail here.

All fruit don't ripen on the vine at the same time!

Develop a Clear Understanding of Adolescent Development

The expedient reaction to children who often break rules is to label them simply as bad children who don't know *how* to behave. Those who are clear about developmental pathways of adolescents understand that *all* students do not mature at the same rates. Indeed there are general developmental differences and gender specific differences in the way children develop. Boys, in particular, generally lag girls in rates of maturity. Neurologists assert that for boys, it's not until their early 20s that the frontal lobe, the portion of the brain partially responsible for decision making, controlling purposeful behaviors, and regulating emotions, is fully developed. Hence, it stands to reason that boys often don't make as prudent decisions as girls. Having an appreciation of knowledge such as this gives one a better understanding that developmental processes account for some of students' ill-timed decisions and immaturity. In turn, the subconscious lowering of expectations may be tempered.

Stay Abreast of Exemplars Who Have Experiences and Backgrounds Similar to Those of Your Students

Stories of the triumphs of individuals whose backgrounds are similar to those of HUMS students often go untold. Becoming more knowledgeable of such individuals not only helps alter lowered expectations of the teacher but also provides concrete evidence of the possibility of students attaining success. It helps engender the understanding that, indeed, their students do have the capacity to produce at high levels of excellence.

Addressing her students, an English media analysis elective teacher put it best:

> If your teachers let you do nothing and get a passing grade, you are being disrespected. . . . You shouldn't be mad at me right now, you should be grateful because I expect something of you, because I know you can do it. (Dockter & Lewis, 2009, p. 15)

EXEMPLARS OF EXCELLENCE

Waiting with bated breath, the sophomores giddily filed into the classroom on a cool autumn Friday morning. They eagerly anticipated interacting with this month's *Exemplar of Excellence*. With almost as much emphasis as he placed on achieving academic outcomes, Mr. King made it a priority to have professionals and those who had conquered challenging conditions come into his classroom to have a fruitful dialogue with his students.

The number one aim of the presentation was to build the belief in his students that current circumstances can be conquered if you defiantly disallow them to define you. He sought to achieve this goal through creating meaningful interactions with individuals who would not only share their triumphant stories but place particular emphasis on specific strategies that helped them endure. To further build belief in realistic possibilities in the minds of his students, he sought individuals who shared the ethnic, racial, and SES experiences his students had. When colleagues asked, he would proudly say,

> It's one thing to invite someone born with a silver spoon in his mouth who's been successful in school and life, but it becomes that much more doable in their minds when someone with shared experiences and background comes to share his or her story.

A second goal for having such invited guests was to introduce students to the wealth of strategies that can be used to overcome obstacles. Thirdly, he aimed to broaden their horizon as it related to the career options available. "Not everyone wants to be a doctor, lawyer, or other run-of-the-mill professional that we typically showcase in front of them."

The guidelines for the presenters who are *Exemplars of Excellence* are simple: They should take no more than 10 minutes to share their story, followed by 10 minutes to outline the strategies that helped them overcome adversity and get to where they are and to share a few of the best lessons they learned from mistakes. This should be followed by dialogue or interactive demonstration with students, where they field questions or have a quick activity that shows students a unique aspect of the exemplar's story, a strategy they can use to emulate the exemplar, or an element of the exemplar's professional practice.

Interestingly enough, Mr. King intimates to colleagues how interacting with such individuals helps him maintain *his own* elevated expectations. As he says, "When doubt inevitably creeps into my mind about what my most behaviorally difficult or struggling learners can become, I quickly think of the stories shared by my exemplars of excellence, who reinforce my belief in the possibilities of *greatness* for all."

Provide Multiple Opportunities for Exposure to Exemplars

When teachers are keenly aware of exemplars from the HUMS communities who have excelled, this awareness facilitates the task of sharing this knowledge with their students. Not only can they share such knowledge, but they can also consistently invite exemplars in to have intimate conversations with students about how to avoid some common pitfalls. They could also work to build ongoing relationships with such exemplars, who, in all likelihood, would freely donate a few hours a month to mentor or positively impact HUMS students in other ways.

Of course, it is not always possible to have exemplars pay your students a visit. With the proliferation of access to information via the World Wide Web and other multimedia formats, showing videos about exemplars or introducing students to literary works about them is more readily accessible and can also have an impact. When students are exposed to people who hail from similar backgrounds and have successfully transitioned to adulthood, it plants the seed that germinates into a belief in the possibility of achieving similar outcomes.

Hearing the inspirational story of Sonia Sotomayor, who overcame juvenile diabetes, experienced the early death of her father, and emerged from impoverished beginnings in the Bronxdale Housing Projects to become the first Hispanic-American female Supreme Court justice, builds belief. The triumphant biography of Rudolfo Anaya, who overcame impoverished beginnings, breaking two vertebrae in his neck (almost dying), and being rejected by dozens of publishers to become an acclaimed award-winning Chicano writer demonstrates the power of perseverance. Having students explore how three African American teens—Sampson Davis, George Jenkins, and Rameck Hunt—committed to each other to stay the course and overcome the daunting odds of their rough Newark, New Jersey, neighborhood broadens perspectives on the possibilities of prevailing. Madame C. J. Walker's story of how she overcame the untimely death of her parents, the presence of an abusive relative, and gender and racial biases to become what's widely recognized as America's first self-made female millionaire is timely.

Envision the Possibilities

Visualize what students can become with your wisdom, care, and pedagogical prowess. Academic and social excellence doesn't spring forth from casual student contact but grows from committing to consistently being warm yet demanding and situating students in situations of success. Use evidence exhibited by exemplars to look beyond the limiting visible images and to create extraordinary visions of excellence of all of your students.

Forming expectations of others is an episode of thought that reairs in the minds of most. The challenge lies in not only forming expectations of excellence but also maintaining them despite the attempts by ill-conceived preconceptions to take hold. Empowering expectations of excellence to prevail is grounded in the notion that all have untapped reservoirs of potential just waiting to be unleashed.

Chapter Summary

Preconceptions of future student capacity, achievement, and behavior formed from current beliefs define teacher expectations. Such pivotal elements of the classroom play a critical role in whether or not all students excel. Teacher expectancy effects are important, as they have been empirically found to account for to up 10% of achievement variance. Whether implicitly or explicitly communicated, such expectations have an even more profound impact in HUMS than in other schools.

Expectations of excellence are maintained when teachers create environments with elevated levels of academic press, challenge students to provide evidence behind their responses, and both embrace and explicitly communicate (to students) a sincere belief in their capacity to excel. Reflective practice and student surveys provide a means of exploring your expectations. Exposing your students to professionals and other exemplars with shared experiences sends the message that you not only desire but *expect* them to be excellent, helps build the belief within them that they can successfully emulate such exemplars, and also helps you maintain high expectations by providing evidence of the possibility of success. Understanding adolescent development of HUMS students helps foster an understanding of some of their counterproductive behavior. First visualizing and then trusting what is envisioned is key in creating and maintaining high student expectations.

ACTIONABLE PROFESSIONAL LEARNING

Please respond individually initially, and then discuss with your collaborative learning team.

1. Being candid with myself, I believe the expectations for all of my students are [high] [average] [low] (choose one). I believe this because . . .

2. Thinking of the interactions with all of my students, I find it at times somewhat difficult to maintain expectations of excellence for all because . . .

3. Specific actions that either implicitly or explicitly indicate lowered expectations are . . .

4. I will introduce my students to exemplars who have shared experiences by (e.g., methods such as multimedia) . . .

5. Resources I will use to personally become more familiar with exemplars who have shared experiences and backgrounds with my students are . . .

6. Identify and contact local exemplars of excellence who share the experiences and backgrounds of your students. Create a plan for consistently inviting them to interact with your students. Provide additional ways (e.g., using the World Wide Web) for students to become more knowledgeable of the stories of these individuals, highlighting strategies that empowered the exemplars to overcome obstacles and additional factors leading to their successes.

Shared Practice

Have each member of your team respond to 1, 2, and 3 above, and then do the following:

1. Identify an element of the expectations you have of your students (e.g., a challenge or something to be improved).

2. Using the questions under the heading "Assess your expectations while reflecting on practice" (p. 170) as a guide, watch a video clip of yourself interacting with students at least three times to begin to uncover more information about a particular element of your teaching (e.g., specific actions, nonverbal emotional cues given, differences in wait time).

3. As a group, watch the video to provide analysis and feedback on the element each member identifies.

4. Engage in rich discussion around *a few* specific strategies that will assist in elevating the identified element of expectation.

5. Implement the suggested strategies (no more than one or two) over the next six to eight weeks.

6. Video-record lessons again, and review the new video with your team to assess improvement and remaining challenges.

Appendix: Interest Inventory

1. What is your favorite school subject? Why?

2. If you were able to choose a topic to learn about, what would it be?

3. Do you work better with others or individually? Why?

4. What types of things do you enjoy doing indoors? Explain.

5. If you had the ability to choose your activity for the weekend, what would it be? Why?

6. Rank the following types of communication you prefer in order from most to least liked: text messaging, instant messaging, telephone calls, e-mail, Twitter, Facebook. Why did you order them that way?

7. What are three characteristics that you think make up a great teacher? Why?

8. Which method of expression do you use to best express yourself: poetry, rap, essay, or song? Why?

9. What is your favorite type of music? What are your three favorite songs? Who are your three favorite artists? What are three favorite music videos? Explain why each is your favorite.

10. If your best friend were to describe you and the things you enjoyed, write that description.

11. What is your favorite outfit? Why?

12. What place(s) in the world would have you visited or would you love to visit most? Explain.

13. What is your favorite way to style your hair (or favorite haircut type)?

14. What way do you like to show others information you have learned in class (group presentation, picture/drawing, project board, skit)?

15. Describe the most enjoyable lessons you ever participated in. What made them enjoyable?

References

Ainley, M., Hidi, S., & Berndorf, D. (2002). Interest, learning, and the psychological processes that mediate their relationship. *Journal of Educational Psychology, 94*, 545–561.

Allen, B. A., & Boykin, A. W. (1991). The influence of contextual factors on Afro-American and Euro-American children's performance: Effects of movement opportunity and music. *International Journal of Psychology, 26*(3), 373–387.

Allen, B. A., & Butler, L. (1996). The effects of music and movement opportunity on the analogical reasoning performance of African American and White school children: A preliminary study. *Journal of Black Psychology, 22*, 316–328.

Alvermann, D. E. (2001). Reading adolescents' reading identities: Looking back to see ahead. *Journal of Adolescent & Adult Literacy, 44*, 676–695.

Anderman, L. H. (2003). Academic and social perceptions as predictors of change in middle school students' sense of school belonging. *The Journal of Experimental Education, 72*, 5–22.

Appleton, J. J., Chrisenton, S. L., & Furlong, M. J. (2008). Student engagement with school: Critical conceptual and methodological issues of the construct. *Psychology in the Schools, 45*, 369–386.

Baker, J. A. (1998). The social context of school satisfaction among urban, low-income, African-American students. *School Psychology Quarterly, 13*, 25–44.

Baker, J. A. (1999). Teacher–student interaction in urban at-risk classrooms: Differential behavior, relationship quality, and student satisfaction with school. *The Elementary School Journal, 100*, 57–70.

Baker, J. A. (2006). Contributions of teacher-child relationships to positive school adjustment during elementary school. *Journal of School Psychology, 44*, 211–229.

Baker, J. A., Grant, S., & Morlock, L. (2008). The teacher-student relationship as a developmental context for children with internalizing or externalizing behavior problems. *School Psychology Quarterly, 23*, 3–15.

Bandura, A. (1986). *Social foundations of thought and action: A social cognitive theory.* Englewood Cliffs, NJ: Prentice Hall.

Bandura, A. (1997). Exercise of personal and collective efficacy in changing societies. In A. Bandura (Ed.), *Self-efficacy in changing societies* (pp. 1–45). New York, NY: Cambridge University Press.

Baumeister, R. F., & Leary, M. R. (1995). The need to belong: Desire for inter-personal attachments as a fundamental human motivation. *Psychological Bulletin, 117,* 497–529.

Black, P., Harrison, C., Lee, C., Marshall, B., & Wiliam, D. (2003). *Assessment for learning: Putting it into practice.* Buckingham, UK: Open University Press.

Black, R. W., & Steinkuehler, C. (2009). *Literacy in virtual worlds.* In L. Christenbury, R. Bomer, & P. Smagorinsky (Eds.), *Handbook of adolescent literacy research* (pp. 271–286). New York, NY: Guilford.

Boekaerts, M., & Corno, L. (2005). Self-Regulation in the classroom: A Perspective on assessment and intervention. *Applied Psychology: An International Review, 54,* 199–231.

Borko, H., Jacobs, J., Eiteljorg, E., & Pittman, M. E. (2008). Video as a tool for fostering productive discussions in mathematics professional development. *Teaching and Teacher Education, 24,* 417–436.

Boud, D. (2001, Summer). Using journal writing to enhance reflective practice. In L. M. English & M. A. Gillen (Eds.), *Special Issue: Promoting Journal Writing in Adult Education. New Directions in Adult and Continuing Education, 90,* 9–18.

Boutte, G. (1999). *Multicultural education: Raising consciousness.* New York, NY: Russell Sage.

Boykin, A. W. (1994). Harvesting culture and talent: African American children and educational reform. In R. Rossi (Ed.), *Schools and students at risk* (pp. 116–138). New York, NY: Teachers College Press.

Brewster, A. B., & Bowen, G. L. (2004). Teacher support and the school engagement of Latino middle and high school students at risk of school failure. *Child and Adolescent Social Work Journal, 21,* 47–67.

Brookhart, S. (2010). *Formative assessment strategies for every classroom: An ASCD action tool* (2nd ed.). Alexandria, VA: ASCD.

Brophy, J. (1983). Research on the self-fulfilling prophecy and teacher expectations. *Journal of Educational Psychology, 75,* 631–661.

Brophy, J. (Ed.) (2004). *Advances in research on teaching, volume 10: Using video in teacher education.* Oxford, UK: Elsevier.

Brown, D. F. (2003). Urban teachers' use of culturally responsive management strategies. *Theory Into Practice, 42,* 277–282.

Brown, M. R. (2007). Educating all students: Creating culturally responsive teachers, classrooms, and schools. *Intervention in School and Clinic, 43,* 57–62.

Brush, T., & Saye, J. (2008). The effects of multimedia-supported problem-based inquiry on student engagement, empathy, and assumptions about history. *Interdisciplinary Journal of Problem-Based Learning, 2,* 21–56.

Buysse, V., Sparkman, K. L., and Wesley, P. W. (2003). Communities of practice: Connecting what we know with what we do. *Exceptional Children, 69,* 263–277.

Byrnes, J. P. (2003). Factors predictive of mathematics achievement in white, black, and Hispanic 12th graders. *Journal of Educational Psychology, 95,* 316–326.

Calder, J. (2006). Chunking as a cognitive strategy: Teaching students how to learn more in less time. *Journal of Teaching in Marriage & Family, 6,* 415–435.

Clarke, A. (1995). Professional development in practicum settings: Reflective practice under scrutiny. *Teaching and Teacher Education, 11,* 243–261.

Connell, J. P., Halpern-Felsher, B. L., Clifford, E., Crichlow, W., & Usinger, P. (1995). Hanging in there: Behavioral, psychological, and contextual factors affecting whether African American adolescents stay in high school. *Journal of Adolescent Research, 10,* 41–63.

Connell, J. P., Spencer, M. B., & Aber, J. L. (1994). Educational risk and resilience in African American youth: Context, self, action, and outcomes in school. *Child Development, 65,* 493–506.

Connell, J. P., & Wellborn, J. (1991). Competence, autonomy, and relatedness: A motivational analysis of self-system processes. In M. Runnar & L. A. Sroufe (Eds.), *Self processes and development. The Minnesota symposia on child psychology* (vol. 23, pp. 43–77). Hillsdale, NJ: Erlbaum.

Covington, M. V., & Omelich, C. L. (1984). Task-oriented versus competitive learning structures: Motivational and performance consequences. *Journal of Educational Psychology, 76,* 1038–1050.

Csikszentmihalyi, M. (1990). *Flow: The psychology of optimal experience.* New York, NY: Harper & Row.

Culver, S. M., Wolfle, L. M., & Cross, L. H. (1990). Testing a model of teacher satisfaction for blacks and whites. *American Education Research Journal, 27,* 323–349.

Darling-Hammond, L. (2008). Teacher learning that supports student learning. In B. Z. Presseisen (Ed.), *Teaching for intelligence* (2nd ed., pp., 91–100). Thousand Oaks, CA: Corwin.

Day, C. (1999). Researching teaching through reflective practice. In J. J. Loughran (Ed.), *Researching teaching: Methodologies and practices for understanding pedagogy* (pp. 215–233). London, UK: Falmer.

Decker, D. M., Dona, D. P., & Christenson, S. L. (2007). Behaviorally at-risk African American students: The importance of student–teacher relationships for student outcomes. *Journal of School Psychology, 45*(1), *83–109.*

Demanet, J., Van Houtte, M. (2012). Teachers' attitudes and students' opposition: School misconduct as a reaction to teachers' diminished effort and affect. *Teaching and Teacher Education, 28,* 860–869.

Dewey, J. (1900). *School and society* (2nd ed.). Chicago, IL: The University of Chicago Press.

Do, S. L., & Schallert, D. L. (2004). Emotions and classroom talk: Toward a model of the role of affect in students' experiences of classroom discussions. *Journal of Educational Psychology, 96,* 619–634.

Dockter, J., & Lewis, C. (2009). Redefining academic rigor: Documentary film making in the new English/language arts classroom. *CURA Reporter, 39*(3–4), 11–17.

Dweck, C. S. (2006). *Mindset: The new psychology of success.* New York, NY: Random House.

Duncan-Andrade, J. M., & Morrell, E. (2008). *The art of critical pedagogy: Possibilities for moving from theory to practice in urban schools.* New York: Peter Lang.

Eccles, J. (1993). School and family effects on the ontogeny of children's interests, self-perceptions, and activity choices. In J. Jacobs (Ed.), *Developmental perspectives on motivation: Nebraska symposium on motivation, 1992* (vol. 40, pp. 145–208). Lincoln: University of Nebraska Press.

Elliot, A. J., & Dweck, C. S. (Eds.). (2005). *Handbook of competence and motivation.* New York, NY: Guilford Press.

Farber, K., & Armaline, W. (1994) Examining cultural conflict in urban field experiences through the use of reflective thinking. *Teacher Education Quarterly, 21,* 59–76.

Farrell, T. (1998). Reflective teaching: The principles and practices. *English Teaching Forum, 36,* 10–17.

Fine, M. (1991). *Framing dropouts: Notes on the politics of an urban high school.* Albany: State University of New York Press.

Finn, J. D. (1989). Withdrawing from school. *Review of Educational Research, 59,* 117–142.

Finn, J. D. (1993). *School engagement and students at risk.* Washington, DC: National Center for Education Statistics.

Finn, J. D., & Rock, D. A. (1997). Academic success among students at risk for school failure. *Journal of Applied Psychology, 82,* 221–234.

Finn, L. (2002). Using video to reflect on curriculum. *Educational Leadership, 59,* 72–74.

Firestone, W. A., & Pennell, J. R. (1993). Teacher commitment, working conditions, and differential incentive policies. *Review of Educational Research, 63,* 489–525.

Fredericks, J. A., Blumenfeld, P. C., & Paris, A. H. (2004). School engagement: Potential of the concept, state of the evidence. *Review of Educational Research, 74,* 59–109.

Freedman, S. W., & Appleman, D. (2009). "In it for the long haul": How teacher education can contribute to teacher retention in high-poverty, urban schools. *Journal of Teacher Education, 60,* 323–337.

Fresko, B., Kfir, D., & Nasser, F. (1997). Predicting teacher commitment. *Teaching and Teacher Education, 13,* 429–438.

Fuchs, D., & Fuchs, L. S. (2006). Introduction to Response to Intervention: What, why, and how valid is it? *Reading Research Quarterly, 41,* 93–99.

Furrer, C., & Skinner, E. (2003). Sense of relatedness as a factor in children's academic engagement and performance. *Journal of Educational Psychology, 95,* 148–162.

Garza, E. A., & Nava, G. N. (2005). The effects of code switching on elementary students in a border area of South Texas: A teacher perspective, Part I. *Journal of Border Educational Research, 4,* 97–109.

Gay, G. (2010). *Culturally responsive teaching: Theory, research, and practice* (2nd ed.). New York, NY: Teachers College Press.

Gill, S., & Reynolds, A. J. (1999). Educational expectations and school achievement of urban African American children. *Journal of School Psychology, 37,* 403–424.

Giroux, H., & Simon, R. (1989). Popular culture as a pedagogy of pleasure and meaning. In H. Giroux & R. Simon (Eds.), *Popular culture, schooling, and everyday life* (pp. 1–29). Granby, MA: Bergin & Garvey.

Goodenow, C. (1993). Classroom belonging among early adolescent students: Relationship to motivation and achievement. *The Journal of Early Adolescence, 13,* 21–43.

Gurian, M., & Stevens, K. (2010). *Boys and girls learn differently! A guide for teachers and parents* (rev. ed.). San Francisco, CA: Jossey-Bass.

Gutstein, E., Lipman, P., Hernandez, P., & de los Reyes, R. (1997). Culturally relevant mathematics teaching in a Mexican American context. *Journal for Research in Mathematics Education, 28,* 709–737.

Hall, L. A., & Piazza, S. V. (2008). Critically reading texts: What students do and how teachers can help. *The Reading Teacher, 62,* 32–41.

Hamre, B. K., & Pianta, R. C. (2001). Early teacher–child relationships and the trajectory of children's school outcomes through eighth grade. *Child Development, 72,* 625–638.

Hamre, B. K., & Pianta, R. C. (2005). Can instructional and emotional support in the first-grade classroom make a difference for children at risk of school failure? *Child Development, 76,* 949–967.

Hamre, B. K., Pianta, R. C., Downer, J. T., & Mashburn, A. J. (2008). Teachers' perceptions of conflict with young students: Looking beyond problem behaviors. *Social Development, 17,* 115–136.

Hargreaves, A. (2001). Emotional geographies of teaching. *Teachers College Record, 103,* 1056–1080.

Hattie, J., & Timperley, H. (2007). The power of feedback. *Review of Educational Research, 77,* 81–112.

Hecht, M. L., Jackson, R. L., & Ribeau, S. A. (2003). *African American communication: Exploring identity and culture.* Mahwah, NJ: Lawrence Erlbaum.

Hembree, R. (1988). Correlates, causes, effects, and treatment of test anxiety. *Review of Educational Research, 58,* 47–77.

Hilliard, A. G. (1992). Behavioral style, culture, and teaching and learning. *The Journal of Negro Education, 61,* 370–377.

Hinnant, J. B., O'Brien, M., & Ghazarian, S. R. (2009). The longitudinal relations of teacher expectations to achievement in the early school years. *Journal of Educational Psychology, 101,* 662–670.

Horowitz, D. F., Darling-Hammond, L., & Bransford, J. (2005). Educating teachers for developmentally appropriate practice. In L. Darling-Hammond & J. Bransford (Eds.), *Preparing teachers for a changing world: What teachers should learn and be able to do* (pp. 88–125). San Francisco, CA: Jossey-Bass.

Hubbs, D. L., & Brand, C. F. (2005). The paper mirror: Understanding reflective journaling. *Journal of Experiential Education, 28,* 60–71.

Hughes, J. N., Gleason, K. A., & Zhang, D. (2005). Relationship influences on teachers' perceptions of academic competence in academically at-risk minority and majority first grade students. *Journal of School Psychology, 43,* 303–320.

Hurley, E. A., Boykin A. W., & Allen, B. A. (2005). Communal vs. individual learning of a math-estimation task: African American children and the culture of learning contexts. *The Journal of Psychology, 139,* 513–527.

Johnson, D., & Johnson, R. (1985). The internal dynamics of cooperative learning groups. In R. E. Slavin, S. S. Sharan, S. Kagan, R. Hertz-Lazarowitz, C. Webb, & R. Schmuck (Eds.), *Learning to cooperate: Cooperating to learn* (pp. 103–124). New York, NY: Plenum.

Jussim, L., & Harber, K. D. (2005). Teacher expectations and self-fulfilling prophecies: Knowns and unknowns, resolved and unresolved controversies. *Personality and Social Psychology Review, 9,* 131–155.

Jussim, L., Eccles, J., & Madon, S. (1996). Social perception, social stereotypes, and teacher expectations: Accuracy and the quest for the powerful self-fulfilling prophecy. In M. P. Zanna (Ed.), *Advances in experimental social psychology* (vol. 28, pp. 281–388). San Diego, CA: Academic Press.

Kelsay, K. (1989). *A qualitative study of reflective teaching.* (ERIC Reproduction Service No. ED 352320).

Killen, L. R. (1989). Reflecting on reflective teaching: A response. *Journal of Teacher Education, 40,* 49–52.

Kissner, E. (2006). *Summarizing, paraphrasing, and retelling: Skills for better reading, writing, and test taking.* Portsmouth, NH: Heinemann.

Klem, A. M., & Connell, J. P. (2004). Relationships matter: Linking teacher support to student engagement and achievement. *Journal of School Health, 74,* 262–273.

Kluger, A. N., & DeNisi, A. (1996). The effects of feedback interventions on performance: A historical review, a meta-analysis, and a preliminary feedback intervention theory. *Psychological Bulletin, 119,* 254–284.

Knight, J., Bradley, B. A., Hock, M., Skrtic, T. M., Knight, D., Brasseur-Hock, I., . . . Hatton, C. (2012). Record, replay, reflect. Videotaped lessons accelerate learning for teachers and coaches. *Journal of Staff Development, 33,* 18–23.

Kolb, D. (1984). *Experiential learning: Experience as the source of learning and development.* Englewood Cliffs, NJ: Prentice-Hall.

Kushman, J. W. (1992). The organizational dynamics of teacher workplace commitment: A study of urban elementary and middle schools. *Educational Administration Quarterly, 28,* 5–42.

Ladson-Billings, G. (1995). But that's just good teaching! The case for culturally relevant pedagogy. *Theory Into Practice, 34*(3), 159–165.

Ladson-Billings, G. (1997). It doesn't add up: African American students' mathematics achievement. *Journal for Research in Mathematics Education, 28,* 697–708.

Ladson-Billings, G. (2001). *Crossing over to Canaan: The journey of new teachers in diverse classrooms.* San Francisco, CA: Jossey-Bass.

LeCompte, M. D., & Dworkin, A. G. (1991). *Giving up on school: Student dropouts and teacher burnouts.* Newbury Park, CA: Corwin.

Lee, J. S. (2012). The effects of teacher-student relationship and academic press on student engagement and academic performance. *International Journal of Educational Research, 53,* 330–340.

LeFevre, D. M. (2004). Designing for teacher learning: Video-based curriculum design. In J. Brophy (Ed.), *Advances in research on teaching, volume 10. Using video in teacher education* (pp. 235–258). Oxford, UK: Elsevier.

Lemov, D. (2010). *Teach like a champion: 49 techniques that put students on the path to college.* San Francisco, CA: Jossey-Bass.

Lieberman, A., & Miller, L. (2011). Learning communities: The starting point for professional learning is in schools and classrooms. *Journal of Staff Development, 32,* 16–20.

Liew, J., Chen, Q., & Hughes, J. N. (2010). Child effortful control, teacher–student relationships, and achievement in academically at-risk children: Additive and interactive effects. *Early Childhood Research Quarterly, 25,* 51–64.

Liu, M. Wivagg, J., Geurtz, R., Lee, S., & Chang, H. M. (2012). Examining how middle school science teachers implement a multimedia-enriched problem-based learning environment. *Interdisciplinary Journal of Problem-Based Learning, 6*, 46–84.

Loughran, J. J. (2002). Effective reflective practice: In search of meaning in learning about teaching. *Journal of Teacher Education, 53*, 33–43.

Lucas, T., & Katz, A. (1994). Reframing the debate: The roles of native languages in English-only programs for language minority students. *TESOL Quarterly, 28*, 537–561.

Lyman, F. (1981). The responsive classroom discussion. In A. S. Anderson (Ed.), *Mainstreaming digest* (pp. 109–113). College Park: University of Maryland College of Education.

Manlove, J. (1998). The influence of high school dropout and school disengagement on the risk of school-age pregnancy. *Journal of Research on Adolescence, 8*, 187–220.

Marks, H. M. (2000). Student engagement in instructional activity: Patterns in the elementary, middle, and high school years. *American Educational Research Journal, 37*, 153–184.

Matsumara, L. C., Slater, S. C., & Crosson, A. (2008). Classroom climate, rigorous instruction and curriculum, and students' interactions in urban middle schools. *The Elementary School Journal, 108*, 293–312.

McDuffie, K. A., Mastropieri, M. A., & Scruggs, T. E. (2009). Differential effects of peer tutoring in co-taught and non-co-taught classes: Results for content learning and student-teacher interactions. *Exceptional Children, 75*, 493–510.

McLaughlin, M., & DeVoogd, G. L. (2003). *Critical literacy: Enhancing students' comprehension of text.* New York, NY: Scholastic.

Mesmer, H. A., & Hutchins, E. J. (2002). Using QARs with charts and graphs. *The Reading Teacher, 56*, 21–27.

Modell, J., & Elder, G. H. (2002). Children develop in history: So what's new? In W. Hartup & R. Weinberg (Eds.), *Child psychology in retrospect and prospect: In celebration of the 75th anniversary of the Institute of Child Development. The Minnesota symposia on child psychology* (vol. 32, pp. 173–205). Mahwah, NJ: Lawrence Erlbaum.

Monroe, C. R. (2009). Teachers closing the discipline gap in an urban middle school. *Urban Education, 44*, 322–347.

Moon, J. (1999). *Reflection in learning and professional development: Theory and practice.* London: Kogan Page.

Murdock, T. B., Anderman, L. H., & Hodge, S. A. (2000). Middle-grade predictors of students' motivation and behavior in high school. *Journal of Adolescent Research, 15*, 327–351.

Nagy, W. E., Herman, P. A., & Anderson, R. C. (1985). Learning words from context. *Reading Research Quarterly, 20*, 233–253.

Nangle, D. W., Erdley, C. A., Carpenter, E. M., & Newman, J. E. (2002). Social skills training as a treatment for aggressive children and adolescents: A developmental–clinical integration. *Aggression and Violent Behavior, 7*, 169–199.

National Council of Teachers of Mathematics (2000). *Principles and standards for school mathematics.* Reston, VA: NCTM.

Nelson, L. J., Hart, C. H., Evans, C. A., Coplan, R. J., Roper, S. O., & Robinson, C. C. (2009). Behavioral and relational correlates of low self-perceived competence in young children. *Early Childhood Research Quarterly, 24,* 350–361.

Newmann, F. M., Wehlage, G. G., & Lamborn, S. D. (1992). The significance and sources of student engagement. In F. Newmann (Ed.), *Student engagement and achievement in American secondary schools* (pp. 11–39). New York, NY: Teachers College Press.

Noddings, N. (1992). *The challenge to care in schools: An alternative approach to education.* New York, NY: Teachers College Press.

Osterman, K. F. (2000). Students' need for belonging in the school community. *Review of Educational Research, 70,* 323–367.

Osterman, K. F., & Kottkamp, R. B. (1993). *Reflective practice for educators: Improving schooling through professional development.* Newbury Park, CA: Corwin.

Patrick, B. C., Skinner, E. A., & Connell, J. P. (1993). What motivates children's behavior and emotion? Joint effects of perceived control and autonomy in the academic domain. *Journal of Personality and Social Psychology, 65,* 781–791.

Pianta, R. C., & Stuhlman, M. W. (2004). Teacher-child relationships and children's success in the first years of school. *School Psychology Review, 33,* 444–458.

Pintrich, P. R., & De Groot, E. V. (1990). Motivational and self-regulated learning components of classroom academic performance. *Journal of Educational Psychology, 82,* 33–40.

Prinz, R. J., Blechman, E. A., & Dumas, J. E. (1994). An evaluation of peer coping-skills training for childhood aggression. *Journal of Clinical Child Psychology, 23,* 193–203.

Prochaska, J. O., Norcross, J. C., & DiClemente, C. C. (1994). *Changing for good.* New York, NY: Avon Books.

Qin, Z., Johnson, D. W., & Johnson, R. T. (1995). Cooperative versus competitive efforts and problem solving. *Review of Educational Research, 65,* 129–143.

Raphael, T. (1986). Teaching question answer relationships, revisited. *The Reading Teacher, 39,* 516–522.

Ready, D. D., & Wright, D. L. (2010). Accuracy and inaccuracy in teachers' perceptions of young children's cognitive abilities: The role of child background and classroom context. *American Educational Research Journal, 48,* 335–360.

Reich, J., & Daccord, T. (2007). *Best ideas for teaching with technology: A practical guide for teachers, by teachers.* Armonk, NY: M. E. Sharpe.

Reschly, A. L., Huebner, E. S., Appleton, J. J., & Antaramian, S. (2008). Engagement as flourishing: The contribution of positive emotions and coping to adolescents' engagement at school and with learning. *Psychology in the Schools, 45,* 419–431.

Rich, P. R., & Hannafin, M. (2009). Video annotation tools: Technologies to scaffold, structure, and transform teacher reflection. *Journal of Teacher Education, 60,* 52–67.

Richards, J. (1990). Beyond training: Approaches to teacher education in language teaching. *Language Teacher, 14,* 3–8.

Romberg, T. A. (1992). Problematic features of the school mathematics curriculum. In P. W. Jackson (Ed.), *Handbook of Research on Curriculum* (pp. 749–788). New York, NY: Macmillan.

Rosenholtz, S. J. (1985). Effective schools: Interpreting the evidence. *American Journal of Education, 93,* 352–388.

Rosenthal, R., & Jacobson, L. (1968). *Pygmalion in the classroom.* New York, NY: Holt, Rinehart, and Winston.

Rubie-Davies, C. M. (2007). Classroom interactions: Exploring the practices of high- and low-expectation teachers. *British Journal of Educational Psychology, 77,* 289–306.

Rudolph, K. D., Lambert, S. F., Clark, A. G., & Kurlakowsky, K. D. (2001). Negotiating the transition to middle school: The role of self-regulatory processes. *Child Development, 72,* 929–946.

Schutz, P. A., & Lanehart, S. J. (2002). Introduction: Emotions in education. *Educational Psychologist, 37,* 67–68.

Scruggs, T. E. Mastropieri, M. A., Berkeley, S. L., & Marshak, L. (2010). Mnemonic strategies: Evidence-based practice and practice-based evidence. *Intervention in School and Clinic, 46,* 79–86.

Schön, D. A. (1983). *The reflective practitioner: How professionals think in action.* New York, NY: Basic Books.

Seiler, G., & Elmesky, R. (2007). The role of communal practices in the generation of capital and emotional energy among urban African American students in science classrooms. *Teachers College Record, 109,* 391–419.

Sherin, M. G., & van Es, E. A. (2009). Effects of Video club participation on teachers' professional vision. *Journal of Teacher Education, 60,* 20–37.

Shernoff, D. J., Csikszentmihalyi, M., Schneider, B., & Shernoff, E. S. (2003). Student engagement in high school classrooms from the perspective of flow theory. *School Psychology Quarterly, 18,* 158–176.

Shuster, K., & Meany, J. (2005). *Speak out: Debate and public speaking in the middle grades.* New York, NY: Idea Press.

Silver, H. F., Strong, R. W., & Perini, M. J. (2007). *The strategic teacher: Selecting the right research-based strategy for every lesson.* Alexandria, VA: ASCD

Sirin, S. R., & Rogers-Sirin, L. (2005). Components of school engagement among African American adolescents. *Applied Developmental Science, 9,* 5–13.

Skerrett, A., & Bomer, R. (2011). Borderzones in adolescents' literacy practices: Connecting out-of-school literacies to the reading curriculum. *Urban Education, 46,* 1256–1279.

Skinner, E., Furrer, C., Marchand, G., & Kindermann, T. (2008). Engagement and disaffection in the classroom: Part of a larger motivational dynamic? *Journal of Educational Psychology, 100,* 765–781.

Skinner, E. A., Wellborn, J. G., & Connell, J. P. (1990). What it takes to do well in school and whether I've got it: A process model of perceived control and children's engagement and achievement in school. *Journal of Educational Psychology, 82,* 22–32.

Steele, C. M. (1992, April). Race and the schooling of black Americans. *The Atlantic Monthly,* 68–78.

Sternberg, R. J. (1987). Most vocabulary is learned from context. In M. G. McKeown & M. E. Curtis (Eds.), *The nature of vocabulary acquisition* (pp. 89–106). Hillsdale, NJ: Erlbaum.

Tatum, A. (2005). *Teaching reading to black adolescent males: Closing the achievement gap.* Portland, ME: Stenhouse.

Tatum, A. W. (2008). Toward a more anatomically complete model of literacy instruction: A focus on African American male adolescents and texts. *Harvard Educational Review, 78,* 155–180.

Taylor, L. K., Bernhard, J. K., Garg, S., & Cummins, J. (2008). Affirming plural belonging: Building on students' family-based cultural and linguistic capital through multiliteracies pedagogy. *Journal of Early Childhood Literacy, 8,* 269–294.

Taylor, R. L. (1991). Poverty and adolescent black males: The subculture of disengagement. In P. B. Edelman & J. Ladner (Eds.), *Adolescence and poverty: Challenge for the 1990s* (pp. 139–162). Washington, DC: Center for National Policy Press.

Tenenbaum, H. R., & Ruck, M. D. (2007). Are teachers' expectations different for racial minority than for European American students? A meta-analysis. *Journal of Educational Psychology, 99,* 253–273.

Terrill, M. C., Scruggs, T. E., & Mastropieri, M. A. (2004). SAT vocabulary instruction for high school students with learning disabilities. *Intervention in School and Clinic, 39,* 288–294.

Thomas, D. E., & Stevenson, H. (2009). Gender risks and education: The particular classroom challenges for urban low-income African American boys. *Review of Research in Education, 33,* 160–180.

Tomlinson, C. (1999). *The differentiated classroom: Responding to the needs of all learners.* Alexandria, VA: ASCD.

Tomlinson, C. (2001). *How to differentiate instruction in mixed-ability classrooms* (2nd ed.). Alexandria, VA: ASCD.

Tournaki, N., & Podell, D. M. (2005). The impact of student characteristics and teacher efficacy on teachers' predictions of student success. *Teaching and Teacher Education, 21,* 299–314.

Tucker, C. M., Zayco, R. A., Herman, K. C., Reinke, W. M., Trujillo, M., Carraway, K., . . . Ivery, P. D. (2002). Teacher and child variables as predictors of academic engagement among low-income African American children. *Psychology in the Schools, 39,* 477–488.

Uekawa, K., Borman, K., & Lee, R. (2007). Student engagement in U.S. urban high school mathematics and science classrooms: Findings on social organization, race, and ethnicity. *Urban Review, 39,* 1–43.

Vadeboncoeur, J. A., & Stevens, L. P. (Eds.). (2005). *Re/Constructing "the adolescent": Sign, symbol, and body.* New York, NY: Peter Lang.

Valenzuela, A. (1999). *Subtractive schooling: U.S.–Mexican youth and the politics of caring.* Albany: State University of New York Press.

Voekl, K. E. (1996). Measuring students' identification with school. *Educational and Psychological Measurement, 56,* 760–770.

Vygotsky, L. S. (1978). *Mind in society: The development of higher psychological processes.* (M. Cole, V. John-Steiner, S. Scribner, & E. Souberman, Eds. & Trans.). Cambridge, MA: Harvard University Press.

Walker-Tileston, D. (2005). *10 best teaching practices: How brain research, learning styles and standards define teaching competencies.* Thousand Oaks, CA: Corwin.

Washor, E., & Mojkowski, C. (2007). What do you mean by rigor? *Educational Leadership, 64,* 84–87.

Webb, N. M., & Farivar, S. (1994). Promoting helping behavior in cooperative small groups in middle school mathematics. *American Educational Research Journal, 31,* 369–395.

Webster-Stratton, C. (2005). The incredible years: A training series for the prevention and treatment of conduct problems in young children. In E. D. Hibbs & P. S. Jensen (Eds.), *Psychosocial treatments for child and adolescent disorders: Empirically based strategies for clinical practice* (2nd ed., pp. 507–555). Washington, DC: American Psychological Association.

Webster-Stratton, C., & Reid, M. J. (2003). Treating conduct problems and strengthening social and emotional competence in young children : The Dina Dinosaur Treatment Program. *Journal of Emotional and Behavioral Disorders, 11,* 130–143.

Weinstein, R. S., Gregory, A., & Strambler, M. J. (2004). Intractable self-fulfilling prophecies: Fifty years after Brown v. Board of Education. *American Psychologist, 59,* 511–520.

Wentzel, K. R. (1997). Student motivation in middle school: The role of perceived pedagogical caring. *Journal of Educational Psychology, 89,* 411–419.

Wentzel, K. R. (1998). Social support and adjustment in middle school: The role of parents, teachers, and peers. *Journal of Educational Psychology, 90,* 202–209.

Wentzel, K. R. (1999). Social-motivational processes and interpersonal relationships: Implications for understanding motivation at school. *Journal of Educational Psychology, 91,* 76–97.

Wentzel, K. (2002). Are effective teachers like good parents? Teaching styles and student adjustment in early adolescence. *Child Development, 73,* 287–301.

Werner, E. E. (1986). The concept of risk from a developmental perspective. In B. K. Keogh (Ed.), *Advances in special education, volume 4: Developmental problems in infancy and the preschool years* (pp. 1–23). Greenwich, CT: JAI Press.

Wheeler, R. S., & Swords, R. (2006). *Code-switching: Teaching standard English in urban classrooms.* Urbana, IL: National Council of Teachers of English.

Wigfield, A., & Eccles, J. S. (1989). Test anxiety in elementary and secondary school students. *Educational Psychologist, 24,* 159–183.

Wigfield, A., Eccles, J. S., Schiefele, U., Roeser, R. W., & Davis-Kean, P. (2006). Development of achievement motivation. In W. Damon (Series Ed.) & N. Eisenberg (Vol. Ed.), *Handbook of child psychology, volume 3. Social, emotional, and personality development* (6th ed., pp. 933–1002). New York, NY: Wiley.

Woolley, M. E., & Bowen, G. L. (2007). In the context of risk: Supportive adults and the school engagement of middle school students. *Family Relations, 56,* 92–104.

Wooley, M. E., Kol, K. L., & Bowen, G. L. (2009). The social context of school success for Latino middle school students: Direct and indirect influences of teachers, family, and friends. *The Journal of Early Adolescence, 29,* 43–70.

Yair, G. (2000). Educational battlefields in America: The tug-of-war over students' engagement with instruction. *Sociology of Education, 73,* 247–269.

Yarrow, F., & Topping, K. J. (2001). Collaborative writing: The effects of metacognitive prompting and structured peer interaction. *British Journal of Educational Psychology, 71,* 261–282.

Yazzie-Mintz, E. (2007). *Voices of students on engagement: A report on the 2006 High School Survey of Student Engagement*. Bloomington: Center for Evaluation & Education Policy, Indiana University. Retrieved from http://ceep.indiana.edu/hssse/pdf/HSSSE 2006 Report.pdf

Yazzie-Mintz, E. (2010). *Charting the path from engagement to achievement: A report on the 2009 High School Survey of Student Engagement*. Bloomington, IN: Center for Evaluation & Education Policy.

Yosso, T. J. (2005). Whose culture has capital? A critical race theory discussion of community cultural wealth. *Race, Ethnicity and Education, 8,* 69–91.

Young, E. (2010). Challenges to conceptualizing and actualizing culturally relevant pedagogy: How viable is the theory in classroom practice? *Journal of Teacher Education, 61,* 248–260.

Zimmerman, B. J., & Schunk, D. H. (2008). *Self-regulated learning and academic achievement: Theoretical perspectives* (2nd ed.). Mahwah, NJ: Lawrence Erlbaum.

Index

Academic content considerations.
  See Inspect to Inspire step; Intersect
  Their Interests and Experiences With
  Instruction step
Academic engagement
  components of, 78
  defined, 4, 9
  See also Engagement
Academic expectations. *See* Expect Nothing
  Short of Excellence step
Academic issues
  engaging educational practices overview, 7
  providing the assist, 106–111
Academic success, instruction and.
  See Sew Success Into Your Instructional
  Fabric step
Achievement gap
  deficit theory and, 36–37
  instructional SOFAs and, 62
Actionable Professional Learning
  engaging educational practices overview,
    17–18
  Expect Nothing Short of Excellence step,
    175–176
  Inspect to Inspire step, 33
  Intersect Their Interests and Experiences
    With Instruction step, 155–156
  Nurture Their Attributes step, 53
  overview of book, xiv, xviii–xix
  Partner to Make Emotional Connections
    step, 113–114
  Reflection on Practice as a Tool of
    Improvement step, 166
  Sew Success Into Your Instructional
    Fabric step, 68–69
Action research
  Intersect Their Interests and Experiences
    With Instruction step, 156
  Partner to Make Emotional Connections
    step, 113–114
  Sew Success Into Your Instructional
    Fabric step, 68–69

Administrator support for teachers, 65–66
Adolescent development, 171
Advocating for students, 93–94
African American students
  engaging educational practices
    overview, 6, 13
  Expect Nothing Short of Excellence step,
    167–170
  Intersect Their Interests and Experiences
    With Instruction step, 118, 120,
    121–128, 140
  MOVE checklist and, 50
  Nurture Their Attributes step, 36, 38
  Partner to Make Emotional Connections
    step, 79–81, 83, 88
Algebra content area, 142
  See also Mathematics
Allen, B. A., 39
Anaya, Rudolfo, 173
Anderson, Mr., 2–3
Animated *Jeopardy* game, 152
Annotating text, 111
Anonymity in surveys, 31, 171
*Any Small Goodness: A Novel of the
  Barrios,* 132
Assist, providing, 106–111
At-risk students
  engaging educational practices
    overview, 6–7
  student-teacher relationships and, 87
  See also HUMS students;
    specific concerns
Attributes, nurturing. *See* Nurture Their
  Attributes step

Bang, 124
Baseball game, 151–152
Baseline data, use of, 63, 64, 66
Basketball examples, 62, 100
Basketball game, 149
Before We Were Four, 129
Begging for Change, 124

Behavioral engagement
  defined, 5
  emotional connections and, 79
  incremental goals and, 63
  See also Engagement
Beliefs, formation of, 167–168
Belles, 130
Biases, critical literacy and, 136
Biggie Smalls, 3
Binder example, 107
Blueford High Series, 121
Blumenfeld, P. C., 5
Book selection. *See* Text, intersecting with
Border Crossing, 130
Borko, H., 162
Boykin, A. W., 39
Brain development, 171
Breakfast, Mrs. T. style, 90
Broccoli example, 117
Brothers Torres, The, 132
Buy-in
  engaging educational practices overview,
    10, 12–15
  Inspect to Inspire step, 32
  Partner to Make Emotional Connections
    step, 73–75

Card arrangement example, 43–44
Care element of student-teacher
    relationships, 89–94
Carmen Browne, 123
Carter, Ken, 104
Celebratory gestures, 99–101
Chain Reaction: A Perfect Chemistry, 133
Challenge, reaction to as engagement
    component, 5
Chemistry lesson example, 48–49
Chest bump gesture, 100–101
Civics/government content area, 146
Classbook game, 149–150
Classroom assist, providing, 106–111
Classroom climate, commitment
    and, 106
Classroom communities
  building of, 83–84
  essential elements of, 82–83
  residential communities comparison,
    81–82
Classroom culture, 60, 61
Closed-ended versus open-ended
    questions, 29
Closure, engagement and, xvii, 153–154
Cognitive engagement
  defined, 5
  elements of engagement, 6
  See also Engagement
Collaborative inquiry, Inspect to Inspire
    step, 33
Collaborative reflection, use of, 160–161
  See also Reflection on Practice as a Tool of
    Improvement step

Collaborative structures
  collaboration versus competition, 60
  engaging educational practices overview, 9
  in reflective practice, 160–161
  See also Peer-interactive strategies
Collective inquiry, Nurture Their Attributes
    step, 53
Commitment element of student-teacher
    relationships, 105–106
Communalism, classroom communities
    and, 83
Communication element of student-teacher
    relationships, 94–103
Communities, classroom
  building of, 83–84
  essential elements of, 82–83
  residential communities comparison,
    81–82
Competition versus collaboration, 60
Connecting versus controlling, xvii, 72–73
Connections, creating
  engaging educational practices overview,
    1–4, 9, 13
  overview of book, xv–xvi
  See also Partner to Make Emotional
    Connections step
Consistency element of student-teacher
    relationships, 60, 103–104
Content considerations. *See* Inspect to
    Inspire step; Intersect Their Interests
    and Experiences With Instruction step
Controlling versus connecting, xvii, 72–73
Conversational questions, 137
Conversations, connecting through, 95–100
Cooperative learning, Nurture Their
    Attributes step, 41
Copper Sun, 126
Critical element of DISC technique, 103
Critical literacy, engaging students in, 136
Cuba 15, 131
Culinary traditions example, 46
Cultural divide, bridging, 77–78
Culturally relevant texts, 136
Culturally responsive pedagogy, 64–65
Culture of classroom, 60, 61

Dancing example, 35
Darkness Before Dawn, 125
Darling-Hammond, L., xviii–xix
Data, baseline, 63, 64, 66
Data and probability content
    area, 143
Davis, Sampson, 173
Debate example, 51
Decision making and development, 171
Deficit theory, xvi–xvii, 36–37
  See also Nurture Their Attributes step
Descriptive element of DISC technique, 102
Development, adolescent, 171
Dewey, J., 115
Dice game, 151

Differentiated instruction, 64–65, 66
DIN (do-it-now) edict, 107, 111
Disabilities, ascertaining, 64
DISC feedback technique, 102–103
Discipline policies, zero tolerance, 66, 86
Dockter, J., 172
Do-it-now (DIN) edict, 107
Drama High Series, 123
Dreamer, The, 131
Dweck, C. S., 61, 68

Earth science content area, 144
　See also Science
Economics content area, xviii, 147
Eiteljorg, E., 162
ELLS (English language learners),
　instructional techniques for, 41
Emako Blue, 127
Emotional armor, surveys and, 31
Emotional connections, creating. *See*
　Connections, creating; Partner to Make
　Emotional Connections step
Emotional engagement
　classroom communities and, 81–85
　defined, 5
　elements of engagement, 5, 6, 9
　priorities, 79–81
　theoretical framework, 80–81
　using connections, 78–79
　See also Engagement; Partner
　　to Make Emotional Connections step
Engagement
　challenge of creating, 6–8
　defined, 4, 79
　elements of, 5–6, 9
　theoretical framework, 13
　See also Emotional engagement
Engaging educational practices
　Actionable Professional Learning, 17–18
　barrage of mismatches, 8
　challenge of creating engagement, 6–8
　definition of engagement, 4
　elements of engagement, 5–6, 9
　elements of practices, xv–xvi, 8–10
　INSPIRE acronym use, xiii, xvi
　introduction, 1–4
　overview of book, xiii–xiv
　rationale for developing, 8, 10–12
　sales situations in the classroom, 12–15
　steps overview, xiii, xvi–xix
　summary, 15–16
　theoretical framework, 13
　See also specific steps
English language arts
　intersecting with. *See* Text, intersecting
　　with
　student personas and, 48
English language learners (ELLs),
　instructional techniques for, 41
Entrées, introducing lessons with, 135
Entry points

Intersect Their Interests and Experiences
　With Instruction step, 135
Sew Success Into Your Instructional
　Fabric step, 62–66
Errors, learning from, 61, 68–69
Excellence, expecting. *See* Expect Nothing
　Short of Excellence step
Exchange of ideas, in MOVE checklist, 50
Exemplars of excellence
　opportunities for exposure to, 173–174
　staying abreast of, 171–173
　vignette, 172–173
Expect Nothing Short of Excellence step
　Actionable Professional Learning, 175–176
　assessing your expectations, 170–171
　exposure to exemplars, 173–174
　importance of expectations, 168
　in INSPIRE acronym, xiii, xvi
　introduction, 167–168
　overview of book, xvii
　staying abreast of exemplars, 171–173
　summary, 174
　surveying student perceptions, 171
　theoretical framework, 169–170
　understanding adolescent
　　development, 171
　vignette, 172–173
　visualizing possibilities, 174
Experienced, in SELF, 141, 155
Experiences, intersecting with. *See* Intersect
　Their Interests and Experiences With
　Instruction step
Exploratory observations, engaging
　educational practices overview, 17–18

Failure, negotiating, 61
Family-like classroom communities,
　82, 83–85, 91
Feedback
　as communication tool, 101–103
　eliciting, 27, 32
　expectations and, 171
　keeping an open line, 96
　positive, affirming statements, 75–77
　video review and, 162–163
　See also Student surveys
Felt, in SELF, 141, 155
Fiction texts. *See* Text, intersecting with
Film production example, 19–20
　See also Videos
First Responders game, 150
5/3 rule, 21, 23, 25
Football example, 101
Forged by Fire, 125
Formative assessment, 64–65, 66
Four Cs of Relationship Building
　Actionable Professional Learning, 113
　care element, 89–94
　commitment element, 105–106
　communication element, 94–103
　consistency element, 103–104

Four Ws, sharing of, 76–77
Fredericks, J. A., 5
Fripp, Patricia, 45
Furrer, C., 79

Gala example, 160
Games, love for as tool, xvii, 148–152
Gender, adolescent development and, 171
Genre choices, 134
Geography content area, 147
Geometry content area, 142
    See also Mathematics
Gestures and lingo, communicating
    through, 97–101
Giroux, H., 46
Global positioning system (GPS) example, 117
Government/civics content area, 146
Grade levels
    entry points below, 63, 66
    vignette use, xviii
    See also Reading levels
Grading, self-growth as barometer, 62
Graphic novels, exposure to, 134
Gutstein, E., 140

Handley, Mr. (vignette), 162
Heat, 132
Highly resistant readers, 135
Hilliard, A. G., 36
Historical fiction, exposure to, 134
History content area, 146
Holley, Mr., 91
Homeboyz, 133
Homerun game, 150–151
Houston, Mr., 1, 3
Howard, Mrs., 7
*How the Garcia Girls Lost Their
    Accents*, 129
HUMS (high-poverty, urban, largely
    minority schools)
    defined, xiii, 6
    mismatches in, 8
    personalized presentations, 49
    See also specific concerns
HUMS students
    deficit theory, xvi–xvii, 36–37
    disidentifying with content, 64
    engaging educational practices overview,
       6–7, 11–12
    focus on, 50–51
    life experience expertise, 45–46
    overview of book, xiii
    pressures on, 63
    realistic texts for, 120–135
    See also specific concerns
Hunt, Rameck, 173
Hurley, E. A., 39

If You Come Softly, 128
Immediate element of DISC technique, 102

Incremental targets, use of, 63–64
Ink, red, 103
Inspect to Inspire step
    Actionable Professional Learning, 33
    creating a pipeline of information, 20–21
    in INSPIRE acronym, xiii, xvi
    organization of book, xvi
    preparing student-centered pedagogy,
       19–20
    summary, 32
    techniques for, 21–27, 177
    utilizing student surveys, 27–32
    vignette, 24–25
INSPIRE acronym, steps in, xiii, xvi
    See also specific steps
Instruction, intersecting with. *See* Intersect
    Their Interests and Experiences With
    Instruction step
Instructional coaches and specialists,
    reflective practice and, 164
Instructional SOFAs
    defined, xiii, 62
    Sew Success Into Your Instructional
       Fabric step, 61–64
Interest inventories, 21, 26–27, 177
Intersect Their Interests and Experiences
    With Instruction step
    Actionable Professional Learning, 155–156
    closure, 153–154
    games, 148–152
    in INSPIRE acronym, xiii, xvi
    laying the groundwork, 115–116
    mathematics, 140–143
    multimedia tools, 148, 153
    overview of book, xvii
    science, 141, 144–145
    social studies, 141, 146–147
    summary, 154
    techniques for, 116–117
    texts (reading), 117, 119–140
    theoretical framework, 118
    vignette, 138–139
Introducing lessons, entrées for, 135
Introductory address to students,
    considerations for, 59–60
Introductory task, format for, 115–116
Issue box, providing, 32

Jacobs, J., 162
James, LeBron, 100
Jason and Kyra, 128
JC Penney, 101
Jenkins, George, 173
Jeopardy game, 152
Jones, Mrs. (vignettes)
    engaging educational practices overview,
       6, 14
    Inspect to Inspire step, 24–25
    Intersect Their Interests and Experiences
       With Instruction step, 138–139

Nurture Their Attributes step, 44–45
overview of book, xviii
Partner to Make Emotional Connections
    step, 76, 83, 92, 95–98, 100–101, 106–107
Reflection on Practice as a Tool of
    Improvement step, 162–163
Journal articles, studying, 155–156
Journal mining, 26
Journal writing, 135, 164
Jumping Tree, The, 131

Kindermann, T., 79
King, Mr. (vignettes)
    engaging educational practices overview,
        6, 14
    Expect Nothing Short of Excellence step,
        172–173
    Nurture Their Attributes step, 51
    overview of book, xviii
    Partner to Make Emotional Connections
        step, 71–72, 83, 96, 111
King Junior High School, 1–3
Klein, Ms. (vignettes)
    engaging educational practices
        overview, 6, 14
    overview of book, xviii
    Partner to Make Emotional Connections
        step, 74, 83, 84–85, 91

Ladson-Billings, G., 140
Lanehart, S. J., 71
Latino/a students
    Expect Nothing Short of Excellence step,
        167–169
    Intersect Their Interests and Experiences
        With Instruction step,
        118, 120, 129–135
    Nurture Their Attributes step, 36, 38–39
    Partner to Make Emotional Connections
        step,
        81, 87–88
Learner entry points
    Intersect Their Interests and Experiences
        With Instruction step, 135
    Sew Success Into Your Instructional
        Fabric step, 62–66
Learning disabilities, ascertaining, 64
Learning Profile Questionnaire: How Do
    You Like to Learn?, 27
Learning profiles, 21, 27
Lee, Spike, 19
Letter posting example, 44
Lewis, C., 172
Library development. *See* Text, intersecting
    with
Lieberman, A., xix
Life experience expertise, 45–46
Life experiences, intersecting with.
    See Intersect Their Interests and
    Experiences With Instruction step

Life science content area, 144
    See also Science
Like, in SELF, 141, 155
Likert-like surveys, 29
Lines of communication, keeping open, 96
Lingo and gestures, communicating
    through, 97–101
Listen—then list technique, 21, 22–23
Live Movie Maker, 153
Loughran, J. J., 158

M. L. King Junior High School, 1–3
Marathon example, 62–63
Marchand, G., 79
Marking of papers, 101–103
Mathematics
    intersecting with, xvii, 140–143
    Nurture Their Attributes step, 46, 48
Measurement content area, 143
Media arts, content in, 51, 136–137
Media technologies. *See* Multimedia tools
Mental health issues, 7
Messed Up, 130
Me versus me, 62–63
Miller, L., xix
Mining of student writing, 21, 23, 26
Mismatches
    barrage of, 8
    deficit theory and, 36
Missteps, learning from, 61, 68–69
M&M candies example, 74
Moment, teaching in the, 61
Money Hungry, 124
Monroe, C. R., 91
Monster, 126
MOVE checklist, 50
Movement, in MOVE checklist, 50
Movement as tool
    Intersect Their Interests and Experiences
        With Instruction step, 149, 151–152
    Nurture Their Attributes step, 41
    overview of book, xiv
Movie production example, 19–20
    See also Videos
Multimedia tools
    Expect Nothing Short of Excellence
        step, 173
    Intersect Their Interests and Experiences
        With Instruction step, xvii, 137, 148,
        152, 153
    Nurture Their Attributes step, 49
    See also Videos
Mystery books, exposure to, 134

Nathan persona, 47, 48, 50
Newscast example, 51
Ni-Ni Simone Series, 123
No Child Left Behind, 117
Noddings, N., 94
Notes, taking, 111

Number cube game, 151
Numbers and operations content area, 142–143
    See also Mathematics
Nurture Their Attributes step
    Actionable Professional Learning, 53
    chemistry lesson example, 48–49
    focus on HUMS students, 50–51
    in INSPIRE acronym, xiii, xvi
    interactive strategies, 40–41
    introduction, 35–37
    life experience expertise, 45–46
    MOVE checklist, 50
    movement as tool, 41, 43–44
    overview of book, xvi–xvii
    personalized presentations, 49
    student personas, 46–51
    summary, 52
    techniques for, 39–43
    theoretical framework, 38–39
    vignettes, 44–45, 51
Nyisha persona, 47, 50

One-of-a-kindness, in MOVE checklist, 50
Open-ended versus closed-ended
        questions, 29
Organization skills, helping with, 106–108

Pacing guide, use of, 66
Paris, A. H., 5
Parrot in the Oven: Mi Vida, 133
Partner to Make Emotional
        Connections step
    Actionable Professional Learning, 113–114
    bridging the cultural divide, 77–78
    buy-in, 73–75
    care element, 89–94
    classroom communities, 81–85
    commitment element, 105–106
    communication element, 94–103
    connecting versus controlling, xvii, 72–73
    consistency element, 103–104
    emotional engagement as priority, 78–81
    in INSPIRE acronym, xiii, xvi
    overview of book, xvii
    power of emotional appeal, 73–74
    providing the assist, 106–111
    student-teacher relationships, 84, 86–106
    summary, 112
    teacher attributes as factor, 78
    techniques for, 75–77
    theoretical framework, 80–81
    vignettes, 71–72, 74, 84–85, 91, 96,
        100–101, 106–107, 111
Payton Skyy Jr. Series, 122
Peer-interactive strategies
    Nurture Their Attributes step,
        40–41, 50, 51
    Partner to Make Emotional Connections
        step, 75, 85, 92
    See also Collaborative structures

Perry Skyy Jr. Series, 122
Personal issues
    engaging educational practices
        overview, 7
    Partner to Make Emotional Connections
        step, 72, 86–87, 103–104, 107,
        109–110
    See also Intersect Their Interests and
        Experiences With Instruction step
Personalized presentations, value of, 49
Personas, student, 46–51
Physical science content area, 145
    See also Science
Pipeline of information, creating, 20–21
Pittman, M. E., 162
Planner example, 107
Play, love for as tool, xvii, 148–152
PLCs (professional learning communities),
        xviii–xix
Popular culture
    connecting example, 3
    content in, 136–137
    Nurture Their Attributes step, 45–48,
        50–51
Positive, affirming statements, 75–77
Powder toss gesture, 100–101
Power structure among students, 91
Practice, reflection on. *See* Reflection on
        Practice as a Tool of Improvement step
Pretests, use of, 63
Prizes, use of, 148
Professional learning, actionable. *See*
        Actionable Professional Learning
Professional learning communities (PLCs),
        xviii–xix
Professional sports leagues, video reviews
        in, 161
Psychological engagement. *See* Emotional
        engagement

Questionnaires. *See* Interest inventories;
        Learning profiles; Student surveys

Raising the roof gesture, 99
Reaction to challenge, as engagement
        component, 5
Read-aloud technique, 135, 139
Reading, intersecting with. *See* Text,
        intersecting with
Reading levels
    Intersect Their Interests and Experiences
        With Instruction step, 120–135
    Sew Success Into Your Instructional
        Fabric step, 64
Realistic fiction texts
    for African American students,
        120, 121–128
    bare essentials, 119–120
    for Latino/a students, 120, 129–135
    See also Text, intersecting with

Redefining Academic Rigor: Documentary Film Making in the New English/Language Arts Classroom, 155
Red ink, use of, 103
Reflection on Practice as a Tool of Improvement step
  Actionable Professional Learning, 166
  collaborative structures, 160–161
  expectations and, 170–171
  in INSPIRE acronym, xiii, xvi
  introduction, 157–158
  overview of book, xvii
  processes utilized in, 164
  reasons to engage in, 159
  reflecting versus reflective practices, 158–159
  summary, 165
  theoretical framework, 159–160
  video as tool, 161–164, 166, 170
  vignette, 162–163
Reflective dialogue, use of, 113–114
Reflective practices, engaging educational practices overview, 10
Relevant, interesting, meaningful things (RIMS), 26
Replay Capture Suite, 153
Research-based practices, engaging educational practices overview, 10
Research frameworks. *See* Theoretical frameworks
Response to Intervention (RtI) framework, 64
Return to Sender, 129
RIMS (relevant, interesting, meaningful things), 26
Rolling Until Right game, 150
Romiette and Julio, 126
RtI (Response to Intervention) framework, 64
Rules of Attraction, 133
Runner example, 62–63

Sales situations in the classroom, 12–15
  See also Student buy-in
Schick, Mrs., 103
Schutz, P. A., 71
Science
  chemistry lesson example, 48–49
  intersecting with, xvii, 141, 144–145
  M&M candies example, 74
Scorpions, 127
Scorsese, Martin, 19–20
Seat incarceration, movement versus, xiv, 41, 43–44
Secret Story of Sonia Rodriguez, The, 133
Seen, in SELF, 141, 155
SELF (Seen, Experienced, Like, Felt), 141, 155
Self-growth, as barometer of progress, 62–64
Self-reflection. *See* Reflection on Practice as a Tool of Improvement step

Sew Success Into Your Instructional Fabric step
  Actionable Professional Learning, 68–69
  barriers to success, 66
  baseline data, 63, 64, 66
  essential pedagogical approaches, 64–65
  incremental targets, 63–64
  in INSPIRE acronym, xiii, xvi
  introduction, 35–36
  missteps, learning from, 61, 68–69
  overview of book, xvii
  SOFAs, 61–64
  success as need, 36–37
  summary, 67
  support for students, 58–60
  support for teachers, 65–66
  supportive structures, 60–61
  theoretical framework, 57–58
Shakur, Tupac, 3
Shared practice
  Expect Nothing Short of Excellence step, 175–176
  Reflection on Practice as a Tool of Improvement step, 166
Shooter, 127
Shoulder bump gesture, 101
Simon, R., 46
Skin I'm In, The, 124
Skinner, E., 79
Slam Dunk! game, 149
Socially significant texts, 136
Social studies
  intersecting with, xvii, 141, 146–147
  student personas and, 48
SOFAs (Success Opportunities For All)
  defined, xiii, 62
  Sew Success Into Your Instructional Fabric step, 61–64
Software tools. *See* Multimedia tools
Sotomayor, Sonia, 173
Spielberg, Steven, 19
Spinner game, 151
Sports leagues, video review in, 161
Standardized test scores
  engaging educational practices overview, 12
  student entry points and, 66
Stop Drop and Read time, 138–139
Strategic element of DISC technique, 103
Student achievement gap
  deficit theory and, 36–37
  instructional SOFAs and, 62
Student attributes, nurturing. *See* Nurture Their Attributes step
Student buy-in
  engaging educational practices overview, 10, 12–15
  Inspect to Inspire step, 32
  Partner to Make Emotional Connections step, 73–75

Student-centered content. *See* Inspect to Inspire step; Intersect Their Interests and Experiences With Instruction step
Student engagement, defined, 4
   See also Engagement
Student entry points
   Intersect Their Interests and Experiences With Instruction step, 135
   Sew Success Into Your Instructional Fabric step, 62–66
Student lingo and gestures, communicating through, 97–101
Student personas, 46–51
Student success, instruction and. *See* Sew Success Into Your Instructional Fabric step
Student support
   engaging educational practices overview, 7, 10
   Sew Success Into Your Instructional Fabric step, xvii, 58–60
   See also Partner to Make Emotional Connections step
Student surveys
   analyzing and using results, 31–32
   collaborative inquiry, 33
   designing, 29, 30–31
   expectations and, 171
   Inspect to Inspire step, 22
   items to include, 30
   open-ended versus closed-ended questions, 29
   overview of book, xvi
   reasons to use, 27–28
   time concerns, 29, 31
Student-teacher relationships
   care element, 89–94
   characteristics of, 84, 86
   commitment element, 105–106
   communication element, 94–103
   consistency element, 60, 103–104
   importance of, 87
   mistakes in, 86–87
   successful classrooms and, 60
   theoretical framework, 87–88
   See also Partner to Make Emotional Connections step
Student writing, mining of, 21, 23, 26
Studying your students. *See* Inspect to Inspire step
Substitute teaching, connecting example, 1–4
Success of students, instruction and. *See* Sew Success Into Your Instructional Fabric step
Success Opportunities For All (SOFAs)
   defined, xiii, 62
   Sew Success Into Your Instructional Fabric step, 61–64

Support for students
   engaging educational practices overview, 7, 10
   Sew Success Into Your Instructional Fabric step, xvii, 58–60
   See also Partner to Make Emotional Connections step
Support for teachers, 65–66
Supportive structures, 60–61
Surveys, student. *See* Student surveys

Tatum, A. W., 140
Teacher attributes
   classroom community and, 83
   emotional connections and, 78
   salespeople example, 12–15
   thermostat example, xiv, 10–11
Teacher expectations, elevated.
   See Expect Nothing Short of Excellence step
Teacher learning communities, xviii–xix
Teacher-student relationships.
   See Student-teacher relationships
Teacher support, 65–66
Teacher vignettes, use of, xiii, xviii
   See also specific steps
Teaching in the moment, 61
Tears of a Tiger, 125, 139
Tell, in Three T Method, 36
Tequila Worm, The, 130
Test, in Three T Method, 36
Tests
   pretests, 63
   standardized, 12, 66
Text, annotating, 111
Text, intersecting with
   African American students, 120, 121–128
   characteristics that engage, 119
   controversial topics, 134
   critical literacy, 136
   cultural and social considerations, 136
   entrée use, 135
   genre choices, 134
   highly resistant readers, 135
   introduction, 117
   knowing when students are engaged, 138, 140
   Latino/a students, 120, 129–135
   overview of book, xvii
   popular culture and media arts, 136–137
   reading level considerations, 134
   realistic fiction, 119–134
Text message example, xiii–xiv, 4
Theoretical frameworks
   engaging educational practices overview, 13
   Expect Nothing Short of Excellence step, 169–170

Intersect Their Interests and Experiences With Instruction step, 118
Nurture Their Attributes step, 38–39
overview of book, xiii
Partner to Make Emotional Connections step, 80–81, 87–88
Reflection on Practice as a Tool of Improvement step, 159–160
Sew Success Into Your Instructional Fabric step, 57–58
Thermostat example, xiv, 10–11
Think-pair-share (TPS) strategy, 40–41, 92
Three strikes discipline policies, 66
Three T Method of Teaching, 56
Time concerns
    Reflection on Practice as a Tool of Improvement step, 157–158
    student surveys, 29, 31
TPS (think-pair-share) strategy, 40–41, 92
Transfer, in Three T Method, 36
Trust concerns
    Partner to Make Emotional Connections step, 72, 75, 84, 89–90, 95
    See also Student-teacher relationships
Turnaround queen example, 44–45

Under the Mesquite, 131
Upshaw, Mr. (vignette), 24–25

Verve, in MOVE checklist, 50
Videos
    Expect Nothing Short of Excellence step, 173, 175–176
    Intersect Their Interests and Experiences With Instruction step, 153
    Nurture Their Attributes step, 49

Reflection on Practice as a Tool of Improvement step, 161–164, 166, 170
Vignettes, use of, xiii, xviii
    See also specific steps
Vision statements, 167–168
Vygotsky, L. S., 37

Walker, Madame C. J., 173–174
Wallace, Christopher, 3
Want, in four Ws, 76
Weaknesses, in four Ws, 76–77
Weight loss example, 63
We Were Here, 132
WHCM (why we have to cover material)
    Partner to Make Emotional Connections step, 73
White flag example, 55–56
Who Am I Without Him, 125
WIFM (what's in it for me) question
    Inspect to Inspire step, 20, 30
    Intersect Their Interests and Experiences With Instruction step, 117
    Partner to Make Emotional Connections step, 73
    Sew Success Into Your Instructional Fabric step, 60
Win, in four Ws, 76
Workload concerns
    providing an assist, 110–111
    reflection and, 157–158
    student surveys, 29, 31
Wreck, in four Ws, 76
Writing, mining of, 21, 23, 26

Zero tolerance policies, 66, 86

CORWIN

A SAGE Company

The Corwin logo—a raven striding across an open book—represents the union of courage and learning. Corwin is committed to improving education for all learners by publishing books and other professional development resources for those serving the field of PreK–12 education. By providing practical, hands-on materials, Corwin continues to carry out the promise of its motto: **"Helping Educators Do Their Work Better."**